TEACHING THE ANCIENT WORLD

SCHOLARS PRESS
GENERAL SERIES

Number 5

TEACHING THE ANCIENT WORLD

Douglas M. Astolfi, Editor

TEACHING
THE ANCIENT WORLD

Edited by
Douglas M. Astolfi

Scholars Press
Chico, California

TEACHING THE ANCIENT WORLD
Douglas M. Astolfi, Editor

© 1983
Scholars Press

Library of Congress Cataloging in Publication Data

Main entry under title:

Teaching the ancient world.

(Scholars Press general series ; no. 5)
Includes bibliographies.
1. Civilization, Ancient—Study and teaching
(Higher)—Addresses, essays, lectures. 2. Bible as
Literature—Study and teaching (Higher)—Addresses,
essays, lectures. 3. Judaism—History—Post-exilic period,
586   B.C.–210   A.D.—Study   and   teaching
(Higher)—Addresses, essays, lectures. 4. Civilization,
Greco-Roman—Study and teaching (Higher)— Addresses,
essays, lectures. I. Astolfi, Douglas M. II. Series.
CB311.T43   1983   930'.07'11   82–10831
ISBN 0–89130–590–4

Printed in the United States of America

Table of Contents

Contributors

Douglas M. Astolfi, Dean, College of Professional and Continuing Education, Director of Summer Schools, Clark University;

Karl Galinsky, Professor of Classics and Chairman of the Department of Classics, The University of Texas at Austin;

James S. Ackerman, Professor of Religious Studies, Indiana University;

Kenneth R. R. Gros Louis, Professor of English and Comparative Literature and Vice President, Indiana University;

Daniel Patte, Professor of Religious Studies and the New Testament, Vanderbilt University;

Gordon Tucker, Assistant Professor of Philosophy, The Jewish Theological Seminary of America;

Mark Morford, Professor of Classics, The Ohio State University.

PREFACE

This volume is the product of two NEH-sponsored workshops held during 1981 and 1982 to improve the teaching of the ancient world on college campuses. The workshops and the material presented here were designed to provide scholars who teach with practical materials about teaching and the application of new knowledge and new classroom aides to the development of exciting courses that would have wide appeal to college and university students. We hope that this material, developed through NEH-funded Institutes, Summer Seminars and Higher Education/Regional and National Projects will stimulate discussions and lead to new courses and new syllabi. We recognize that the material we are presenting does not address all areas of interest to classical scholars and teachers. We have chosen this material because it is interrelated and because, when viewed as a whole, it represents areas of general interest and application to biblical scholars, historians, philosophers, and others teaching about the ancient world. We were guided in our selection by evaluations of prior NEH projects. We have selected materials that college and university teachers felt had the broadest application to the variety of disciplines and courses which are taught in relation to classical civilization.

The material presented here is organized in four basic sections. The first section is designed to provide the reader with a general and concise overview of the study of the classics and of the new techniques and materials available to scholars who teach. In his introduction, Karl Galinsky, Professor of Classics at The University of Texas at Austin, challenges classicists and others who teach about the ancient world to capitalize on the inherent breadth of their disciplines and to regain the central role in the liberal arts curriculum. Through a brief examination of the state of the academy, new teaching approaches, cultural history and the uses of various media, Professor Galinsky sets the framework for the three remaining sections of this volume. To clarify his general comments, Professor Galinsky's introduction is followed by course syllabi illustrating his meaning for the reader through specific examples.

Section II deals with literary approaches to biblical literature and to ancient texts. Kenneth Gros Louis, Professor of Literature and Academic Vice President of the Bloomington Campus at Indiana University, begins this section with a discussion of methodological considerations relating to the Bible as narrative text and with a critical analysis of the Song of Songs. His two articles are followed by bibliographical materials developed during the NEH-funded 1979, Institute for College Teachers held at Indiana University. The bibliographical materials include a syllabus for literary critics dealing with Ancient Mesopotamian Thought and Culture, The Patriarchal Age, The Mosaic Age, The Bible as Literature, and Monarchy in Israel.

Professor Gros Louis's articles are followed by an investigation of the application of semiotics and structuralism to the study of ancient texts. In this article, Professor Daniel Patte of Vanderbilt University examines the ways these fields of research can "contribute to a better understanding of the way in which the Humanities, in general, and the Ancient World, in particular, should be taught in the present cultural situation." Professor Patte provides a clear and concise analysis of structuralism and semiotics and gives concrete examples of their application to undergraduate courses in Biblical Studies and Classics. His notes provide an excellent brief bibliographical aide to those wanting to know more about structuralism, semiotics and their application to scholarship and teaching.

Section II concludes with a biblical scholar's view of the Bible as Literature. In this article, James Ackerman, Professor of Religious Studies at Indiana University, talks about the need to develop an interdisciplinary framework for the study of the Bible. His comments have broad application to the whole field of classical studies and demonstrate the ways a single discipline can, without compromising academic excellence, expand to perspectives not commonly found in narrowly defined courses. Professor Ackerman's article is followed by a bibliography or "Institute Reader" developed after seven years of NEH-sponsored Summer Institutes held at Indiana University.

The third section of this volume was compiled by Gordon Tucker of the Jewish Theological Seminary of America in New York City. This section, an outgrowth of NEH-sponsored Summer Seminars at JTS, probes the place of post-Biblical, Hellenistic Judaism in the study of the Ancient World. Professor Tucker and others at JTS have clearly demonstrated that an understanding of Judaism immediately before and during the early Christian period is important to a full understanding of the development of early Christian thought and the Roman world. Like the previous two sections, this section includes syllabi and bibliographical material which we hope will be useful to scholars seeking to add new material and new life to the courses they teach.

The final section deals with courses in Greek and Roman Civilization and Mythology and contains materials developed by Mark Morford of The Ohio State University. The materials presented were developed for use at Ohio State and are easily adapted to other large institutions. As importantly, the workshops have demonstrated how these materials and approaches can be useful at institutions with as few as one classics course.

The section contains a general descriptive essay prepared by Professor Morford, description and catalogue of individualized materials useful for teaching Roman and Greek Civilization, sample pages from his study guide treating the same subject, and a bibliography of useful texts. Again, we have attempted to blend a brief theoretical framework with a description of practical materials useful for teachers.

Those of us who have worked on this volume and the staff of the NEH Higher Education Regional and National grants program hope that the material will prove stimulating for teachers interested in improving their courses. We also hope that, despite the fact that we offer no panacea, the ideas generated will encourage students to pursue the classics and the study of the ancient world with a new vigor.

THE CHALLENGE OF TEACHING
THE ANCIENT WORLD

Karl Galinsky
The University of Texas

I would like to set the tone for this conference and its published version by striking a note of optimism, of Toynbeean challenge and successful response. We are fortunate to be in fields like classics, biblical studies, and ancient history and religion. These fields are not expendable, but expandable. In contrast to many other disciplines, they have an inherent breadth on which we need to capitalize. They constitute the very basis of the western humanistic tradition, and therefore have wide applications. Besides this inherently broad base, they have the additional advantage of being classics in the sense of being susceptible to different interpretations by different people at different times. This flexibility is not to be confused with Sophistic relativism or rampant modern-day subjectivity, but the study of the ancient world has an inbuilt dynamism which many other fields are lacking.

Compare how much more fortunate we are in this regard than our colleagues in modern language departments where compartmentalization is most acute and the study of literature, for one, still goes by the century clock. Specializations are conveniently arranged by centuries –your 18th century man (or woman) is virtually guilty of arrogant trespass if he or she encroached on New Year's Eve of 1699. Organic laws of literature and culture are thus easily ignored and yield to the aridity of mathematical periodization. We are blessed that we fell on hard times earlier than the modern languages and that we are now dealing with much more than languages and literatures and have become veritable area studies programs.

There is a gap, of course, between this reality in our teaching and the graduate training which most of the practitioners of our discipline have received or are still receiving. Concomitant with the thesis-oriented approach of graduate work there is still a tendency to pigeonhole people as early as possible in their careers, to type them by the title of their dissertation, and to view them with discomfort when they open up new areas of inquiry for themselves. Ironically, of course, we cite the latter activity as one of the most desirable rationales to our students when advocating the need for humanistic components in their curriculum. The resultant discrepancy, more pronounced in other humanistic fields than ours, has not gone unnoticed, as is clear from

Dr. Allen's description in the *Wall Street Journal* of February 2, 1982. There is an increasing recognition, however, which is indicated by the huge number of applications to this Conference, that specialization in research is fine, but outdated in our daily work of teaching where more and more of us need to be generalists. And more than that: there is the realization that continuing education is not simply the preserve of doctors, managers, and engineers; our discipline needs it just as vitally in terms of meeting ongoing challenges. The world does not stand still; the teaching of the ancient world does not either.

The NEH Conference was designed to do something about this need, which is real enough, but I want to define the expectations that can reasonably be placed on the conference and these proceedings. First the negative sort of definition: do not expect that the Conference, the materials, and the essays will immediately solve all your problems, provide instant nuts and bolts, and furnish a *vademecum* for troubled curricula or courses. There is no genie in this bottle, nor are there antiseptically packaged lesson plans that can conveniently be unwrapped back in the classroom. For, to turn to the positive aims, the conference and proceedings are there to provide long-term stimulation about underlying problems and ideas. They represent different ways of looking at things. They furnish a sub-stratum of ideas that can generate different kinds of courses or course units. And yes, the combination of seemingly disparate approaches and subjects may bring home to you the increased realization of the flexible boundaries of our field and the approaches to it. A think-tank excercise, then, with practical applications.

My own bias, carefully honed by a scholarly and temperamental predilection for the Romans and by years of administrative preoccupation with the bottom line, is practical. Before surveying some of the main areas of curricular innovation and recent methodologies, I want to offer a few more general caveats and observations.

The first concerns the limitations placed on the transferability of curricular models from one program to another. While all applicants to the Conference expressed their own special plight with the eloquence normally reserved for academicians pleading for a merit increase, the stark fact is that there is no ideal *locus* where ancient world programs will flourish effortlessly. Concerning the success of the program at The University of Texas, for instance, it should not be assumed that it was the automatic result of the irrigation of the soil of the Southern tradition with oil; more than one-fourth of our 48,000 students are enrolled in the Business School, and the combined enrollment in all the professional schools completely outnumbers that in arts and sciences. Within the Department there are the competing claims of the "service courses," the undergraduate major program, and the graduate program. As in any program, however, these are not drawbacks or "problems," but challenges. All I am saying is that there are different logistics and academic environments and that courses and programs cannot simply be copied, but need to be adapted to each individual setting.

Related to this issue is the fact that the most effective representative of our discipline is the teacher who is sensitive to the idiosyncracies of the academic ecology on his or her campus—one who is attuned to the *genius loci*. It pays to be attentive to the changes in one's academic environment, and that refers not only to the inevitable turnover in administration. More significantly, our students change—in terms of preparation, social outlook, academic interests, etc.—and on our part there needs to be a sense of responsiveness instead of an attempt to impose the same old molds of ten or twenty years ago. While the substance and the goals of our teaching should remain the same, the packaging often needs to change. I am not advocating trendiness, but responsiveness and the chance to make an impact. Academic and curricular leadership may be defined not only as giving to students what they need, and not what they want, but also in making them feel that what they need is what they want. On our campus, e.g., any course called literature in translation will guarantee one a nice small class; if the same reading is integrated into a course called mythology or cultural history, the number of takers increases exponentially. The same is not true of other campuses.

To be effective on their campuses the teachers in our discipline need to do yet more than have this kind of sensitivity; he or she must develop outreach and be a *zoon politikon*. Instead of expecting mankind to pay its cultural debt in the form of their salaries and bemoaning their isolation, teachers of the ancient world can improve their lot substantially by breaking out of this isolation and participating fully in the administrative, political, and committee life of their schools. Contrary to up-front appearances, curricular and budgetary decisions often are not made on the basis of academic virtue or the selfless application of objective educational ideals, but they are often made on the basis of the way of the least resistance. When a department or program is invisible, the resistance it offers can be counted on to be invisible also. In a more constructive spirit, teachers in our fields, especially in one- or two-person programs, need to make contact with colleagues in related disciplines, with students, student newspapers, and all the rest of the campus world. They often are isolated, not because of the wrongly perceived limitations of our field, but because of their failure to establish such contacts. For instance, among the 641 applicants to the NEH Conference there were several from different departments at the same, and often small, colleges or universities, who vouched individually for being the only applicant from that campus. Coming out of the cocoon and getting to know, as a first step, your colleagues in related disciplines is not even entrepeneurism, it is simply a life skill. And keep in mind that the ideal of the teacher with a personal following was the operative model of the universities of late antiquity and that the phrase *zoon politikon* was coined by one of the most effective teachers of all times, when one looks at the result—even if the Persians might not necessarily agree.

In no particular order of priority, let me comment on some of the new approaches and techniques pertinent to courses in our area. After that survey, I will conclude with a few concrete do's and don't's that apply to our teaching situation, regardless of its locale. In keeping with the intent of the Conference, my remarks are not meant to be exhaustive, but simply to highlight and open up some new perspectives.

I. *Computer-Assisted Instruction*

Computer use is by no means the preserve of large universities, but even small campuses often possess surprisingly large resources in this regard. In advocating the utility of this technology, I want to start with the external and political reason; it is often helpful to assuage guilty administrative consciences (there are still a few) by having CAI thrown as a bone to the humanities when the lion's share of computer funds usually goes to the sciences and engineering. Such requests, coming from nontechnical and supposedly just paper-and-pencil fields like the humanities, favorably impress some administrators because they are indicative of a willingness to supplement time-honored teaching methods with some degree of innovation. And if you do not do this now, ten years from now the computer resources on your campus may be solidly allocated to the technical and scientific fields, and your efforts will come too late. Now is the time to get the foot in the door.

Needless to say, the primary rationale for CAI courses is intrinsic and educational and there has to be a clearly defined need that CAI would be able to fill. In classics, terminology courses (the Greek and Latin element in English; medical and scientific terminology) are a good case in point and so are elementary language courses; the drill sessions at the terminals are the equivalent of the old language lab. But there are applications—sometimes just in terms of a few learning units that require extensive memorization—to courses in history, mythology, and art as well. CAI is not naively to be used as a panacea, nor will requests for it legitimatize the unimaginative teacher as a model of innovation, but it is important for teachers in our field to utilize this new resource whenever feasible. Resource persons in classics are Professor Richard Scanlan (University of Illinois), Professor Gerald Erickson (University of Minnesota), Professor Joseph Tebben (Ohio State University), and Professor Lee Pearcy (University of Texas).

II. *Self-Paced Courses*

They are not necessarily linked to CAI, but generally follow the so-called Keller method. Programs of this kind are easier to staff in departments with a relatively large number of faculty or teaching assistants, but they are modifiable for small departments, too. Resource contacts: among larger classics departments, The University of Texas at Austin and Ohio State University; for smaller classics programs, you might want to share information with the University of Idaho and San Diego State University (Edward Warren) and, for koine Greek, Southwest Missouri State University at Springfield, Department of Religious Studies (Robert Hodgson).

III. *Film Courses*

Since most of this introduction is based on my personal experience with one program aspect or another, I might as well put the personal element up front here. It continuously amazes me how quickly one can get a reputation in our field for doing things just a little bit differently; I certainly did not lack for a reputation previously, for better or for worse, but after incorporating films on a regular basis into one of my introductory civilization classes last fall—and that was publicized quite well—I have received a steady stream of inquiries and invitations for speaking engagements on the subject. All this is rather disproportionate to the actual significance of the "innovation," but the genesis of the course is another case example of the combination of idiosyncratic and general principles.

Idiosyncratic: I simply wanted to experiment for no better reason than that I was bored with my "standard" Greek and Roman civilization courses, which already contained a large visual component in the form of slides and even short movies—e.g., Walter Cronkite in "You Are There" on the death of Socrates. Those courses were doing well, but I had taught them year after year.

General: There is just no doubt that most of our students now come from a visually oriented culture. That does not mean illiteracy, a word that is grossly overused by inert faculty members, but for us specifically it means that many of our students come into prolonged (i.e., over two minutes) contact with the world of the Bible, and Greece and Rome, not in Sunday school or high school, but on TV or VCR's through the likes of Ben Hur, The Ten Commandments, The Robe, Cleopatra, Helen of Troy, Steve Reeves's Hercules, etc. Their curiosity is aroused not by reading, but by seeing. This is the elemental form of "being there," as exemplified by Peter Sellers in the movie of the same title; he "likes to watch." Instead of assuming a traditional and actually decreasing model of prior knowledge for our students, we should just sometimes start with where they are and lead them from there to our exalted level of knowledge. The course was basically a recombination of segments from my other courses on Greek and Roman civilization and there was a fair amount of reading and essay tests. True to the title of the course (Film and Reality), the films were often used as a starting point for and foil to the presentation of the historical, social, and cultural issues of a given period. Sometimes the discussion of the films in this context took longer, and sometimes (depending on the merits of the films) it took very little time indeed. It was not a course in film criticism, but it was helpful to demonstrate that cliches and stereotypes were just that and to provide a more solid background knowledge. The films are not expensive to rent (and there is a comprehensive rental guide available on virtually every campus); on our campus the movie theater in the Student Union showed them as part of its regular offerings. Anyone, therefore, and not just the 160 students and auditors (including several museum docents and professional people in Austin) could attend and the venture was very profitable (i.e., for the theater; I wish I had guaranteed the Department a percentage of the gate receipts). There is usually some mechanism on any campus to procure film rentals and to furnish projectionists and equipment. The model here provided for a weekly showing; in other culture courses it might be a useful supplement to show one movie every two or four weeks. I have no apostolic fervor about this type of course format. The main rationale is simply what I said about the students' changing backgrounds.

IV. *Courses in Cultural History*

Again, I am not interested in abstract, conceptual models here, but I would define such courses as emphasizing the interrelation of various factors that make up a given culture: art, literature, social and political history, religion, philosophy, architecture, etc. It is the kind of synoptic course—whether Greek, Near Eastern, or Roman—that transcends the typical limitations of our graduate training.

Few teachers in our field are experts in all these different areas of civilization, and yet this area studies approach is a vital humanistic counterweight to carrying excessive specialization over into our undergraduate teaching. And such courses generally are very successful.

How should they be taught if you typically are well trained in the relevant language and literature, but less so in art, archaeology, or architectural history? One answer is to go the way many inter-disciplinary courses are taught and use team teaching. This is fine, so long as the operative criterion is the cohesiveness of the course, and the students are not left holding a bag of *disiecta fragmenta*. There needs to be a good coordination among the teaching team; if at all possible, everybody involved should sit in on the others' lectures. A bit past its prime, the term "interdisciplinary" still is used extensively for *vita* building, but the equation of interdisciplinary with qualitatively good is a simplistic anachronism. There is nothing wrong, for instance, with a good disciplinary course on Shakespeare, which is infinitely more valuable than something called "Shakespeare and the Human Condition," with a rogues gallery of academic disciplines—anthropology, literature, psychology, classics, etc.—vying to convey extraneous knowledge to illuminate an artificially created background that will remain even murkier than that in Plato's cave. The teaching situation of a cultural history course, then, will simply depend on the availability and personal suitability of good colleagues in related disciplines. When in doubt, do it yourself and simply use those colleagues as resource persons for your own preparation of the lectures and discussions. You will need to personify the area studies approach and you may even write your old graduate school to train its current Ph.D.'s in ancient studies more broadly. My favored, though somewhat sad, example of the long road we sometimes still have to travel involves the selection of three areas of general teaching interest which job applicants using the American Philological Association Placement Service are asked to list near the top of their *vita*. This particular young lady, a Ph.D. from an institution which I will let you guess, bravely listed: (1) Early Minoan Archaeology, (2) Middle Minoan Archaeology, and (3) Late Minoan Archaeology. The need for continuing education in our field was never demonstrated more conclusively.

V. *New Theoretical and Critical Approaches*

What is good is that there has been a great deal of activity in this area (structuralism, semiotics, deconstructionism—although it might be said that there were several people in our field who practiced deconstruction, mostly on their own programs, before the name was invented). What is bad is that, as can be seen from Mr. Allen's observations in the *Wall Street Journal*, this can easily degenerate into the new jargon which, so far from broadening our field, reinforces the tendency endemic to humanistic academe to create new in-groups, with restricted access, within the academic subculture of narcissism, to use Christopher Lasch's term. New theories and new critical approaches should genuinely deepen and enrich our understanding of mythology, the Bible, classical literature, etc. and they need to be more than academic status symbols and esoteric exercises in cerebral acrobatics.

I doubt that many students are turned on by the theorizing of Claude Levy-Strauss, whom they might confuse, at any rate, with the inventor of blue jeans; at the same time, it is important to convey to students the realization that myth is not something cut and dried, but is the subject of continuing intellectual discussion. Knowledge of new theoretical constructs does not relieve us, however, from applying judiciousness and good sense. The healthy American tendency, which is rooted in the pluralism of our society, to be undoctrinaire and unimpressed with ideologies should not be confused, by the European originators of these marvelous constructs and by their apostolic successors, with a lack of sophistication. We should not turn to such systems because we are troubled by the lack of hermeneutics in many fields and subfields of our disciplines, such as Roman literature. To plug into a ready-made system, thus avoiding the critically humanistic task of being sensitive to nuances and making individual judgments, often degenerates into mechanical schematizing that has little to do with intellectual brilliance, originality, or imagination. The bottom line, as Mr. Allen notes, often is a writing style so tedious that it drives off students and the lay public in general.

It should be stressed to students that the study of the ancient world is not a stagnant, timeless repository of well-known evidence and ageless wisdom. A sense of the new is not provided merely by new models of interpretation, but also by the obvious progress of our purely factual knowledge about the ancient world. A few recent examples are the relationship between the ancient Near East and Greek mythology, the excavations at Ebla, work on the Gnostics, and the archaeological discoveries pertaining to the history of early Rome. At the same time, there are some subjects, certainly in Greek and Roman literature, that have been so tortuously belabored that they would benefit immensely from an at least decade-long moratorium on further publication—Greek tragedy and Vergil's *Eclogues*, for example.

We certainly should not be intellectually lazy and not make theories such as structuralism and semiotics part of our repertoire. We should do so in the spirit of the eclectic *homo ludens* and the Sophistic relativist. And we should never lose sight of the fact that such interpretive models are the means to an end and not an end in themselves.

Finally, I have two more items of advice and one desideratum. First, in our teaching of the ancient world it is important to stress the *differences* between their civilization and ours, as well as the similarities. True enough, there is a timeless continuum of humanistic issues and the availability of translations in the modern idiom is more than welcome. Still, the Greeks and Romans were not simply like us. If the Greeks invented democracy, it was not like the democracy we practice today. And they also should be credited with inventing tyranny, oligarchy, ochlocracy, and all the rest. Without proper understanding of the different definition of innovation in ancient times and of the Roman hang-up on the *mos maiorum* in particular the promulgation of the gospel by St. Paul and the Church fathers is obscured by the misapplication of modern values and concepts to antiquity and becomes ahistorical nonsense. The simplistic parallels between the decline of the Roman empire and the supposed decline of our civilization are another case in point, as is, even more centrally, the definition of humanism. My own feeling is that Edith Hamilton would have been greatly shocked if a real ancient Greek had walked in amid all the doilies of a Main Line sitting room.

Secondly, and in connection with the outreach function I mentioned earlier: you must use local resources to the fullest possible extent. That means your local (often non-campus) museum and library and their lecture and film services, local architecture, and the nearest chapter of the Archaeological Institute of America. Just as essential is work with the local and area high schools, and even elementary and junior-high schools.

Now the desideratum. It is the kind of course that would comprehensively deal with the major aspects of the classical influence on American civilization, a course that would document the richness of the classical legacy in American culture—art, architecture, constitution and law, literature, and thought. In connection with the Bicentennial the American Philological Association laudably established a Committee on the Classics and the American Republic, and several lectures and presentations have resulted from it over the years. Figuratively speaking, there have been a lot of trees, branches, stumps, shrubs, and even some deadwood, but there has not been a forest. A fragmented prosopography of apostles of classical learning from Maine to Wyoming in bygone centuries is not suitable for instilling in students a sense of the sweep and vitality of the Greco-Roman tradition in our country. My remarks are not meant to be carping, but simply to point out the fact that there is still much to be done. In keeping with the whole tenor of this essay and the Conference, I would prefer to end not on the note of completion and satisfaction, but of ongoing challenges now and in the years ahead.

o o o

Reprinted from *The Wall Street Journal*, February 2, 1982
James Sloan Allen

The Humanists Are Guilty of Betraying Humanism

The annual gatherings of professional humanists, like the members of the Modern Language Association (MLA) who met in New York recently, have become occasions not just for fraternizing, sharing scholarship and job seeking but for lamentations over the state of the humanities. Classes in the humanities dwindle as students turn to the social and physical sciences; thousands of aspiring humanists scramble for fewer jobs; the proficiency of students in reading, writing and reasoning wanes.

Humanists usually blame their troubles on the hegemony of science and on an economy that measures education only by its "cash value." There is some truth in this. But a little experience among the humanists, attending their conventions, listening to their speeches, reading their books and articles and interviewing job-seekers discloses another cause of their plight: they have betrayed humanism.

The humanists have betrayed humanism by converting education—and most egregiously the teaching of literature—into a pseudo-scientific labor over technical issues set forth in a jargon that baffles common understanding. One does not talk about novels or stories, poems or plays any more; one "decodes" or "deconstructs texts." One does not explore and evaluate an author's thoughts and perceptions for the purpose of strengthening mind and illuminating life; one seeks clues to "performative linguistic acts" for the purpose of achieving "critical enablement." Literature, after all, we are told, is "primarily about language, and not much else."

The infatuation with esoteric questions and cant has turned the MLA convention into a circus of professional hokum, which may be no great loss, but it is also turning humanistic education into a funhouse mirror's image of science comprehensible only to an initiated elite. This is a loss. By rendering the study of literature (as well as history and culture generally) arcane and exclusive the humanists deprive us of the education we most need—an education in mental discipline, intellectual autonomy, moral judgment, emotional response and the like. Worse, they set perverse standards of language and thought that become the norm for ambitious scholars, intimidated educators and unsuspecting students. The result is the proliferation of an ill-education in technical skills, ponderous analysis and pretentious jargon that feeds on self-doubt and intellectual dishonesty.

This conclusion does not rest on casual impressions alone. Several recent studies confirm it. One group of researchers, at the University of Chicago, discovered that the grading pattern of English teachers in a number of colleges and secondary schools consistently favored student papers written in a turgid, intellectually inflated style over those written simply and lucidly, even when both contained the same ideas. Why? Because teachers routinely take as their models of writing and intellect the publications in their professional journals. How can students be expected to think and write intelligibly when their teachers, often unsure of themselves and awed by abstract language, lack the ability or will to teach them how?

A similar failure is evident in the teaching of reading. Base reading scores have been rising lately—after years of decline—but, as many a college teacher could say (and as reported last fall by the Department of Education in its National Assessment of Educational Progress), students read with ever more inactive minds. They draw few inferences from what they read; they see few relations among ideas; they discern few connections between the written word and life experience.

Again, it is easy to blame forces outside academe for this—particularly the video culture that makes a fetish of moving images and a habit of passive response. But blame also belongs to educators who, on the one hand, equate reading all the way through high school with mechanical "skills development" and who, on the other hand, treat books in college as "texts" to be technically deciphered according to abstruse theory.

Rarely are reading, writing, thinking taught with any bearing on the common life any more. How very vulgar that would be: how very unproductive; how very unprofessional. No wonder young people divorce humanistic learning from their life and turn to more practical studies. And no wonder so many aspiring humanists find no teaching jobs; their profession has ceased to serve anyone but the professionals.

Just try, as I have been trying, to find a young Ph.D. capable of teaching courses in writing, "great books," and history in a truly humanistic way. It can hardly be done. Candidates come forward in abundance, but scarcely one with a properly and sufficiently responsive mind. It is enough to convince anyone not already under the sway of The Profession that humanistic education is not so much imperiled by enemies from the outside, such as science, popular culture and vocationalism, as it is by the treason of the humanists themselves.

o o o

SYLLABAI

Fall 1981   TTH 10–30–12   EDB 104
INTRODUCTION TO THE ANCIENT WORLD:
FILM AND REALITY

CC 301 (28370)   CC 342 (28540)
CC 302 (28380)   CC 347 (28550)

Instructor: Karl Galinsky, Professor of Classics
Office Hours: TTH 9–10:30 and by appointment

REQUIRED BOOKS:

H. D. F. Kitto, *The Greeks* (Penguin)
Homer, *The Odyssey*, Transl. by R. Fitzgerald (Anchor)
D. Grene and R. Lattimore, eds., *Sophocles I* (Chicago)
Chester Starr, *The Ancient Romans* (Oxford)
W. Shakespeare, *Julius Caesar* (Pelican)
Suetonius, *The Twelve Caesars*, Transl. by R. Graves (Penguin)
Petronius, *The Satyricon*, Transl. by W. Arrowsmith (Mentor NAL)

LECTURES AND FILMS:

September   1:   Introduction; The Age of Homer
             2:    ULYSSES (with Kirk Douglas)
             3:    Odysseus and the *Odyssey*
                   Reading: Kitto, 44–64; Homer, *Odyssey*, Books 1, 6, 9,
                   10, 11, 22, and 23 (optional: as many books of the
                   Odyssey as you can read)

             8:    Greek Mythology: Its Origins and Functions
             9:    HERCULES (with Steve Reeves)
            10:    The Adaptability of Mythological Heroes
                   Reading: Kitto, 194–204, 7–43

            15:    The Persian Wars
            16:    THE 300 SPARTANS
            17:    Sparta and Athens
                   Reading: Kitto, 109–152

            22:    The Origins and Nature of Greek Tragedy
            23:    OEDIPUS REX (with Tyrone Guthrie)
            24:    The Meaning of Sophocles' *Oedipus*
                   Reading: Sophocles, *Oedipus*

            29:    The Role of Women in Greek Society
            30:    MEDEA (with Maria Callas)

October   1:   Euripides and his *Medea*
                     Reading: Euripides, *Medea* (handout); Kitto, 219–236
               6:    Alexander and his World
               7:    ALEXANDER THE GREAT (with Richard Burton)
               8:    FIRST HOUR EXAM
                     Reading: Kitto, 169–194

               13:   The History and Character of the Romans: an
                     Overview
               14:   A FUNNY THING HAPPENED ON THE WAY TO
                     THE FORUM (with Zero Mostel)
               15:   Roman Comedy and Roman Life
                     Reading: Starr, 9–39; 48–53

               20:   Rulers and Slaves
               21:   °SPARTACUS° (with Kirk Douglas)
               22:   The End of the Republic
                     Reading: Starr 70–85, 115–21

               27:   Julius Caesar: The Man and the Legend
               28:   JULIUS CAESAR (with James Mason)
               29:   From Caesar to Augustus
                     Reading: Shakespeare, *Julius Caesar*; Suetonius, *Julius
                     Caesar*

November   3:   The Augustan Age
               4:    °CLEOPATRA° (with R. Burton and E. Taylor)
               5:    Roman Women
                     Reading: Starr, 86–119; Suetonius, *Augustus*

               10:   Cruelty and Civilization: The Roman Games
               11:   °BEN HUR° (with Charlton Heston)
               12:   Christians and Romans
                     Reading: Starr, 185–94

               17:   SECOND HOUR EXAM
               18:   THE LAST DAYS OF POMPEII
               19:   Life in a Roman Town: Hygiene, Health, and Low
                     Life-Expectancy
                     Reading: Selected Satires of Juvenal (handout); Starr,
                     162–70; Petronius, *Satyricon* 21–38

               24:   The "Mad" Emperors: Tiberius, Caligula, Claudius,
                     and Nero.
                     Reading: Suetonius, *Lives of Caligula and Nero*

December   1:   Petronius and the Question of Roman Decadence
               2:    FELLINI'S SATYRICON
               3:    Decline and Fall—Part I
                     Reading: Petronius, *Satyricon* 38–84 (*Dinner with
                     Trimalchio*)

               8:    Decline and Fall—Part II
               9:    THE FALL OF THE ROMAN EMPIRE

Reading: Starr, 142–49
12:      9 A.M.: *FINAL HOUR EXAMINATION*

FILMS:

All movies will be shown on Wednesdays in the Texas Union Theater. With the exception of the asterisked movies (Spartacus, Ben Hur, and Cleopatra), all movies will be shown twice, i.e., on Wednesday afternoon and Wednesday evening or night. For exact show times, please contact the Texas Union. A season pass for the Classical Civilization Film Series is available during business hours at the Union Theater. It costs $15 and will admit you to all the movies required for this course. Attendance at the weekly screenings is a required part of the course.

READINGS:

Please try to do these in advance of the lectures in which they will be discussed and bring the texts to class. This applies especially to the readings in the ancient authors and Shakespeare.

EXAMS:

There will be three 75-minute exams, consisting of both essays and "objective" questions (with some latitude of choice). The tests will be on each third of the course and there will be optional review sessions before each exam.

PAPERS:

Papers are optional and for extra credit. The topic needs to be approved by me; there are a variety of good topics and we have some bibliographical aids even on the films. Students who have taken one or two of my CC courses are required to write a paper for this course.

OTHER EVENTS:

A major art exhibit, entitled "Caesars and Citizens," will be on display from September 17 to December 6 on the second floor of the Humanities Research Center. Also to be found there is a large collection of Greek and Roman plaster casts, Greek vases, and smaller artifacts. *I, CLAUDIUS*, the thirteen-part BBC production, will be shown September 27 through December 6 on Thursdays at noon and Sundays at 2 P.M. in the HRC. This is free and open to the public, as are several gallery talks and lectures connected with "Caesars and Citizens." Check the *Texan* for details.

DEPARTMENT OF CLASSICS   FALL 1981

SELF-PACED LATIN 506
Unique No. 28980
GUIDELINES FOR STUDENTS

TEXTBOOK: F. M. Wheelock, *Latin: An Introductory Course Based on Ancient Authors*, Barnes & Noble College Outline Series (paperback); plus individual study units available in the Self-Paced Latin Center.

SELF-PACED LATIN CENTER: Waggener Hall 14, open Monday–Friday, 10–3 and Monday–Thursday 7–9 p.m. *No tests may be begun after 2:30 p.m. or 8:30 p.m.*

COURSE COORDINATOR: Karl Galinsky, WAG 123-B; Assistant, Mark Damen, WAG 119.

°° FORMAT °°

There are 28 units to this course. You will pick up each unit at the Self-Paced Latin Center and complete the exercises. Then return to the Self-Paced Latin Center, discuss the materials and any questions with the assistant on duty, and, if you are sufficiently prepared, take a readiness test on the unit. We will grade the test at once and discuss it with you. If you pass the readiness test with a score of less than 80, you will restudy the materials and then take another readiness test at your convenience. There is a maximum of three readiness tests for each unit; if you receive less than 80 even the third time around, you will be allowed to proceed so long as your receive a passing grade (60 or more). That, however, is the exception; with a reasonable effort, you should receive 80 or more points on each unit. The final grade will be the average of your best readiness test scores on 28 units. *THERE WILL BE NO INCOMPLETES* given for this course; *you must complete all the work by December 11, or drop the course by October 23.*

Units need to be completed by certain deadlines. These deadlines are:

Sept.	17	Unit	5
Oct.	5	Unit	10
Oct.	21	Unit	15
Nov.	5	Unit	20
Nov.	24	Unit	25
Dec.	11	Unit	28

One point will be subtracted from the final grade for each day of late completion of these units.

Several tapes are available in the Tape Checkout Library (Batts 225) of materials from Wheelock and the Study Units. The numbers of the tapes are LT-0-1 and LT-0-2.

VIVAT LINGUA LATINA! VIVANT STUDIOSI!

CLASSICAL CIVILIZATION
301 (00110) / 342 (00285)

INTRODUCTION TO THE ANCIENT WORLD /
THE CULTURAL HISTORY OF GREECE

Fall Semester 1978

TTH 10:30–12 HRC 4.252

Instructor: G. K. Galinsky, Professor of Classics
Office Hours: T 1:30–3, W 8:15–9:45

REQUIRED TEXTS:

Homer, Odyssey, trans. by Robert Fitzgerald (Anchor paperback)
Aeschylus I, Sophocles I, Euripides V (all University of Chicago paperbacks)
Plato: any edition containing the *Republic* and the *Apology* (e.g., Mentor paperback 302)
A. R. Burn, *The Pelican History of Greece* (Penguin paperback A 792)

LECTURES AND READINGS:

Sept.	5:	Aims and Methods of the Course; Modern Views on Greece
Sept.	7:	Minoans and Myceneans *Reading:* Burn 26–30, 35–48; *Odyssey,* Books 1, 5.1–227, 6, 9.
Sept.	12:	Troy and Homer
Sept.	14:	The *Odyssey* and its hero *Reading: Odyssey,* Books 10, 11, 13, 22, 23 (optional: 7, 17, 18, and all the rest).
Sept.	19:	Greek Colonization; cultural life in early Greece
Sept.	21:	Early Greek art and architecture *Reading:* Handouts on Greek Lyric Poetry, Burn 83–110
Sept.	26:	Sparta and the Spartan myth
Sept.	28:	Athens to the Persian Wars *Reading:* Burn, 112–25, 146–62, 167–92.
Oct.	3:	The origins of tragedy; the Greek theater
Oct.	5:	Aeschylus' *Oresteia*
Oct.	10:	HOUR EXAMINATION
Oct.	12:	Apollo, Delphi, and the Delphic Oracle *Reading:* Aeschylus, *Oresteia*
Oct.	17:	Eleusis and the Eleusinian Mysteries
Oct.	19:	Athens in the 5th century: art and monuments *Reading:* Burn, 213–57.
Oct.	24:	Sophocles and Oedipus
Oct.	26:	Oedipus at Colonus. *Reading:* Sophocles, *Oedipus the King, Oedipus at Colonus.*
Oct.	31:	Classical sculpture
Nov.	2:	HOUR EXAMINATION
Nov.	7:	Early Greek Philosophy
Nov.	9:	The sophists and Euripides *Reading:* Euripides, *Orestes;* Burn, 126–45.
Nov.	14:	Socrates; Socrates' trial, as narrated by Walter Cronkite (film)

Nov.	16:	Plato and his ideal state *Reading:* Plato, *Apology of Socrates*; Plato, *Republic*, Books 5, 7, 10.
Nov.	21:	Another view of the 5th century—Thucydides *Reading:* Handout on Thucydides
Nov.	28:	The role of women in Greece
Nov.	30:	Alexander the Great *Reading:* To be arranged
Dec.	5:	Hellenistic civilization—Part I
Dec.	7:	Hellenistic civilization—Part II *Reading:* Burn, 326–62
Dec.	12:	Dionysus triumphant: the *Bacchae* *Reading:* Euripides, *Bacchae*.
Dec.	16:	FINAL HOUR EXAMINATION (room to be announced)

TESTS will comprise three hour exams, consisting of both essays and "objective" questions (with some latitude of choice). The tests will be on the material covered since the previous test.° The *READINGS* are a vital part of this course and there may be a few, usually announced *QUIZZES* of 5 to 10 minutes in length on the contents of the reading assignments. It is essential that you read the assignments, especially from Greek literature—Homer, Aeschylus, etc.—BEFORE they are discussed in class. *OPTIONAL PAPERS* for extra credit are welcome. They cannot, however, be used as a substitute for a bad exam and you must see the instructor for approval of the topic. The choice of the topic is yours.

°There will be optional review sessions before each exam.

DEPARTMENT OF CLASSICS   SPRING 1981

Instructor:	Karl Galinsky	Classical Civilization 302/347
	Professor of Classics	Unique Numbers: 27690/27855
Office Hours:	TTH 9–10:30	TTH 10:30–12 noon
Office:	Waggener Hall 123-B	WEL 2246

INTRODUCTION TO THE ANCIENT WORLD:
ROME AND EARLY CHRISTIANITY /
THE CULTURAL HISTORY OF ROME

REQUIRED TEXTS:

L. P. Wilkinson, *The Roman Experience* (Knopf paperback)
Plutarch, *Lives of the Noble Romans* (handouts)
Terence, *The Brothers*, transl. by F. O. Copley (handout)
Vergil, *The Aeneid*, transl. by C. Day Lewis (Anchor paperback A20)
Suetonius, *The Twelve Caesars*, transl. by Robert Graves (Penguin L72)
Seneca, *Thyestes*, transl. by Moses Hadas (Bobbs-Merrill paperback)
Gore Vidal, *Julian* (Signet paperback Q2563)

LECTURES AND READINGS:

Jan. 20:   Aims and Methods of the Course; Sources and
                Approaches
Jan. 22:   Etruscan Civilization - Part 1
                Reading: Wilkinson 5–15; Plutarch, *Romulus.*
                Optional Reading: D. H. Lawrence, Etruscan Places
                11–12, 65–102, 111–33 (on reserve in Classics Library,
                WAG 1).
Jan. 27:   Etruscan Civ. - Part 2; Rome's Etruscan heritage
Jan. 29:   Rome to the Punic Wars
                Reading: Plutarch, *Numa Pompilius*; *Wilkinson 25–
                32.*
Feb.   3:   Grecizing Innovators vs. Roman Conservatives: The
                Shaping of Roman Culture
Feb.   5:   The old vs. the new in Roman religion; the Villa of
                Mysteries at Pompeii
                Reading: Plutarch, *Marcus Cato*; Wilkinson 19–25,
                33–47.
Feb. 10:   Greek vs. Roman in Pompeian Painting
Feb. 12:   Greek and Roman Elements in Comedy
                Reading: Wilkinson, 51–66; Terence, *The Brothers*
Feb. 17:   The Age of Reform: The Gracchi
                Reading: Wilkinson 71–84

Feb. 19:   FIRST HOUR EXAMINATION

Feb. 24:   The Collapse of the Republic
Feb. 26:   Catullus' Poetry
                Reading: Suetonius, *Life of Caesar*; Catullus (handout)
Mar.   3.   From Caesar to Augustus
Mar.   5:   The Augustan Program: Vergil's *Aeneid* - Part I
                Reading: Aeneid 1, 2, 4, 6–12
Mar. 10·   Vergil's *Aeneid* - Part 2
Mar. 12:   Augustan Art and Monuments
                Reading: Suetonius, *Life of Augustus*; Wilkinson 95–
                107.
Mar. 24:   Roman women: their status, habits, social role, etc.
Mar. 26:   Stoics and Epicureans
                Reading: Wilkinson 111–33.
Mar. 31:   From Tiberius to Nero
                Reading: Suetonius, *Life of Nero.*

April 2:   SECOND HOUR EXAMINATION

A syllabus for the final part of the course will be distributed later. The focus
will be on the interaction and conflict between early Christianity and the
classical tradition, as exemplified by Constantine and Julian the Apostate, and
on the fall of the Roman Empire.

Policy on exams, etc.: There will be three 75 minute examinations, including
the final. They will be non-comprehensive, i.e., they will be on the materials
covered since the previous exam. The format will comprise both objective and
essay questions, with some choice in either. Each exam will count for one-third

of the final grade, though slightly more weight may be given to markedly improved exams in the computation of the final grade. Generally, there will be no make-up of exams except under particularly stringent and well-documented circumstances. There will be optional review sessions before each exam.

Optional papers (8-9 pages double-spaced) are encouraged and will count for extra credit. They will not exempt you, however, from satisfactory performance on the exams. The choice of topic is yours, but needs to be approved by the instructor.

CLASSICAL CIVILIZATION 303/352 K:
Mythology and Art.

W. R. Nethercut   117 Waggener Hall   T, Th. 10:30-NOON

FALL TERM 1981

September   1:   Pre-History: the Neolithic and early Bronze Ages: the Myths of Narcissus, Hyacinth, and Cypress (*Cyparissos*). READ *Mayerson*: pp. 222–25 and 138–40.

3:    Crete, Europa, the Minotaur. READ *Mayerson*: p. 16 (OVID) and pp. 316–22.

8:    Atlantis: Crete and Thera (San Torini).

10:    Introduction to the Trojan War. READ *Mayerson*: pp. 375–97.

15:    The *Illiad* of Homer. The Fall of Troy. READ *Mayerson*: pp. 397–418.

17:    Homer and Hesiod. Collections, catalogues, summaries. The vocabulary of early Greek. Non-literate ("oral") and literate psychology. READ *Mayerson*, pp. 2–3.

22:    Creation Myths. Cronus (Saturn) and Uranus, the birth of Aphrodite (Venus); monsters: Gorgons (Medusa) and the Cyclops (Polyphemus), Typhoeus. THE ORDER OF ZEUS. READ *Mayerson*, pp. 19–87.

24:    A contrast of the landscapes and mythologies of Greece and Egypt.

29:    FIRST HOUR EXAMINATION

October   1:   THE GODS. Hera and the Earth. Zeus. READ *Mayerson*, pp. 88–98.

6:    Poseidon (Neptune), Demeter and Persephone (Proserpina).

READ *Mayerson*, pp. 98–114.

8:    Apollo.
      READ *Mayerson*, pp. 117–49.

13:   Artemis (Diana).
      READ *Mayerson*, pp. 150–68.

15:   Athena and Hephaistos (Minerva and Vulcan); Ares
      and Aphrodite (Mars and Venus).
      READ *Mayerson*, pp. 179–209.

20:   Hermes and the Underworld (Mercury).
      READ *Mayerson*, pp. 210–47.

22:   Dionysus (Bacchus) and Mystery Religions.
      READ *Mayerson*, pp. 248–79.

27:   SECOND HOUR EXAMINATION

October   29:   HEROES: Check Bibliography of Anthropological and
                Psycho-analytical approaches to Mythology, p. 458
                Freud, Jung, Campbell. THE STORY OF ACHILLES,
                PERSEUS pp. 280–98.

3:    Homer's story of Odysseus.
      READ *Mayerson*, pp. 436–38.

5:    Heracles.
      READ *Mayerson*, pp. 298–316.

10:   Theseus.
      READ *Mayerson*, pp. 358–74.

12:   Thebes and Oedipus.
      READ *Mayerson*, pp. 322–42.

17:   Jason and the Argonauts.
      READ *Mayerson*, pp. 342–58.

19:   Roman Vergil and the story of Aeneas.
      READ *Mayerson*, pp. 459–81.

24:   Greek Vase Painting: Geometric, Black Figure, Red
      Figure, Polychromatic. The Rise of the Individual.

CC 303/352M   Fall 1981
Myth and Magic in Antiquity   MWF 9–10:00

Instructor: Teri Marsh   Hours: MWF 10–11:00 and
Office: Wag 107   by appointment

This course is designed as an introduction to the study of myth and magic.
The first part of the course will focus on the social and psychological functions of myths in general and of magical *mythoi* in particular. Since the

primary sources for classical mythology are literary, the literary "intentions" of the authors will not be ignored. The second part of the course will be more concerned with the actual practice of magic in Antiquity and elsewhere. We will examine the corpus of Greek and Roman literary and non-literary evidence and cross cultural anthropological evidence to determine the following: (1) the attributes of magical activity; (2) the nature of magical thinking; and (3) the socio-political and psychological motives for and functions of magic. Finally, the ways in which particular cultural conditions affect the practice of magic (e.g., by transforming it into a form of seduction) will be examined through an analysis of three very different historical periods in Antiquity.

Written work will consist of three hour exams (the last of them given during the final exam period) and an optional paper. Each exam will count for 30% of your grade. The paper will allow you to increase your grade by a maximum of 5 points. The remaining 10% of your grade will be determined by your attendance.

Texts

Fitzgerald (ed.), Homer, *The Odyssey*
Sophocles, *Sophocles II*
Euripides, *Euripides I*
Apuleius, *The Golden Ass*
Seneca, *The Medea*
Freud, *Totem and Taboo*
°°° Leach, *Culture & Communication* (optional)

Assignments (subject to change)

9/31	Introduction: Myth and Magic	_____
10/2	Myth: Definition and Functions I	*Erga*, 42–105, *Th.* 510–617 (a handout)
10/4	Functions of Myth II	Handout: The Theban Cycle
10/9	Myth, Fiction, and Truth	Handout: The House of Atreus
10/11	Magical Mythoi in Greece: A Historical Survey	_____
10/14	Perseus and the Phallic Mother	Handout: Perseus and Andromache
10/16	Magic & the Hero II: Odysseus	*Odyssey* 1, 4, 12 up thru p. 216
10/18	The hero & the witch	*Od.* Book 10
10/21	The centaur's magical charm	Sophocles, *Women of Trakhis*
10/23	Magic and the Heroine I: The "Other"	"
10/25	Magic and the Heroine II: Victims and Victimizers	Euripides' *Medea*
9/28	Women & Magic in Mythology	_____
9/30	Magical *Mythoi* in Rome A Historical Survey	
10/2	The Evil Witch	Seneca's *Medea*

10/5	Just a Good Story	The Golden Ass: to be assg. (_____)
10/7	EXAM I: NO MAKEUPS	
10/9	Literature & Anthropol- ogy	Handout: Theok. *Idyll* II
10/12	The Papyri: a survey of sources	Handout: Magical Papyri
10/14	Drugs & Potions: The "in- between	Review: Helen's drug; centaur's drug; Medea's drug. Handout: Magical Drugs & Amulets
10/16	The Evil Eye	Handout: the eyes in magic, seduction, and animal behavior.
10/19	Symbolic Implements	Handout: Magical and commu- nicative implements/review *Od.* 10.
10/21	Spells, Symbolic Behavior & Ritual	Od. pp. 364–68—the scar; Handout: the rain dance and the eating of the gods.
10/23	The attributes of magic: magic and communic.	review date
10/26	Magical Thinking I: The Mythic Mind	_____/attend class!
10/28	The Mythic Mind.	begin reading Freud, chapt. II
10/30	Pollution, Contagion & the Taboo	Freud, Chapt. II
11/2	"	
11/4	The Omnipotence of Thoughts	Freud, chapt. III
11/6	The psychological func- tions of and motives for magic.	Handout: Desire and the desire to repeat
11/9	Socio-political functions of and motives for magical practices.	_____
11/11	Exam II. no makeups!	
11/13	Magic or Seduction: An operational Theory	review Papyri
CASE STUDIES		
11/16	The archaic age: Animism, the gods, and nature	handouts
11/18	Archaic age: the mind, the body and language	handouts
11/20	The Classical age: the emergence of *logoi* and *techne*	handouts
11/23	The Classical Age II	handouts
11/25	The Classical Age III	handouts
11/30	Magic and Superstition in Rome	handouts
12/2	"	
12/4	The Persistence of Magic	
12/7	Concluding Remarks	

12/9   Review: How to Cast a
            Spell!

CC 303 / 352 : Classical Mythology   The University of Texas at
                                            Austin
E. D. Francis   WAG 14B / 471–5742
                                            Office Hours : MWF 12–1

SYLLABUS

January 14th: The Riddle of the Sphinx

            Morford and Lenardon (abbreviated M & L), "Introduc-
            tion," 1–17; Ch. 3, "The Twelve Olympians," 59–72; for
            the myth of Pelops, see pp. 300 and 303.

See Policy Statement for a list of course texts; note that all readings from
Rose's *Handbook* are optional and that assignments from G. S. Kirk's
Nature of Greek Myths are only required of those students registered
for Upper Division credit, that is, students enrolled in CC 352.

NOTE that readings listed under the title of each lecture are assigned
FOR THE NEXT CLASS MEETING. The pages I have just cited from
Morford and Lenardon therefore represent the preparation for
WEDNESDAY'S class.

January 16th: The Myths of Ancient Greece: an Introduction

            (for CC 352 students) Kirk, Ch. 1, 13–29; (for all students)
            M & L, Ch. 19, "Perseus and the Legends of Argos," 341–
            52; Aeschylus, *Prometheus Bound* lines 640–886, espe-
            cially 640–86 and 822–77 (in *Greek Tragedies I*, pp. 88–
            97; brief passages from Herodotus, Bacchylides, and Ovid
            to be handed out in Wednesday's class.
            (optional) Rose, 271–72

January 18th: Greek Mytholoolgy and the Near East I: Legends of Argos and
            the Myth of Io
                                        Simonides' "Danae" (handout)
            Kirk, 147–50
            Rose, 272–74

January 21st: Greek Mythology and the Near East II. Perseus and the
            Beauty of the Medusa
            M & L 286–89; Meschus' *Rape of Europa* (handout) Rose,
            182–86

January 23rd: Greek Mythology and the Near East III: Europa, Minos,
            Cadmus, from Asia to Europe
            M & L, Ch. 12, "Demeter and the Eleusinian Mysteries,"
            218–37; the Homeric *Hymn to Demeter* (handout) and
            notes on Homeric Hymns, Demeter, and Mysteries (hand-
            out)

Kirk, 95–112; 249–53
(optional) Callimachus' *Hymn to Demeter* (3rd century B.C.; handout)

January 25th: Myth and Ritual: Demeter and Eleusis
M & L, Ch. 7, "Aphrodite and Eros," 105–32; the Homeric *Hymn to Aphrodite* (handout), and selections from Hesiod and Rilke on the Birth of Aphrodite (handout)

January 28th: The Cult of Love: Divine Aphrodite
M & L, Ch. 17, "The Trojan Saga," 306–27; Ch. 18, "The Returns," 328–40; Homer's *Odyssey* 1–4; Rose, 243–48

January 30th: Homer's ODYSSEY: Telemachus, Fighting at a Distance
Odyssey 5–8; G. Dimock, "The Name of Odysseus" (handout)

February 1st: Homer's ODYSSEY 5–8: From Ogygia to Skherie
Odyssey 9–12

February 4th: Homer's ODYSSEY 9–12 Part I: "I am Odysseus, the man of resource and sacker of cities"
Odyssey 9–12 reviewed

February 6th.   Homer's ODYSSEY 9–12 Part II: Underworld and Otherworlds
Odyssey 13–16; John Chadwick, "Homer the Psueudo-Historian" (handout)

February 8th: Homer's ODYSSEY 13–16: Return to Ithaka
Odyssey 17–20

February 11th: Homer's ODYSSEY 17–20: The Beggar, the Suitors and the Seer
Odyssey 21–24

February 15th: FIRST HOUR EXAMINATION
M & L, Ch. 1, "Myths of Creation," 23–35; handouts of American-Indian creation myths and *Silmarillion*; Kirk, Ch. 6, 113–44

February 18th: The Creation of the Universe
Hesiod, *Theogony* lines 1–506 (handout); Rose, Ch. 2, 17–42; Kirk, Ch. 6 (review)

February 20th: The Making of Gods and Men
M & L, Ch. 2, "Zeus' Rise to Power," 36–58; Ch. 5, "Poseidon, Sea Deities, Group Divinities, and Monsters," 91–97; Hesiod, *Theogony* lines 507 to end (handout)

February 22nd: Zeus' Rise to Power
Aeschylus *Prometheus Bound* (in *Greek Tragedies I*, 62–105); Kirk, Ch. 5, 95–112 (review); Rose, Ch. 3, 43–77

February 25th: Prometheus defies Tyranny
                M & L, Ch. 17, 306–27 (review); Rose, Ch. 8 Pt. 2, 230–43

February 27th: Homer's ILIAD: an Introduction to the Trojan War
                Iliad 1–5 (omitting the Catalogue of Ships in Book 2)

February 29th: Homer's ILIAD 1–5: The Wrath of Achilles and the Limita-
                tion of Mortality
                Iliad 6–10; Kirk, 150–52 (Bellerophon); Rose, 270–71 (Bel-
                lerophon) and 257–59 (Meleager)

March 3rd: Homer's ILIAD 6–10: The Will of Zeus
                Iliad 11–15

March 5th: Homer's ILIAD 11–15: The Will of Hera
                Iliad 16–20

March 7th: Homer's ILIAD 16–20: The Death of Patroclus and the
                Arming of Achilles
                Iliad; M & L, Ch. 4, "Anthropomorphism and Greek
                Humanism," 73–90

SPRING VACATION

March 17th: Gods and Men in Homer
                Iliad 21–24

March 19th   Homer's ILIAD 21–24: The Will of Achilles and the Fall of
                Troy

March 21st: SECOND HOUR EXAMINATION
                M & L, Ch. 10, "Hermes," 169–85; Ch. 13, "Views of the
                Afterlife, the Realm of Hades," 238–69; selected texts
                from ancient authors (handout); Rose, Ch. 4, 78–101, 257
                (Ixion), Sisyphus, 270–71, 294

March 24th: Greek concepts of Death and Afterlife
                M & L, Ch. 18, "The Returns," 328–40 (review); Ch. 16,
                "The Mycenaean Saga," 300–305; Pindar, *First Olympian
                Ode*

March 26th: Mycenaean Legends I: The Feast of Tantalus and the House
                of Atreus
                Aeschylus, *Agamemnon* (in *Greek Tragedies I*, 2–60);
                Kirk, 165–67 (Agamemnon)

March 28th: Mycenaean Legends II: The Homecoming of Agamemnon
                M & L, 186–211; The Homeric *Hymn to Dionysus* (hand-
                out); Euripides, *Bacchae*; Pindar, *Third Pythian Ode*
                (handout); Rose, Ch. 6, 134–64

March 31st: Theban Legends I: The Return of the Native: Dionysus and
                Apollo
                M & L, Ch. 15. "The Theban Saga," 283–99; Sophocles,
                Oedipus the King (in *Greek Tragedies I*, 108–76);

Callimachus *Fifth Hymn: The Bath of Pallas* (handout);
Kirk, 156–60 (Cadmus), 163–65 (Oedipus), Ch. 4, 69–91;
Rose, 186–89, 195–96

April 2nd: Theban Legends II: Blindness and Insight
Aeschylus, *Seven Against Thebes* (handout); Kirk, Ch. 1
and 2, 13–37 (review); Rose, 189–93

April 4th: Theban Legends III: The Sons of Oedipus
Sophocles, *Antigone* (in *Greek Tragedies I*, 179–228);
Rose, 193–95

April 7th: Theban Legends IV: Antigone and the Nature of Law
M & L, Ch. 22, "The Argonauts," 399–412; Pindar,
Fourth Pythian Ode (handout); Apollonius of Rhodes, *The
Voyage of Argo* (selections; handout); Kirk, 160–63
(Jason); Ch. 5, 95–112 (review)

April 9th: The Argonauts: Journey to Colchis and the Golden Fleece
Euripides, *Medea* (handout); M & L, Ch. 9, "Apollo,"
144–68; Rose, 198–205, 292

April 11th: Jason and Medea
M & L, Ch. 6, "Athena," 98–104; Ch. 21, "Theseus and
the Legends of Attica and Crete," 357–73; Bacchylides,
Dithyrambs 17 and 18 (handout); Catullus 64 (selections;
handout); Kirk, 152–56

April 14th: Athenian Legends: The Kings of Attica and the Coming of
Theseus
M & L, Ch. 8, "Artemis," 133–43; Euripides, *Hippolytus*
(in *Greek Tragedies I*, 231–91); Theocritus, *Idyll* 1 (handout); Rose, 261–69, 102–33

April 16th: Hippolytus and the Perils of Chastity
M & L, Ch. 20, "Herakles," 353–75; Bacchylides, *Fifth
Ode* (handout); *Iliad* 19 (The ATE of Zeus, review); Kirk,
Ch. 8 and 9, 176–219; Rose, 205–19

April 18th: Herakles: Birth, Madness, and Toil
Theocritus, *Idyll* 13 (handout)

April 21st: The Glory of Hera
Odyssey 9 (The Cyclops revisited); Euripides, *Cyclops*
(handout); Theocritus *Idylls* 6 and 11 (handout)

April 23rd: The Cyclops Theme: From Brute to Blighted Lover
M & L, Ch. 14, "Orpheus and Orphism," 270–79; M & L,
213–17 (Narcissus and Echo), and selections from Virgil,
Ovid, and Rilke (handout); Rose, 254–55, 295–96

April 25th: Orpheus and Eurydice and other Antique Lovers
Apuleius, *Amor and Psyche* (handout); M & L, Ch. 24,
"Roman Mythology," 431–61; Kirk, Ch. 3, 38–68; Ch. 10
and 12, 224–53, 276–303; Rose, 286–88

April 28th: Amor and Psyche
                 M & L, Ch. 24 (review); Kirk, Ch. 11, 254–75

April 31st: The Cult of Isis
                 M & L, Ch. 25, "The Survival of Classical Mythology,"
                 462–81; E. D. Francis, "Bull-Slaying at Manchester"
                 (handout)

May 2nd: The Rise and Fall of Roman Mithras

TO STUDENTS IN CC 353: You may wish to read the assigned chapters
from Kirk's *Nature of Greek Myths* in an order different from the one I have
suggested: I have simply tried to space these reading assignments in a man-
ageable fashion, concentrating them towards the end of the course since you
will be addressing an essay question on the Final Examination derived from
this book.

POLICY STATEMENT

I.   Course Texts:

     A.   Required for all students:

                      M. Morford and R. Lenardon, *Classical Mythology* (2nd
                      edition); D. Grene and R. Lattimore (editors), *Greek
                      Tragedies, Volume I*; Texts of Homer's ILIAD and
                      ODYSSEY: Robert Fitzgerald's translations are available
                      in the Coop, but if you already own another translation
                      you are not required to buy Fitzgerald's. I shall, however,
                      quote from Fitzgerald's version in class.

     B.   Required for students registered for Upper Division credit
                      (CC 352); optional for Lower Division students (CC 303):

                      G. S. Kirk, *The Nature of Greek Myths*, Penguin A1783

     C.   Optional for all students:

                      H. J. Rose, *A Handbook of Greek Mythology*. Morford
                      and Lenardon's text is not an especially rewarding one,
                      though its simplicity commends it for use in so general a
                      course as this. For students who are seriously intrested in a
                      more detailed account of the evidence I suggest Rose's
                      useful handbook.

ALL THESE TEXTS ARE AVAILABLE IN THE UNIVERSITY COOP

II.   Course Requirements:

     A.   *Examinations*: Three hour examinations will be set, one
                      after approximately each third of the course. The third
                      examination will be non-comprehensive (i.e., you are
                      responsible only for the last third of the course after
                      March 21st) and will be set at the time advertised for the
                      Final. No make-ups, except for those exceptions provided

for in the University's *General Information Handbook*. In any case, only one make-up will be allowed and will not be administered until Finals Week.

B.   *Term Papers*: Students enrolled in CC 352 are required to submit ONE term paper of no less than 8 pages no later than Noon, May 2nd. Students enrolled in CC 303 (Lower Division) are not required to submit any work beyond the three exams, but any student may also offer a term paper for extra credit. The effect of this extra credit paper upon a Lower Division student's grade will be as follows: if the grade for the paper is one letter grade higher than the course grade based on examinations, the final grade will be raised to that higher grade. Otherwise the grade based on performance in the examinations will stand.

I shall circulate guidelines and suggestions regarding paper topics, etc. following the first hour examination.

C.   *Reading Assignments for Class*: my lectures are based on the assumption that all students will have completed the reading assignments from Morford and Lenardon and the Greek texts BEFORE COMING TO CLASS. The lectures will only be concerned with interpreting the material you have read; I do not often intend to spend class time merely rehearsing the basic story.

III. UPPER AND LOWER DIVISION and the OPTION OF PASS/FAIL

A.   The ONLY differences between the requirements for CC 303 (Lower Division) and CC 352 (Upper Division) are as follows:

Students enrolled for Upper Division credit are required
(a) to present a term paper; and
(b) to answer AN ADDITIONAL ESSAY QUESTION (from a choice of three) on the last examination which will be derived from G. S. Kirk's *Nature of Greek Myths*

B.   The mean grade in this course over the last three years has been fairly high (a mid to low B). IF, HOWEVER, ANY STUDENT IS UNDULY ANXIOUS ABOUT THEIR GRADE, then PLEASE CONSIDER CHANGING YOUR REGISTRATION IN THE COURSE TO PASS/FAIL. It really makes a lot of sense if you are apprehensive about this voyage into a strange land.

IV.   GRADING: Grades for this course will be assessed on the following basis:

CC 303 (Lower Division): an equal third of the final grade will be assigned to each of the three examinations. Remember that you are entitled to apply for extra credit on the basis of submitting an optional term-paper (see II B, above).

CC 352 (Upper Division): an equal 25% of the final grade will be assigned to each of the three examinations and the term-paper.

V.　　HANDOUTS: You will be receiving handouts (lecture outlines, etc.) in each class. I recommend that you buy a fairly sizeable FOLDER so that you can keep these papers in order. Believe me, from past experience, I know that it will be worth the small investment involved.

CLASSICS　　　　　　　　　　　　　　　　　　　　　FALL 1981

CC 306/336:　　LATIN & GREEK ELEMENT IN ENGLISH

Unique No.:　　See Course Schedule

Instructor:	G. Morgan	Parker	Hitt	Armstrong
Time:	MWF 10–11	TTH 9–10:30	MWF 10–11	MWF 1–2
Place:	WAG 201	GAR 313	BEB 261	BEB 251

This course provides a systematic approach to vocabulary building based upon Latin and Greek roots, prefixes, suffixes, and other combining forms. Deals directly with hundreds of common but frequently misunderstood, misused and otherwise difficult words encountered daily. Attention also given to common Latin phrases and quotations found in all disciplines and professions. The history of many colorful and pithy words will be explored. The direction of the course will be general and the needs of students with varied backgrounds and interests will receive prime consideration.

Homework includes a careful study of the textbook, along with completion of assignments contained in the text, or in handouts. There will be a short project, optional for CC 306, but required for CC 336. Class participation is expected, based on homework assignments and discussions. There will be two quizzes and two exams, and a comprehensive final which counts 25%.

There are no prerequisites. This course counts towards fulfilling elective or Area D requirements.

TEXT

Donald M. Ayers, *English Words from Greek and Latin Elements* (1974), University of Arizona Press

CLASSICS　　　　　　　　　　　　　　　　　　　　　FALL 1981

CC 306M/336M:　　MEDICAL AND SCIENTIFIC TERMINOLOGY

Unique No.:　　See Course Schedule

Instructor:	Lee Pearcy
Time:	TTH 12–1:30
Place:	ECJ 1.202

This course provides an introduction to medical and scientific terminology—to what words mean, how they are made, and how to make them. Students will not only learn the meaning of many hundreds of medical and scientific terms, but they will also learn how to analyze an unfamiliar word and discover its meaning without using a medical dictionary, and how to form new words for new concepts. CC 306M/336M will be taught with computer-assisted instruction. Students will meet with the instructor as a class for 1-1/2 hours per week for lectures, discussion, and examinations. Each student will also be expected to complete at least two computer-assisted lessons each week. Terminals will be available in Waggener Hall, and students will be able, within broad limits, to set their own pace for completion of the course. The CAI programs have been designed to be easy to run.

Students registered for upper division credit (336M) must complete a special project, usually a short essay. All students must complete 26 computer-assisted lessons. There will be three examinations and a final examination. For students in CC 306M, exams count 60%, the final exam 40%. For students in CC 336M, exams count 50%, and project 20%, and final exam 30%.

There are no prerequisites. No background in Latin, Greek, or computer science required. Course counts toward Area "D" or elective requirements.

TEXTS

O. E. Nybakken, *Greek and Latin in Scientific Terminology*
T. Brunner & L. Berkowitz, *The Elements of Scientific and Specialized Terminology* (workbook)

GENERAL INFORMATION

OFFICE HOURS: MWF 10:30–12:00, and you're welcome to come in at other times as well— just knock. Waggener Hall 14–A.

This is a course in *language* and in *classical civilization*. It has two goals: to increase your knowledge of words, language, and the ways in which they are formed, and to increase your knowledge of medical and scientific terminology. We will consider the special language of medicine and science as an example of language in general. A good part of our class time will be spent talking about the general principles of this special language, about its sources in Greek and Latin, and about its history. But you will also find, I hope, that at the end of the term you will know several thousand new medical and scientific terms, and—more importantly—that you can recognize or form an almost limitless number of additional terms.

Hence memorization becomes almost inevitable. You will be assisted in the task of memorizing words and their components by the DEC-10 computer, and terminals dedicated to the use of this class are located in Waggener Hall 14–E. Programs for the use of this class may be run on any DEC-10 terminal, but I strongly recommend that you use the terminals in WAG 14–E, where proctors are available to help you. If at any time you have a question about the computer-assisted instruction, please feel free to ask me about it.

Two textbooks are required for this course: Oscar E. Nybakken, *Greek and Latin in Scientific Terminology* (Ames, Iowa, 1959), and Theodore F. Brunner and Luci Berkowitz, *The Elements of Scientific and Specialized Terminology* (Minneapolis, 1967).

I have scheduled two one-hour examinations, one on October 1 and one on November 5. A final examination will be given at the time and place announced by the Registrar. In addition, those who are registered for upper-division credit (CC 336M) will have to submit a special project, either a term paper or some equivalent piece of work. A list of suggested projects will be distributed soon. For students in CC 306M, the two one-hour examinations will count 25% of the final grade each, and the final examination will count 50%; for students in CC 336M, the two one-hour examinations will each count 20%, the special project will count 20%, and the final examination will count 40%. One point will be deducted from your final average for each computer-assisted lesson not completed with credit by midnight on the day of the final examination.

I am in general very reluctant to schedule make-up examinations unless circumstances entirely beyond your control prevent you from attending an examination. Lack of time to prepare or other examinations on the same day are *not* grounds for making up an examination.

READING AND LECTURE SCHEDULE

Please note that except for the first two weeks of the term and the weeks of September 28, October 26, and November 2, students will attend this course only on Tuesday. The time that would have been spent in a second weekly class meeting is to be used for completing the computer-assisted lessons or for other course-related purposes.

September	1:	Organizational meeting.
	3:	Introduction: General Language and Scientific Language.
	8:	Introduction continued. Nybakken 1–23.
	10:	Tracts for the Times: Digestive, Urinary, and Genital.
	15:	The Greek Alphabet, and Other Matters.
	22:	Elementary Greek. Nybakken 24–29; 44–61.
	29:	Rosh Hashanah—no class meeting.
October	1:	First Examination, *covering B & B 1–9 and readings and lectures to date.*
	6:	The Nervous System.
	13:	Elementary Latin. Nybakken 30–44.
	20:	The Grammar of Prescriptions.
	27:	The Respiratory Tract.
	29:	The Greeks and Professor Sagan.
November	3:	Election Day—no class meeting.
	5:	Second Examination, *covering B & B 10–18 and readings and lectures to date.*
	10:	Where the System Breaks Down: Semantic Change. Nybakken 231–307.
	17:	Where the System Breaks Down: Malformations & Misnomers.
	24:	The Skeletal System.
December	1:	The Circulatory System.
	8:	Concluding Unscientific Postscript.

BASIC DEFINITIONS

1. ROOT	The fundamental element of a word which expresses the basic meaning common to all words of the related group (e.g., FAC-[to make, to do]: fact, effect, efficient).
2. PREFIX	(LAT. pre-: before, fix-: fasten) One or more letters or syllables placed at the beginning of a word in order to modify its meaning (e.g., ad-, con-, epi-).

3: SUFFIX — (LAT. sub-: under, fix-: fasten) An element at the end of a word which serves as a derivative, formative, or inflection (e.g., -osis, -ia, -or, -al).

4: AFFIX — (LAT. ad-: to, fix-: fasten) A collective term for prefixes, suffixes and infixes.

5: NOUN — (LAT. nomen, name) A word designating an object, thing, or living being (e.g., ant, moron, chair, cruelty).

6: VERB — (LAT. verbum: word) A word which expresses an action, process, or state of being (e.g., run, convert, am).

7: ADJECTIVE — (LAT. ad-: to, ject-: throw) A word which modifies a noun by denoting a quality or specifying a distinction (e.g., wise, green, this).

8: SYLLABLE — (GK. syn-: together, lab-: take) One or more speech sounds constituting an uninterrupted unit of utterance (e.g., an-ten-na).

9 DIPHTHONG — (GK. di-: two, phthong-: sound) The pronunciation of two vowels in one syllable (e.g., -ou-, -oi-).

10: DIAERESIS — (GK. dia : apart, (h)aere-: take) The conversion of one syllable into two by separating vowels of a diphthong (e.g., Zoë /Zo-e/ vs. Zoë /Zō/).

11: HYPHEN — (GK hypo-. under, hen : one) A punctuation mark (-) used between the syllables of a divided or compound word (e.g., anti-infective, salpingo-oophoritis).

12: ORTHOGRAPHY — (GK. ortho-: correct, graph-: write) The art and rules of spelling according to accepted standards.

13: TRANS- LITERATION — (LAT. trans-: across, litter-: letter) The representation of the words or sounds of one language with the symbols of another language (e.g., χθών: chthon).

14: VOWEL GRADATION (ABLAUT) — (GER. ab-: off, laut-: sound) The change in the internal vowels of a word in order to indicate certain distinctions (e.g., sing, sang, sung, song).

15: ASSIMILATION — (LAT. ad-: to, simil-: resemble) A process in which two adjacent sounds acquire common or identical characteristics (e.g., con- + -bine = combine; ad- + -lusion = allusion).

16: ELISION — (LAT. ex-:, laed-: strike, harm) The omission of a final vowel of a word or stem before another word or stem beginning with a vowel (e.g., nycto- + -aphonia = nyctaphonia).

17: SYNCOPE   (GK. syn-: together, cop-: cut) The loss of one or more sounds or letters from the middle of a word (e.g., ne'er for never).

18: HAPLOGRAPHY   (GK. haplo-: simple, graph-: write) The simplification of a word by elimination of a letter or syllable similar to an adjacent letter or syllable (e.g., rotator $\longrightarrow$ rotor).

19: ETYMOLOGY   (GK. etymo-: true, log-: word) The origin and derivation of a word as shown by reducing it to its components.

20: FOLK ETYMOLOGY   The popular change in words so as to give them an apparent relationship to other better-known words (e.g., pentice $\longrightarrow$ penthouse).

21: ANALOGY   (GK. ana-: up, log-: proportion) The tendency or process of modifying or creating words on existing patterns (e.g., *hydromatic* on the basis of automatic).

22: COGNATES   (LAT. con-: together, (g)nat-: born) Two or more words in different languages which have the same root (e.g., mater: meter: mother; duo: dyo: two).

23: DOUBLET   Two words of the same language which are derived from the same original word (e.g., *fragile* and *frail* from LAT. *fragilis*).

24: HYBRID WORD   (LAT. hibrida: mongrel) A word composed of elements of two or more languages (e.g., microteeth, television).

25: CLIPPED WORD   A word which has lost the initial and/or final part (e.g., *flu* for *influenza*, *polio* for *poliomyelitis*).

26: NEOLOGISM   (GK. neo-: new, log: word) A new word or expression in a language or a new usage of an old word or expression.

27: CALQUE   (FR. calque: copy) A word or expression whose meaning or form is modelled upon that of a word or expression in another language (e.g., GER *Sauerstoff* for GK *Oxygen*).

28: SYNONYM   (GK. syn-: together, onym-: name) A word having the same meaning as another word (e.g., old: aged).

29: ANTONYM   (GK. anti-: opposite, onym-: name) A word having the opposite meaning to another word (e.g., old: young).

30: ACRONYM   (GK. acro-: end, point, onym-: name) A word formed from the abbreviation of two or more words (e.g., SCUBA = Self-Contained Underwater Breathing Apparatus).

31: PALINDROME   (GK. palin-: back, again, drom-: run) A word, phrase or sentence which reads the same either forward or backward (e.g., Madam, I'm Adam).

32: EPONYM (GK. epi-: upon, onym-: name) A proper name which is so prominently associated with something that it becomes the description for it (e.g., Mesmerism, Bright's Disease).

33: DIMINUTIVE (LAT. di-: apart, minu-: lessen) A suffix or derivative denoting "smallness" (e.g., animalcule, gosling, bacillus).

34: INCHOATIVE (LAT. incoh-: begin) An affix which indicates that an action is beginning or coming into being (e.g., -esce- in sen*esce*nce or conval*esce*).

35: VERNACULAR (LAT. vernacul-: native) The current spoken daily language of the people of a given geographical area.

36: THESAURUS (GK. "treasure house") A dictionary of synonyms and antonyms.

37: ONOMATO- (GK. onomato-: name, poe-: make) The formation of
POEIA words imitating sounds (e.g., moo, plop, fizz).

38: ARTICULATION (LAT. art-: joint, cul-: little) The formation of sounds by the vocal organs.

SPECIAL PROJECT: QUESTIONS AND ANSWERS

Q. What is the special project?
A. An essay, usually, of from 750 to 1500 words (3-6 typed pages) on some topic related to the language of science or medicine, or to the history of science or medicine before A.D. 1700.

Q. What are you after, really?
A. Clear thinking and good writing, that's all.

Q. Are you going to hand out a list of topics?
A. No.

Q. Why not?
A. Because I want you to think up your own topic.

Q. How on earth am I going to think up my own topic?
A. Look at yourself first. What are you interested in? Do your interests have any relation to the subject matter of this course? Is there anything in this course that confuses, puzzles, or irritates you? What? Can you solve the problem or clarify it? Have you come across anything in the lectures or reading for this course that you would like to know more about? If after this self-examination you still don't have a glimmer of an idea, come by WAG 14-A during my office hours and I'll try to help.

Q. What are the criteria on which you will grade this essay?
A. In this order:

1. Is it THOUGHTFUL; that is, has the author formulated an hypothesis

or asked a question with care and accuracy, and has he tested his hypothesis or considered his question with respect for the facts as he knows them and in accordance with the rules of logic?

    2. Is it WELL-WRITTEN; that is, has the author expressed his meaning clearly, using an organization that is easy to follow and language that is easy to read?

    3. Is it MECHANICALLY CORRECT; that is, does it follow standard practice in grammar, punctuation, and spelling?

Q. When is this paper due?
A. If your last name begins with A-L, your project is due before 4:00 P.M. on Tuesday, November 24. If your last name begins with M-Z, your paper is due before 4:00 P.M. on Tuesday, December 1.

Q. What is your policy on late papers?
A. Unless I have authorized in advance and in writing late submission of a paper, I shall reduce the grade of the paper by one-third of a mark (e.g., A to A-, A- to B+, and so on) for each day the paper is late.

RESERVE READING LIST

    I intend these readings to supplement the lectures, to expand on ideas contained in them, or to contrast with them. In no case have I assigned a reading which merely repeats the material in a lecture. *Required readings* are marked with an asterisk; other readings are optional. As a general rule, students enrolled in CC 306M will probably want to read only the required readings, while those enrolled in CC 336M may want to do one or more of the optional readings. *On examinations* some questions may require knowledge of the *required readings only*. All books on this list are on reserve in the Undergraduate Library, except for the American Heritage Dictionary, several copies of which are permanently shelved in the reference section of that library.

Week 1.   °Lewis Thomas, "How to Fix the Premedical Curriculum," from *The Medusa and the Snail*.
(Propaganda for the first week.)

     2.   °*The American Heritage Dictionary*, pp. xix-xx, 1496-1502.
(Calvert Watkins writing on Indo-European.)

     3.   Herodotus Book VII, chapters 175-233.
(The story of Thermopylae; note that this reference is to *book* and *chapter* not pages.)

     4.   °Hippocrates, *Oath* and *Canon*.
(In a folder, with study questions.)

     7.   Ovid, *Metamorphoses*, Book VI.

     8.   Otto Jespersen, *Growth and Structure of the English Language*, pp. 106–39.

     9.   °T. H. Savory, *The Language of Science*, pp. 47–64.
(A chapter on "The Growth of the Language of Science.")

    10.   °Lavoisier, "Preface" to *Elementary Treatise of Chemistry*.

    12.   °Thomas, "On Etymons and Hybrids," *Medusa and the Snail*.

13.   C. S. Lewis, *Studies in Words*, pp. 24–74.
(Highly recommended as a model of how to talk about words.)

14.   °Savory, *Language of Science*, pp. 112–42.
(Two chapters on "The Character of the Language of Science" and "The Nature of Scientific Prose." Written several years ago for British readers, but still useful.)

Lecture Outline 1

GENERAL LANGUAGE AND SCIENTIFIC LANGUAGE

I.   What do we mean by "the language of science"?

A. Vocabulary?
B. Rhetoric or style?
C. A way of matching the Word with the World?

II.   What is the language of science like?

A. Overwhelmingly Greek and Latin

1. Greek	Latin	Gk/Lat	Other
58.5%	21.77%	13.23%	6.5% ("Dorland's" 1965)

B. Mechanistic and constructive
C. Precise, restrained, and specific
D. Stable

1. Democritus
2. Harvey

> The kidney had a hard compact substance very much like that of the heart; of obscure red colour; temperature hot and moist inasmuch as sanguineous flesh.

E. Sanctioned

III.   Where did the language of science come from?

A. It did not exist in ancient times.

1. Hippocrates
2. Plato
3. Galen

B. It originated in the fusion of Cartesianism, Neoplatonism, and early modern experimental science in the seventeenth and eighteenth centuries.

WARNING
This may not
be true!

1. Descartes
2. Leibniz
3. Lavoisier

Lecture Outline 2

TRACTS FOR THE TIMES
Words and Stories Connected With
The Digestive System
And Its Nomenclature

I. The *pyloric sphincter*

   A. Pylorus
      1. The Greek words *pule* and *pyloros*
      2. The Latin word *porta*
      3. The pylorus and the portal vein
                          a. pylethrombosis
                          b. pylephlebitis
      4. The Battle of Thermo*pylae*

   B. Sphincter
      1. The Greek word *sphingo*
      2. Sphinxes
      3. Oedipus

II. The *duodenum*

   A. How it got its name
   B. Some observations on Roman numerals
   C. 1. dodecahedron
      2. dodecamerous
      3. duodecimal

III. The *jejunum*
   A. How it got its name
   B. What "jejune" means

IV. The *caecum* or *cecum* (and why there are two spellings).
V. The *sigmoid coln*

The physician ought to know literature, to be able to understand or to explain what he reads. Likewise also rhetoric, that he may delineate in true arguments the things which he discusses; dialectic also so that he may study the causes and cures of infirmities in the light of reason. Similarly also arithmetic, in view of the temporal relationships involved in the paroxysms of diseases and in diurnal cycles.

St. Isidore of Seville

WORDS AND THE MACHINE
A Student's Guide to the University of Texas
Programs of Computer-Assisted Instruction in
Medical and Scientific Terminology.

Lee T. Pearcy, Jr.
Assistant Professor of Classics
December 1, 1978

Part I
Some General Considerations

"In my first year of medical school I had to learn a whole new Language." These words were spoken not by an American studying overseas, or by a foreigner studying in this country, but by a doctor who was born and educated in Texas. Every profession, in fact, has its own special language, and anyone who hopes to practice any profession has to spend a good deal of time learning that profession's technical terms. Medical and scientific professionals deal routinely with sentences like this: "Tracheostomy rather than laryngeal intubation is indicated when respiratory obstruction is imminent or when the dyspnea is so great as to exhaust the patient."

There are two ways to learn the unfamiliar words in this sentence. One is to learn each word—'tracheostomy,' 'laryngeal,' 'dyspnea'—and its meaning—'formation of an opening into the trachea,' 'pertaining to the larnyx,' 'difficulty in breathing.' The other, and far better, way is to learn the elements of terminology and decode words instead of memorizing them. If '-ostomy' is a suffix meaning 'formation of an opening' then 'tracheostomy' must mean 'formation of an opening into the trachea'; if ' al' is a suffix meaning 'pertaining to' then 'laryngeal' must mean 'pertaining to the larynx'; if 'dys' means 'difficulty' and 'pnea' means 'breathing' then 'dyspnea' must be difficulty in breathing.

Computers learn words the first way. To a computer, each word is a string of letters and must be associated with another string of letters, its meaning. People—who are far more intelligent than computers—can learn words in the second way. Most people find it easier to master a technical vocabulary by learning the elements of words than by learning each word separately, but 'easier' is not the same as 'easy,' and a fair amount of memorization is necessary. Even so, there are far fewer word elements than words. This series of computer-assisted lessons has been designed to help you learn the elements of words and how to recognize these building blocks when they occur in technical terms.

The Romans had a proverb: Repetitio mater memoriae. "Repetition is the mother of memory." We all know that if we hear a song often enough, we can repeat the lyrics without ever having made a conscious effort to memorize them, or that if we have a list of formulae to learn we learn it more quickly if a friend drills us on it. In these lessons the computer will play the role of the friend who helps us drill or the radio that plays a song again and again.

Many people believe that computers are complicated machines that require special training to use. Some are, but anyone can learn to use a computer with only a little study. The key word here is 'use'; as you take these computer-assisted lessons, remember that YOU ARE USING THE COMPUTER, the computer is not using you. You are in charge, and it is up to you to make the most of the machine. The computer cannot teach you anything, but you can learn with the computer's help.

Part II
How to Talk to a Machine

This section of this manual will explain the commands and procedures used in operating the program called CLASSY. You will need to know how to log in; that is, how to connect your terminal to the main computer. Your instructor will explain how to do this, and how to call up CLASSY and run it.

After you have logged in and asked the computer to run CLASSY for you, the computer will ask for your social security number. This number identifies you to the program and helps the program to keep track of your records.

TYPE YOUR SOCIAL SECURITY NUMBER AND HIT THE RETURN KEY

It is important to remember that the computer will not respond to any command until you have hit the return key. When you type something, it is stored at the terminal until you send it to the computer by hitting the return key.

What if you make a mistake in typing? There are two ways to rub it out: one is to hold down the SHIFT key (at the bottom left- and right-hand corners of the keyboard) and hit the key marked RUB (above and to the right of the right-hand shift key) once for each character you wish to erase. This will cause the erased characters to appear between reverse slashes. If, for example, you typed 'dat' for 'cat' and erased it by this method, the screen would show 'dat \ tad \ '. Many people prefer to erase by holding down the CONTROL key (above the right-hand shift key) and simultaneously hitting the H key once for each character to be erased. CONTROL-H moves the cursor (the mark of light that shows where you are typing) to the left, back over what you have typed. When you type the correct characters, your mistake will be automatically erased.

TO ERASE A MISTAKE, TYPE EITHER:
1. SHIFT + RUB;
2. CONTROL-H.

After it has found out who you are, the computer will print a request for Course Name, Lesson Name. Once you have run the program a few times, you will know that the quickest way to get directly to the drill program is to type both names together, separated by a comma, like this: CC306M,CC8. It does not matter if your type upper-case or lower-case letters, but there must be no spaces, and the two parts of the command must be separated by a comma. If you aren't sure what to do, simply type "list" and a list of available courses (or available lessons, if you've already selected a course) will be printed. As you are selecting a course, you can type "<course name>,report" and the computer will type a report of the lessons taken, how many times you have attempted them, and the date, time, and score of your most recent attempt. You can also type "help" to get an explanation of what to do next.

WHEN THE COMPUTER ASKS FOR 'COURSE NAME' TYPE ONE OF FOUR THINGS:

1. The course name in this format: CC306M
2. The course name followed by a lesson name (which will be the letters 'CC' followed by a number from 1 to 27): CC306M,CC8
3. <course name>,REPORT; e.g. CC306M,REPORT
4. HELP

If you select a course without selecting a lesson, the computer will type a request for

Lesson Name. Type the lesson name, which will be the letters CC followed immediately—no spaces, no punctuation—by the number of the lesson you want, thus: CC12. You may also type "list" for a list of available lessons.

Once you have selected a course and lesson, the program will go directly to the drill section. Each drill lesson can have up to six parts. The first four parts ask you to give the meaning of word components: prefixes, suffixes, word roots, and combining forms. A lesson may have any, all, or none of these first four parts. The fifth part of the lesson will ask you to give the meaning of a scientific word, and the sixth part will ask you to give the word corresponding to a definition printed by the program. In the first four parts the computer will ask you to define all the items stored in its memory; in the fifth and sixth sections the computer will ask you to respond to up to twenty items drawn from a longer list. In all six parts the program will evaluate your answer and try to decide if it is right, wrong, or partially correct.

Remember that the computer is not as intelligent as you are; it is, in fact, no more intelligent than an automobile or any other complicated piece of machinery that we use. It has been told to treat your answer as a string of letters and to compare that string with another string which it has stored in its memory. If your answer doesn't match that string EXACTLY, the computer concludes that your answer is either wrong or partially correct. It then searches through your answer to see if it can find a certain group of character strings. It has been instructed to accept any answer containing this group as partially correct, and if it finds the group it types a message telling you so. If it doesn't find either the correct answer or the group of strings which it will accept as partially correct, it concludes that your answer is wrong—and tells you so.

What does this mean in practice? Suppose that the computer has been programmed to ask you for the meaning of ' itis' and has been programmed to accept the answer 'inflammation' as correct and the character string 'inflam' as partially correct. It will type '-itis?' and wait for an answer. If you type 'inflammation' and hit the return key, it will respond with VERY GOOD or some similar message. If you type ANYTHING containing the letters 'inflam'—anything at all—the computer will respond with a message telling you that your answer is partially correct. 'Inflamation', 'Inflamed', 'when something becomes inflamed' are all partially correct; so is "Today I saw a gasoline truck labeled INFLAMMABLE." The computer cannot evaluate these answers; all it can do is match one string of letters with another.

Now that you know this, you should be able to make more effective use of the computer as a learning tool. If the computer can't do more than make a rough evaluation of your answer, it follows that YOU and YOU ALONE can judge whether your answer is really correct, and whether you have learned anything by typing it for the computer to evaluate. Machines can compare strings of letters and type; people can read and decide.

But if the computer's response to your answer seems impossibly wrong-headed, tell someone—your instructor, or the terminal-room proctor. You can also use the CLASSY program to leave a message for your instructor by typing $COMMENT after it has asked you a question. The program will then tell you how to leave a message.

There are other commands which can be used after the program has asked you for an answer. If these commands are used after you have selected a course, they must be preceded by a dollar sign ($) like this: $EXIT. They are

1. TIME	causes the time of day to be printed;	
2. DATE	causes the date to be printed;	
3. EXIT	stops execution of the program and allows you to log off or run the program again;	

5. HINT		gives you a hint by typing one letter of the answer and spaces for the remaining letters. You may get additional letters by typing $HINT again, but the computer will not give you credit for an answer on which you have received more than 50% of the letters as hints.
6. TERMINATE		stops execution of the program and logs you off automatically.

Information on other available commands will be printed in response to the HELP command.

After you have finished with all six sections of the drill lesson, the computer will type your score and the percentage of questions you have answered correctly. Partially correct answers are recorded as though they were fully correct. If you have answered less than 70% of the questions correctly, the computer will suggest that you take the lesson again and will not record in its memory that you have attempted the lesson. The computer will then ask you if you want to take another lesson.

WHEN THE COMPUTER ASKS IF YOU WANT TO TAKE ANOTHER LESSON TYPE 'YES' OR 'NO'.

If you type 'no,' the computer will stop running the CLASSY program and log you off. If you type 'yes,' the computer will return to the point in the program at which it asked you to select a course. You may then select a different course and lesson or the same course and lesson.

Part III
How to Make the Most of
Your Machine

In the jargon of professional educators, the third section of this manual would be about "learning strategies." Perhaps it's better to talk about ways to use the computer intelligently and efficiently. To be effective, computer-ASSISTED instruction must have people using it with thought and judgement. You are responsible for the quality of your experience at the terminal; the best-designed program stupidly used is like a book held upside-down.

Speaking of books—even in an age of electronic data processing, they are a highly efficient and portable means of information storage and retrieval. This series of programs in computer-assisted instruction, in fact, is designed to be used with a book, *The Elements of Scientific and Specialized Terminology*, by Theodore F. Brunner and Luci Berkowitz, published by the Burgess Publishing Company, Minneapolis, Minnesota, in 1967. Each lesson in this program corresponds to a chapter in the book, and you will probably find that your time at the terminal will go more efficiently if you study the appropriate chapter before attempting the computer-assisted lesson. After you have studied the chapter and think you know the material in it, come to a terminal and take the drill lesson. As soon as you finish the lesson the computer will show you how many questions you have answered correctly, and this information should help you decide how well you have learned the material in the lesson.

Set a goal for yourself. The computer will not record any lesson on which you answer less than 70% of the questions correctly, but you may decide that you want to answer 80% or even 90% of the questions correctly. Don't give yourself credit for less; take the lessons again and again until you reach your goal. The computer will record only your most recent attempt.

Many people find that they learn while taking the drill lessons, and that by repeating a lesson several times in succession they learn the material in it. Others, however, learn more efficiently by returning to the book between attempts at the computer-assisted drill. You will have to decide what proportion of your learning will be assisted by the computer and what proportion by the book.

Keep track of your progress. One advantage of computer-assisted instruction is that it allows you to proceed at your own pace. You can do all 27 lessons in a few weeks, or one lesson a week for 27 weeks. Most people, however, learn best by proceeding at a regular pace and by setting aside a regular time each week for the computer-assisted lessons. The REPORT command will help you to monitor your progress in the course; use it often.

When the computer tells you that an answer you have typed is right, wrong, or partially correct, it is, in a way, pretending to be human, for the ability to tell right from wrong is a human characteristic. So think about what the machine types. Is it true? Are you satisfied with your answer? Since the computer can't really distinguish right from wrong, don't be afraid of making mistakes. There is a sense in which it is impossible to make mistakes on a computer. The machine can't condemn you, and if you get a low score—which means only that your answers did not match the answers stored in the machine—the computer will ignore it. If YOU are dissatisfied with your score, you can take the lesson again.

Part IV
List of Commands

When the computer asks you for:	Please type:
Your social security number	Your social security number (dashes aren't needed)
Your name	Your name, first name first, last name second. Don't use middle initials, and remember to capitalize the first letters of your names.
Your instructor's last name	Your instructor's last name (again, remember to capitalize the first letter)
Course Name	1. The course name in the form CC306M 2. The course name followed by the lesson name, separated by a comma, thus: CC306M,CC12 3. <course name>,REPORT 4. LIST 5. HELP
Lesson Name	1. The lesson name, thus: CC3 (for lesson 3) 2. LIST 3. HELP
The meaning of a term (e.g. "post- ?")	1. The meaning of the term 2. $HINT 3. $TIME 4. $DATE 5. $EXIT 6. $TERMINATE 7. $COMMENT
Whether you want to take another lesson	1. YES 2. NO (if you type no, you will be logged off automatically)

THE BIBLE AS LITERATURE
An Interdisciplinary Perspective

James S. Ackerman
Department of Religious Studies
Indiana University

This material on "The Bible As Literature" gives some of the results of an inter-disciplinary institute that began at Indiana University in 1970, culminating in an N.E.H. Summer Institute in 1979. In the beginning we did not realize that we would be doing pioneering work that would start to bridge the gap between two disciplines that have long been isolated from one another. Our goals were much more modest: to provide historical-cultural background and helpful literary analyses, along with classroom teaching techniques, to help secondary school teachers in Indiana develop units or courses on biblical literature in their English curriculum. We had no idea that we would receive over 2500 application requests in the first five years, and that teachers from all 50 states and from four foreign countries would attend.

It did not take us long to discover that, whereas there was an over abundant supply of material on the historical–cultural background of the biblical world, there were virtually no helpful *literary* analyses of biblical texts. Literary scholars had apparently been intimidated by the new complexities of biblical studies that had resulted from the ever-increasing data uncovered by ancient Near Eastern archaeology during the past century.

Biblical scholars have traditionally had no interest in literary interpretation of the text. We are trained as historians and linguists. For us the biblical material provides data which, combined with archaeological information, help us to reconstruct the cultural history of ancient Israel. Therefore one goal of our analysis is to move behind the final form of the text, reconstructing its antecedent sources. If we can properly date and situate these sources, as well as trace the process of their redaction, we gain valuable insights into various periods of Israel's cultural history. Furthermore, if we can compare biblical texts with ancient Near Eastern parallels, we are better able to elucidate the manner in which ancient Israel interacted with her larger cultural environment.

Since our methodologies were oriented primarily toward the goal of historical reconstruction, we had little use for the ahistorical kind of literary criticism described in Ken Gros Louis's enclosed essay on methodology. For our purposes the text has only one meaning—the meaning it had to the writer and his/her original audience. One pursues that meaning by attempting to reconstruct the text, by purging it of editorial accretions, by using comparative linguistic data; and our understanding is guided by our general knowledge of the time period of that text. Even though I was an undergraduate English major, I had developed a fairly negative attitude toward what literature scholars did when they approached the Bible. Some studied and taught the Bible as a major source for the Western literary imagination (Milton, Melville, etc.)—not as great literature worthy of study in and of itself. Others were more interested in the aesthetics of the style and rhythms of the beautiful King James translation. Still others studied and taught the Bible by replicating what biblical scholars had concluded. That is, even though they did not have the linguistic and historical–critical competencies to assess the conclusions of biblical scholars, they faithfully taught our source criticism and historical background instead of concentrating on the literature itself.

During the past decade a long overdue rapprochement has begun to take place between biblical scholars and literary scholars. As soon as I heard Ken Gros Louis give his first lecture (it was on Genesis 1), I realized that here was a scholar who approached a text using a completely different methodology from the historical–critical method in which I had been trained. And yet it was abundantly clear to me that he was reaching valuable insights into the text which the historical–critical tradition, despite our voluminous biblical commentaries, had not perceived.

We have been trained to search the text for historical data, including religious perspectives that can be ascribed to a certain group in a certain region during a certain period of time. We look for discrepancies in style and viewpoint, attributing them to variant sources or to later redactors and editors. Our discipline has made enormous advances in reconstructing the ancient Near Eastern world, including the history and culture of early Israel. But until recently we have not paid sufficient attention to the final form of the text and to the stylistic devices through which the text expresses meaning.

Several biases contributed to that neglect. First, as historians we worked through a text to recover the "original tradition" because it could usually provide more reliable historical data. Editors and redactors were interesting to us only because they showed how later generations reinterpreted the tradition. Secondly, our methods were shaped by scholars (e.g. Gunkel) who were heavily influenced by nineteenth-century Romanticism; thus the quest for more accurate historical data was accompanied by a fascination for coming closer to the age of the originally inspired poet. Redactors and editors could only becloud the early pure expression. And third, our historical–critical methods came into being, amidst much controversy, in reaction to what we regarded as the amusing and fanciful (i.e. non-scientific) musings of Jewish and Christian interpreters throughout the past two millennia. We realized that they did not have access to the archaeological data and historical knowledge we now possess, so they couldn't be blamed. But the pre-scientific approaches to the Bible, as perhaps epitomized by the allegorical readings of Philo and Origen, gave us a deep suspicion of any method other than the historical that claims to tell what the text means. For us, the only correct meaning is what it meant to the original writer and audience. The rest—the question of what it means today—we leave to theologians and homilists.

That was ten years ago. In the past decade biblical studies has entered what the noted New Testament scholar Dominic Crossan terms a "second revolution," equally as significant in shaping the future of biblical studies as the historical–critical method had been for the past century. Literary scholars have convinced us that their methods are not purely a subjective imposing of their meanings on the text. They have helped us to see that a proper appreciation of such elements as style, point of view, and imagery do bring us deeper insights into the meaning of a text. Gradually, we are learning to move away from a flat reading—for historical data and/or abstract theological viewpoint—to a more complete appreciation of the resonances and subtle nuances in the text. For example, Ken Gros Louis's essay on the Song of Songs (in this section), adheres to one of the traditional interpretations long held by biblical scholars: the "Three Character" drama theory. But none of us had ever seen the rich texture that he finds: the subtle psychological portrait of rural woman and urban king that sets up a series of opposing images and values:

> The Song of Songs presents us with totally different ways of viewing reality, different perspectives on love, and different perceptions of human experience. The tensions are characterized in terms of various oppositions: the private vs. the public, the country vs. the courts, the natural vs. the artificial, the simple vs. the sophisticated. The young woman whose story this is cannot get away from her own roots, nor does she want to. The young lovers are one with nature; they live in it, they describe each other according to its terms, they participate in its cycles. By contrast, Solomon and his court are inside, and inside in many different ways. They are literally inside, as seen when the women in the king's chambers gaze at the young woman's sunburned complexion. They are inside the city, enclosed by walls, guarded by watchmen supported by sixty mighty men protecting it against alarms by night. They are inside figuratively, within their limited perception of nature and its cycles, in their inability to create images and metaphors without using for comparison the artificial works of master hands or the well-known buildings and sites of other cities. Because they are inside they are limited, enclosed unto themselves and their world.
>
> The dominant image pattern of the Song is, in fact, that of enclosure.

I am not inferring that literary criticism is destined to replace the historical emphasis that has dominated biblical studies. But it is clear that this methodology, new to us, will bring a valuable corrective that will complement the historical–critical method.

In 1979 Gros Louis and I directed an N.E.H. Summer Institute that was aimed at developing interdisciplinary approaches to the Bible as literature. The participants were ten biblical scholars (who learned to read poetry, drama, and fiction by studying Herbert, *King Lear*, and *A Portrait of the Artist as a Young Man*) and ten literary scholars (who were introduced to biblical Hebrew and biblical background). Each week we also met together to work on biblical texts (see the syllabus in the enclosed packet), and gradually we learned to appreciate and make increasing use of the methods and insights developed within the other discipline.

As background for Institute participants we prepared a bibliography of earlier work on literary analysis of the Bible that we had found helpful. To show how rapidly this new field is developing I will close with further bibliography, most of which has appeared since 1979.

Alter, Robert, *The Art of Biblical Narrative* (New York, 1981)

Fishbane, Michael, *Text and Texture* (New York, 1978)

°Fokkelman, Jan P., *Narrative Art in Genesis: Specimens of Stylistic and Structural Analysis* (Assen, Holland, 1975)

°Fokkelman, Jan P., *Narrative Art and Poetry in the Books of Samuel* (Assen, 1981).

Frye, Northrop, *The Great Code: The Bible and Literature* (New York, 1982).

Good, Edwin M., *Irony in the Old Testament*, 2nd edition (Sheffield, England, 1981)

Gros Louis, Kenneth R. R. et. al., *Literary Interpretations of Biblical Narratives.* Vols. 1 and 2. (Nashville, 1974 and 1982)

Gunn, David M., *The Story of King David* (Sheffield, 1978)

Gunn, David M., *The Fate of King Saul* (Sheffield, 1980)

Kugel, James L., *The Idea of Biblical Poetry: Parallelism and Its History* (New Haven, 1981)

Long, Burke O. ed., *Images of Man and God: Old Testament Short Stories in Literary Focus* (Sheffield, 1981)

Magonet, Jonathan, *Form and Meaning: Studies in Literary Techniques in the Book of Jonah* (Bern, 1976)

°O'Connor, M., *Hebrew Verse Structure* (Winona Lake, IN, 1980)

Robertson, David, *The Old Testament and the Literary Critic* (Philadelphia, 1977)

Williams, James G., *Those Who Ponder Proverbs: Aphoristic Thinking and Biblical Literature* (Sheffield, 1981)

Crossroads Press is initiating a series of commentaries and monographs devoted to literary criticism of the Bible.

°Only these books require some knowledge of biblical Hebrew.

SOME METHODOLOGICAL CONSIDERATIONS[*]

Kenneth R. R. Gros Louis
Indiana University

Much has happened in the new field of literary analysis since *Literary Interpretations of Biblical Narratives* was published in 1974. The present essay is very much a personal assessment of how one literary critic proceeds in analyzing a biblical text. I am aware of, but do not discuss, the excellent work of Robert Alter, Michael Fishbane, Menakhem Perry and Meir Sternberg, David Robertson, and Leland Ryken (among others) who, I believe, share many of my basic assumptions about literary criticism of the Bible. The gap between literary critics and biblical scholars, however, even scholars who say they are endorsing this new approach to the study of the Bible, remains very great. Part of the reason for this gap results from the traditional definition of "literary criticism" in biblical scholarship, which is why I will discuss several of these definitions in this essay. But the main reason for the gap, in my opinion, is that some biblical scholars simply reject the notion that the Bible can be analyzed in the same manner as Shakespeare, Goethe, or Zola. These scholars have explained their position and will, I am sure, explain it again. Their emphases on the sacredness of the Bible and on the necessity of studying it in its historical contexts, however, are rejected by me, as they must, I believe, be rejected by any student of literature.

A literary interpretation of the Bible in no way replaces or invalidates other approaches—source analysis, anthropology, sociology, theology, archaeology, comparative religion—nor does it seek to rival in authority the centuries of interpretations in commentaries, or the more recent scholarly contributions of form criticism. Literary critics, in considering the Bible primarily and fundamentally as a literary document, believe in the creative power of language to affect our lives, and we deeply appreciate the Bible's portrayal of human situations and characters. The questions literary critics ask differ from those asked by biblical scholars. While we are certainly aware of the findings of biblical scholarship, we do not seek to explain any aspects of the text with the help of extraliterary information. The text to us

---

[*]To appear in *Literary Interpretations of Biblical Narratives*, Vol. II, Abingdon Press, 1982. (Copyright © Abingdon. Reprinted by permission.)

is not sacred, and whether the events it describes are historical is not relevant to our purposes. The traditional disciplines of biblical criticism, important as correctives to flights of critical fancy, are not called upon to document
any conclusions we might make. Our approach is essentially ahistorical; the
text is taken as received, and the truth of an action or an idea or a motive, for
literary criticism, depends on its rightness or appropriateness in context. —Is it
true, we ask, not in the real world, but within the fictive world that has been
created by the narrative?

I would like to outline my own critical assumptions in approaching the
Bible as literature, describe the kinds of questions I ask myself in preparing
to teach or write about biblical passages, and summarize how I deal with a
specific text. Let me begin in the most general terms, with my most basic
assumptions:

1.   Not everything in the Bible is literary in nature.
2.   Literary analyses of the literary aspects of the Bible are
     virtually non-existent.
3.   What has been called "literary criticism" of the Bible is not
     the kind of literary criticism teachers of literature do.
4.   In fact, the biblical scholar's definition of "literary criticism"
     is virtually the opposite of the literary critic's definition.
5.   Teachers of literature are *primarily* interested in the liter-
     ary reality of a text and not its historical reality.
6.   The literary reality of the Bible can be studied with the
     methods of literary criticism employed with any other text.
7.   Approaching the Bible as literature, then, means placing
     emphasis on the text itself—not on its historical and textual
     backgrounds, not on the circumstances which brought the
     text into its present form, not on its religious and cultural
     foundations.
8.   The literary critic assumes unity in the text. To quote
     Northrop Frye: "a purely literary criticism . . . would see
     the Bible, not as a scrapbook of corruptions, glosses, reduc-
     tions, insertions, conflations, misplacings, and misunder-
     standings. . . ."
9.   The literary critic assumes conscious artistry in the text.
10. The literary critic, then, explores such topics as narrative
     structure, scene placement, selection and ordering of epi-
     sodes, plot conflicts, image patterns, thematic emphasis,
     character development, and so on.
11. Literary criticism of the Bible is not biblical scholarship, it
     is literary criticism; the two are complementary.

(These assumptions underlie the essays in the 1974 volume; see especially Leland Ryken's "Literary Criticism of the Bible: Some Fallacies.")

Several of the most recent and widely used introductions to the Old Testament document my third and fourth assumptions. I am not trying to attack these views, but simply to illustrate the gulf which exists between biblical scholars and literary critics. Bernhard Anderson, for example, in the third edition (1975) of his *Understanding the Old Testament*, writes: "We cannot begin to understand the Old Testament as long as we regard it merely as great literature, interesting history, or the development of lofty ideas. The Old Testament is the narration of God's action: what he has done, is doing, and will do." Now whether or not I believe this statement, I feel obliged as a student of literature to alter Anderson's last sentence to read something like this: "*The basic assumption of the Old Testament is that it describes* the narration of God's action, what he has done, is doing, and will do." There is a world of difference between my sentence and Anderson's— for him, the Old Testament *is* the narration of God's actions; for me, that is the *fiction* which the Old Testament lays down as its basic premise. In using the word *fiction*, of course, I do not mean that it is necessarily *untrue*.

J. Kenneth Kuntz, in his very fine 1974 book, *The People of Ancient Israel*, describes a literary approach to the Bible as being concerned with genres, oral traditions, authors, editorial changes, dates, the intended audience, relation to historical events, chief rhetorical features, and the author's purposes. Kuntz here outlines a very respectable list of what literary scholars have long been interested in, but the list is appropriate to historical critics of literature, not to literary critics of literature.

Another good study, by James King West, *Introduction to the Old Testament*, published in 1971, reiterates Kuntz's understanding of what literary criticism is: "Higher criticism—is the interpretation of the text. Also called 'historical criticism' and roughly synonomous with 'literary criticism,' this discipline is concerned with the historical circumstances out of which the Biblical books developed—their authorship or the processes through which they were composed, the sources employed, their provenance (time and place of origin), and the purposes of their composition." West, like Kuntz, does not make any distinction between literary *scholarship* and literary *criticism*.

The gap between teachers of literature and biblical scholars can be seen even more strikingly in earlier, though highly respected studies. Gerald A. Larue, for example, in his 1969 book, *Old Testament Life and Literature*, writes that the literary approach to the Bible "may ignore the intention of the authors of the Bible and the relevance of what they said to their own time, or, in stressing literary characteristics, may slight the religious convictions of the writers." We know, as students of literature, that the author's intention, his goals in writing for his contemporary audience, and his religious convictions, play a small role indeed in literary criticism and, more importantly, in the analysis of literary texts. We may be familiar with all of this information, but we do not depend on it for interpretation, even with an avowedly religious poet such as Milton. For us, in fact, Milton's Satan, Adam, Jesus, God, and Samson, are much more interesting than Milton himself. It is *their* views of themselves and their worlds, and not Milton's of his, on which we focus.

A final example also illustrates another of the chief difficulties in studying the Bible as literature. L. Berkhof's 1952 *Principles of Biblical Interpretation* might have been retitled "Principle of Biblical Interpretation," for the overriding thesis is that the Bible is divinely inspired. One result of this view is that there is no room for the literary notion of the persona in biblical criticism. Berkhof points out, for example, that the prophets often shift from the third to the first person and speak *as if they were God*. "This," says Berkhof, "would be unexampled boldness on the part of the prophets, if they were not absolutely sure that God was putting the words, which they were speaking, into their mouths as their own." Such a statement not only ignores the notion of persona, but also the possibility that an author could create a character whom he then identified as a prophet. Berkhof's extreme view also prevents him from acknowledging the existence of another crucial critical concept, that of the unreliable narrator: "The interpreter," writes Berkhof, "should gladly accept the explanations which the authors themselves give of their own words or of the words of the speakers whom they introduce. It goes without saying that they are better qualified to speak with authority in this respect than anyone else." What Berkhof seems unaware of is that writers develop specific strategies for presenting their material, and that these strategies often intentionally lead us astray.

I have not selected these examples perversely or hostilely. They accurately represent, it seems to me, biblical scholars' notion of what literary criticism is, as well as many biblical scholars' concern that literary critics are undermining the authority of the Bible as a sacred text. The issue, in a sense, may be whether we see literary criticism of the Bible as a further extension of its secularization and therefore as damaging; or whether we see literary criticism as a new means for introducing readers of the Bible to its richness. It may also be, of course, that by making the Bible more accessible, by teaching it like any other literary text, we may indeed be demystifying it in a way that will permanently damage its authority as Scripture. My own opinion is that this risk—if it exists at all—is worth taking.

It might be useful to go through the kinds of questions which a literary critic considers in approaching a work of literature. Many of these questions will be known to readers; there is nothing unusual about the approach which I am about to describe. Nevertheless, it seems to me that it is an approach which is rarely applied to biblical narratives. A literary critic begins by being primarily interested in how a work is structured or organized. Why, for example, does it begin the way it does? (It is sometimes helpful to consider alternate beginnings.) What are the identifiable breaks in the text, either marked as such (chapters, verses, stanzas) or occasioned by changes in action, thought, language, setting? How does the ending differ from the beginning? In considering various breaks or units, we should be alert to parallels and contrasts, through reiterated speeches, reiterated actions, echoes of language, image, scene. The ending of a work of literature usually involves changes in characters, imagery, setting, tone, point of view. If, in fact, some of these do not change, the narrative may thus emphasize those which *do* change.

A literary critic is also concerned about tone; that is, the narrative's relation to its subject or its attitude to its subject, as well as the narrative's relation to us as audience. Is the narrative condescending or apologetic? Does it seek to arouse our interest in a topic, to excite our emotions, to compel us to action, to make us sad or happy? What information does the narrative give us and with what nuances? How much does the narrative intrude on the language of the characters and their conversations or actions? What information is not known to us or not given to those in the narrative? Do the omissions make a difference? Is there some information, for example, that we would like very much to know? There are major differences between first person and third person narration—first person narration obviously involves limited knowledge in that the "I" teller is able to tell us about and comment on only what is within his or her vision. Third person narration, however, can have complete knowledge, not only of the actions of the major characters, but of actions and incidents taking place far away from the primary events. In some instances, particularly in biblical narrative, we may not have a narrative voice distinct from the voice or voices of the speakers or characters. This situation presents a particular problem with regard to biblical narrative and the question of narrative voice.

A literary critic is alert to changes in characters which occur during the progress of a work. We ask if characters feel different at the end towards certain people or topics or issues than they did in the beginning. We ask how their situation has changed, if it has—their physical situation, material, geographical, psychological, spiritual. In what specific ways have the changes occurred? What events or characters occasioned or forced or contributed to the changes? With whom and with what, in other words, did the characters come into contact, and to what end? In biblical narrative, for example, answers to some of these questions are often provided by parallel episodes or parallel incidents which help direct us to the issues of character development. At what point in the narrative do the characters change, if they do? In considering this question, we need to look carefully not only at what the characters say, but at how they say it. What images or metaphors do they use? What is their tone of voice? What words become more pronounced in their vocabulary or shift in meaning or are rejected or are emphasized? The assumption here is that characters in a work of literature—like us—reveal themselves and their backgrounds, their concerns, biases, attitudes, by what they say and how they say it. It is also important to note how characters react to one another, what they say and do.

The action of a narrative is in many ways less meaningful than how that action comes into being. We ask whether the action or pronouncement or decision is plausible in the context of a particular narrative. Is David's affair with Bathsheba, for instance, prepared for in the narrative? Is it plausible for David to call Bathsheba from the roof top on which she is bathing? Is it plausible, given the terms of the story, that Cinderella gets to the ball? Is it plausible, given what we know of Hamlet, that he should not immediately or indeed perhaps ever obey the instructions of the ghost? Part of our job, in other words, is to explain why we believe in the plausibility of a narrative, no matter how fantastic its action or its "plot" might be. If the narrative is not plausible, than we should be prepared to consider the reasons for its very implausibility.

Literary critics also consider how readers respond to a work, how it affects them, what it makes them think about. Critics are concerned with exploring why it is that a work leads us to specific responses and specific thoughts, how it directs our reactions, guides and limits them. In this instance, literary critics frequently turn their attention to rhetorical devices and consider their effect on the work and on us as readers. The list of rhetorical devices, of course, is very long, and many of them are prominently used in biblical narrative.

All of these questions, it seems to me, are directed towards answering the question: How does this work of literature gain whatever meaning it has for us? If we do not answer this question, then we are not dealing with literature as literature, but rather with literature as philosophy, or as history, or as theology, or psychology, and so on—all of which disciplines are related to literature, influence it, and are influenced by it.

For all of the questions I have suggested above, it may be more important to be able to demonstrate how we arrive at the answers rather than to know the answers themselves. The demonstration usually involves an awareness of a narrative's alternatives, choices, options: in terms of scene placement, choice of speaker, length of a character's speech, imagery, metaphors used by a character, individual words which a character may emphasize and thus become associated with, and so on. We must constantly be asking: why does the narrative include this scene at this moment? Why does the narrative have this particular character saying these particular words at this moment? Why does the narrative remind us of an earlier scene or character or speech at a particular moment in the course of the narrative itself?

The crucial question of options and choices and alternatives is very well illustrated by the four gospels. Here after all are four narratives essentially about the same subject; but clearly the narratives have made different choices, selected different options, worked with different narrative strategies. The gospel of Mark, for example, whatever the sources, has selected and arranged narrative units in a particular order and to a particular end. As we know from reading the four gospels, the narrative of Mark has designs and strategies which differ from those of Luke, Matthew, and John. In a concern with Mark's gospel as literature, then, we are less immediately interested in sources, theology, philosophy, world view or whatever. Instead, we ask questions having to do with narrative technique, organization and selection of material, character development, character motivation, character ambiguities. We ask why Mark decided to order his material in the way he did; why particular scenes or incidents are described and placed where they are in the text; in what directions the narrative is moving, towards what end; why certain incidents are repeated; what connections or transitions exist between one narrative unit and another; what relationships exist among the characters. And on such a list could go.

Of particular interest in the gospel of Mark is the use of parables. A literary critic would ask why they are used at all. What do we learn from them that we would not learn from straightforward narration? We also wonder why the narrative selected these particular parables for inclusion in this particular narrative. We ask how they function, what their relation is to the narrative as a whole; why they appear in the specific narrative contexts in which they occur. We ask what the effect would be of moving them elsewhere in the narrative? All of these questions are directed to the gospel's narrative strategy—selections have been made, we must assume, for many parables, options and alternatives have been rejected, both in terms of the material and in terms of its placement in the narrative as a whole.

As I consider these questions about the parables or indeed about any aspect of a biblical narrative, I also feel the need to be aware of what other disciplines have contributed to the issues. I must find out at some point, for example, the definition and use of parables in Jesus' historical setting as well as the historical circumstances, if any, which they reflect. For parables, I would discover in scholarship and criticism two divergent trends. Some scholars seek to discover the original form of the parable and the original meaning of its internal historical references (to persons, customs, cultural factors). Other scholars treat the parables as aesthetic objects and analyze them with the methods of structuralism or with the aid of the perspective of existentialism. Clearly a tension exists between these approaches—historical critics run the risk of leaving the parables in the past, with nothing to say to the present; and those who treat them as metaphors or as autonomous aesthetic objects perhaps do less than justice to them as parables, and particularly as parables of Jesus. My own approach, as is certainly evident by this time, attempts to view the parables as literary devices in a literary narrative. And yet I am aware that the assumption of this narrative is unique. I can never forget that the narrative believes it is describing the life of the Messiah, the son of God. The gospel, from a literary point of view, is creating a fictional world—but the word fictional is not meant to connote that the world may not be a true one. The fictional world of Mark, in other words, is based on specific narrative assumptions and intentions which a critic cannot ignore.

The scholarship and criticism on parables illustrates the continuing gap which exists between biblical scholars and literary critics. Various essays tell us that we need to decide what class of parable a particular parable belongs to. Is it a figurative saying? A similitude? A parable of advent? Of reversal? Of action? All of this may be useful information, but I am not sure that it is useful to me as a literary critic, any more than it is useful in understanding a particular sonnet to identify whether an image is a Petrarchan image or a Neoplatonic one. Another set of essays on parables might explain that parables tease us into thought. As a literary critic, I feel compelled to ask precisely how this occurs and why. Yet other essays say that Jesus uses parables because truth in a tale is more readily remembered. Even if I accept this statement, I still need to demonstrate how it functions and whether it functions successfully in the narratives which make use of parables. More generally, biblical scholarship points out that Jesus obviously uses parables to illustrate his teachings. As a literary critic, I must ask why Jesus uses parables at all. He surely had at his disposal, as do we, many other ways and means of illustrating what it is he wanted to convey. Finally, it is generally agreed that parables appeal to readers because there is something in them which touches on broad areas of human experience. This again may be an accurate statement, but it seems to me that the job of the literary critic is to uncover precisely what experience is being touched on and what the relation then is between that experience, the parable, the narrative context in which the parable appears, and the narrative of Mark as a whole.

I have dwelled for a long time, perhaps too long, on parables and a literary critic's concerns and questions about them. I would like to close this essay on methodology by describing my own approach to a biblical narrative.

I begin by reading the narrative six or eight times, at various intervals. I then write an elaborate summary of it, a summary which frequently is longer than the narrative itself. I will then construct several summaries of the summary. What I am trying to do (and what may sound like a very mechanical process) is to familiarize myself so thoroughly with the text that I can detach myself from it and approach it as an object totally familiar to me but at some remove from me. Once I have this full knowledge of the text and the ability to separate myself from it, I can look at the narrative from a distance to see when one action or speech is an echo of another, when one scene is related to another or repeats a previous scene, and so on. It is at this point that I can begin to take notes, either mentally or on paper, of such things as repetitions in the narrative—repetitions of situations, of scene, of a motif or a word, of individual phrases, particularly when they are attributed to a single character. This enables me to begin to understand the small changes which might occur in the repetitions and thus begin to answer the question: why is there repetition at all? Is it used for emphasis?

to accelerate the action? to emphasize attitudes? to reveal a new aspect of a character or of the action? to foreshadow later action? In pondering the summary of my summaries, I am also looking for the kinds of concerns I described earlier—development of character, changes in a character's situation or attitude, tone or language, motives for a character's action or a narrative intrusion or digression, reasons for placing a scene where it is (by looking at what comes before it and at what comes after it). I am always thinking about alternatives, choices, options, always asking why a scene, a word, a phrase, a speech, occurs in a particular context and at a particular moment in the narrative.

At this point I read everything I can in biblical scholarship about the biblical narrative. I believe it is crucial to do this only after I have totally assimilated the narrative and identified most of its strategies. In reading through biblical scholarship, I am of course seeking background information; perhaps more importantly, I am also attempting to discover what has been of particular interest to biblical scholars and critics. I want to know what issues they have identified as crucial in the text, what emphases they have placed in their analyses of the narrative. This will lead me to make a list of the major issues as perceived from the perspective of biblical scholarship. The list will often coincide with the list of issues I have found important from a literary point of view. In preparing for my essay on David, for example, I became aware during the first part of my analysis and before I had read biblical scholarship that there was a seeming inconsistency in the narrative in that Saul on two occasions has to ask who David is. I later discovered, as most readers will be aware, that biblical scholarship has been concerned with the very same issue. I also was aware during the course of my analysis from a literary point of view that David's relationships with Saul and Absolom dominated the narrative. I later discovered, again as most readers know, that biblical scholars devote much attention to David's relationships with these two characters. After I have finished my review of biblical scholarship and compared it with my own initial analysis from a literary perspective, I am prepared to make a list of questions which, it seems to me, are central to an understanding of the narrative as a work of literature. These questions may range in number from 15 to 20 to as many as 40 or 50. Usually, it will be possible to cluster the questions into certain groupings. From this list of questions, the organization or structure of the lecture or essay that I hope to prepare emerges.

There is really no way to end an essay on methodology other than to say that the methodology I have described has led to the essays which I have written for this particular volume. Since we are dealing with biblical narratives, however, there may be questions which any consideration of methodology must take into account. These include the issue of divine inspiration, the problem of making value judgments about the Bible and its narratives; the question of what the text is—that is, is our text the entire Old and New Testament? one of the narratives within one of the testaments? a unit within one of these narratives? and so on. Behind all of the present work on the Bible as literature there remains the question of the authority of the Bible as scripture. I have stated my own opinion about the issue earlier and it may be helpful to close by repeating it here. The Bible is one of the great works of western culture. As a student and teacher of literature, I believe it is important to make the text of the Bible as accessible as possible to as many people as possible. In interpreting the biblical narratives as literature, and I believe many of them are great literature indeed, my hope is that the texts are being made more accessible, that the Bible will exert its proper influence in our culture, that the values which it endorses and promulgates will, as they should, affect us all.

THE BIBLE AS LITERATURE
N.E.H. Institute for College Teachers
Indiana University
Summer 1979

Syllabus for Literary Critics

Ancient Mesopotamian Thought and Culture
Reading:
> Bright, John, *A History of Israel* (Westminster, 1972) pp. 23–66.
> Jacobsen, Thorkild, "Formative Tendencies in Sumerian Religion," *Toward the Image of Tammuz*, (Harvard, 1970), pp. 1–15.
> —————, "Ancient Mesopotamian Religion: The Central Concerns," *Toward the Image of Tammuz*, pp. 39–47.
> "The Creation Epic," in James B. Pritchard, *Ancient Near Eastern Texts Related to the Old Testament*, (Princeton, 1969), pp. 60–72.
> Jacobsen, T., "Reflection of the World View in Later Myths: 'Enuma Elish,'" in H. Frankford (ed.), *The Intellectual Adventure of Ancient Man* (Chicago, 1946), pp. 168–84.
> Sandars, N. K., *The Epic of Gilgamesh* (Penguin), pp. 61–71,97–117.

The Jesus Birth Stories
Reading:
> Matthew 1–2; Luke 1–2

The Patriarchal Age
Reading:
> Bright, J., *A History of Israel*, pp. 67–102.
> deVaux, *The Early History of Israel* (Westminster, 1978), pp. 221–56, 267–87.
> Gunkel, *The Legends of Genesis* (Schocken, 1964), pp. 37–87.
> Speiser, E. A., "The Biblical Idea of History in its Common Near Eastern Setting," in *The Jewish Expression* ed. by J. Goldin (Yale, 1976), pp. 1–17.

The Mosaic Age
Reading:
> Bright, John, *A History of Israel*, pp. 105–39.

deVaux, *The Early History of Israel*, pp. 99–117, 453–72, 673–80.

Campbell, E. F., "The Amarna Letters and the Amarna Period," *The Biblical Archaeologist Reader*, Vol. 3, pp. 100–120.

Alt, A., "The Settlement of the Israelites in Palestine," *Essays on Old Testament History and Religion* (Doubleday, 1970), p. 175–221.

Anderson, B. W., "Martin Noth's Traditio-Historical Approach in the Context of 20th Century Biblical Research" and M. Noth, "The Major Themes of the Tradition in the Pentateuch and their Origins," in *A History of Pentateuchal Traditions*, by M. Noth (trans. by B. W. Anderson) (Prentice-Hall, 1972), pp. xvii–xxviii, 46–62.

Buber, M., *Moses: The Revelation and the Covenant* (Harper, 1958), pp. 13–19, 101–9.

Newman, M., *The People of the Covenant* (Abingdon, 1962), pp. 39–71.

Riemann, P., "Covenant, Mosaic," *Interpreter's Dictionary of the Bible Supplement* (Abingdon, 1976), pp. 192–97.

Greenberg, M., "Some Postulates of Biblical Criminal Law," in *The Jewish Expression* ed. by J. Goldin (Yale, 1976), pp. 18–37.

Jonah
Reading:
  Jonah 1–4

Canaanite Culture and the Period of the Judges
Reading:
  Bright, John, *A History of Israel*, pp. 140–75.

  McKenzie, John, *The World of the Judges* (Prentice-Hall, 1966), pp. 34–43, 94–120.

  deVaux, *The Early History of Israel*, pp. 139–52.

  Pritchard, James B., *Ancient Near Eastern Texts Related to the Old Testament* (Princeton, 1969), pp. 129–31, 138–40.

  Frankfort, H. A., "Myth and Reality," in *The Intellectual Adventure of Ancient Man* (Chicago, 1946), pp. 3–27.

  Eliade, M., *The Sacred and the Profane* (Harcourt Brace, 1959), pp. 68–113.

  Anderson, B. W., "Myth and the Biblical Tradition," *Theology Today* 27 (1970–71), pp. 44–62.

  Cross, F. M., "The Divine Warrior in Israel's Early Cult," in A. Altmann (ed.), *Biblical Motifs* (Harvard, 1966), pp. 11–30.

The Song of Songs
Reading:
  Song of Songs 1–8

Monarchy in Israel
Reading:
  Bright, John, *A History of Israel*, pp. 179–224.

  Alt, A., "The Formation of the Israelite State," in *Essays on OT History and Religion* (Doubleday, 1968), pp. 225–309.

  Cross, Frank M., "The Ideologies of Kingship in the Era of the Empire: Conditional Covenant and Eternal Decree," in *Canaanite Myth and Hebrew Epic* (Harvard, 1973), pp. 219–73.

  Guthrie, H. H., "God as Cosmic King: Hymnic Praise, Temple and King" in *Israel's Sacred Songs* (Seabury, 1966), pp. 59–117.

Anderson, B. W., "Creation and Covenant: Zion Theology," in *Creation Versus Chaos* (Association, 1967), pp. 60–77.

von Rad, G., "The Beginnings of Historical Writing in Ancient Israel," in *The Problem of the Hexateuch and Other Essays* (McGraw-Hill, 1966), pp. 166–76, 189–204.

Nelson, H. H., A. L. Oppenheim and G. E. Wright, "The Significance of the Temple in the Ancient Near East," in G. E. Wright and D. N. Freedman, *The Biblical Archaeologist Reader*, Vol 1 (Quadrangle, 1961), pp. 145–84.

Weinfeld, M., "Covenant, Davidic," in *Interpreter's Dictionary of the Bible Supplement* (Abingdon, 1976), pp. 188–92.

Eliade, M., *The Sacred and the Profane* (Harcourt Brace, 1959), pp. 20–65.

Sacred History and Prose Fiction
Reading:

Genesis 2:18–25; 25:29–34

Judges 3:12–30

I Samuel 24:1–23

Alter, R., "A Literary Approach to the Bible," *Commentary* 60 (December 1975), pp. 70–77.

The Poetics of Biblical Parallelism I
Reading:

Deuteronomy 32:1–43

Hrushovski, "Hebrew Prosody," *Encyclopaedia Judaica*, Vol. 13 (Macmillan, 1971), pp. 1200–1203.

Job 3

Prophecy and the Divided Kingdom
Reading:

Bright, J., *A History of Israel*, pp. 225–339.

Paul, S., "Prophets and Prophecy," *Encyclopaedia Judaica*, Vol. 13 (Macmillan, 1971), pp. 1150–75.

Muilenburg, J., "The 'Office' of the Prophet in Ancient Israel," in J. Philip Hyatt (ed.), *The Bible in Modern Scholarship* (Abingdon, 1965), pp. 74–97.

Ross, J., "The Prophet as Yahweh's Messenger," in B. W. Anderson and W. Harrelson (ed.), *Israel's Prophetic Heritage* (Harper, 1962), pp. 98–107.

Huffmon, H. B., "The Covenant Lawsuit in the Prophets," *Journal of Biblical Literature* 78 (1959), pp. 285–95.

von Rad, G., *The Message of the Prophets* (Harper and Row, 1965), pp. 15–49.

Heschel, A., *The Prophets* (Jewish Publication Society, 1962), pp. 351–66.

Scott, R. B. Y., *The Relevance of the Prophets* (Macmillan, 1968), pp. 1–39, 60–89.

Crenshaw, J., *Prophetic Conflict* (Berlin, 1971), pp. 24–38, 62–86.

Spiegel, S., "Amos vs. Amaziah," in J. Goldon (ed.) *The Jewish Expression* (Yale, 1976), pp. 38–65.

Napier, B. D., *Prophets in Perspective* (Abingdon, 1963), pp. 36–57.

Malamat, A., "Prophetic Revelations in New Documents from Mari and the Bible," *Vetus Testamentum Supplement 15* (Brill, 1965), pp. 207–27.

The Book of Job
Reading:
>   Job 1–42

Theocratic Judaism and the Exile
Reading:
>   Bright, H., *A History of Israel*, pp. 343–92.
>   Bickerman, E., *From Ezra to the Last of the Maccabees* (Schocken, 1962), pp. 3–40.
>   Freedman, D. N., "Pentateuch," *Interpreter's Dictionary of the Bible* (K–Q volume) (Abingdon, 1962), pp. 712–27.
>   Weinfeld, M., "Theological Currents in Pentateuchal Literature," *Proceedings of the American Academy for Jewish Research* 37 (1969), pp. 117–39.
>   von Rad, G., "The Deuteronomic Theology of History in I and II Kings," in *The Problem of the Hexateuch and Other Essays* (McGraw-Hill, 1966), pp. 205–21.
>   Cross, F. M., "The Themes of the Book of Kings and the Structure of the Deuteronomistic History," "The Priestly Work," in *Canaanite Myth and Hebrew Epic* (Harvard, 1973), pp. 274–89, 293–325.
>   Freedman, D. N., "The Chronicler's Purpose," *Catholic Biblical Quarterly* 23 (1961), pp. 436–42.
>   Kapelrud, A. S., "The Role of the Cult in Old Israel," in J. P. Hyatt (ed.) *The Bible in Modern Scholarship* (Abingdon, 1965), pp. 44–56.
>   Guthrie, H. H., *Israel's Sacred Songs* (Seabury, 1966), pp. 5–25.

Genesis
Reading:
>   Genesis 1–11

Wisdom in Israel
Reading:
>   Bickerman, E., *From Ezra to the Last of the Maccabees* (Schocken, 1962), pp. 41–90.
>   Williams, R. J., J. L. Crenshaw and H. Conzelmann, "Wisdom in the Ancient Near East, Old Testament, and New Testament," *Interpreter's Dictionary of the Bible Supplement* (Abingdon, 1976), pp. 949–60.
>   Gordes, R., "The Social Background of Wisdom Literature," *Hebrew Union College Annual* 18 (1944), pp. 77–118.
>   Scott, R. B. Y., "The Study of the Wisdom Literature," *Interpretation* 24 (1970), pp. 20–45.
>   Murphy, R. E., "The Interpretation of Old Testament Wisdom Literature," *Interpretation* 23 (1969), pp. 289–301.

Apocalyptic in Israel
Reading:
>   Bright, J., *A History of Israel*, pp. 407–67.
>   Bickerman, E., *From Ezra to the Last of the Maccabees*, pp. 93–186.
>   Hanson, P. D., "Apocalypse, Genre" and "Apocalypticism," *Interpreter's*

Dictionary of the Bible Supplement (Abingdon, 1976), pp. 27–34.

————————, "Old Testament Apocalyptic Reexamined," *Interpretation* 25 (1971), pp. 454–79.

Cross, F. M., "The Early History of the Apocalyptic Community at Qumran," and "A Note on the Study of Apocalyptic Origins," in *Canaanite Myth and Hebrew Epic* (Harvard, 1973), pp. 326–46.

Gaster, T. H., "Analytical Index," in *The Dead Sea Scriptures* (Doubleday Anchor, 1956), pp. 327–42.

The Abraham Story
Reading:
   Genesis 11:27–25:11

New Testament Background: Jesus
Reading:
   Reicke, Bo, *The New Testament Era* (Fortress, 1968), pp. 82–188.

   Cullmann, O., "The Significance of the Qumran Texts for Research into the Beginnings of Christianity," and W. H. Brownlee, "John the Baptist in the New Light of Ancient Scrolls," in K. Stendahl (ed.) *The Scrolls and the New Testament* (Harper, 1957), pp. 18–53.

   Fuller, R. H., "The New Testament and Mythology," "The New Quest of the Historical Jesus," *The New Testament in Current Study* (Scribner's, 1962), pp. 1–53.

   Davies, W. D., "The Strength and Weakness of Form Criticism" and "Recent Emphases in Gospel Criticism," in *Invitation to the New Testament* (Doubleday, 1969), pp. 109–35.

   Bornkamm, G., "The Dawn of the Kingdom of God," *Jesus of Nazareth* (Harper, 1960), pp. 64–95.

   Jeremias, J., *The Parables of Jesus* (Scribner's, 1963), pp. 90–114.

   Fuller, R. H., "Synoptic Studies," *The New Testament in Current Study* (Scribner's, 1962), pp. 70–85.

   Beare, F. W., "The Baptism of Christ" and "The Temptation," *The Earliest Records of Jesus* (Blackwell, 1962), pp. 40–43.

   Bultmann, R., *Form Criticism* (Harper, 1962), pp. 32–63.

Wilderness and Sinai
Reading:
   Exodus 15:22–34:35
   Numbers 10:20–20:29

New Testament Background: Paul
Reading:
   Reicke, Bo, *The New Testament Era* (Fortress, 1968), pp. 188–224.

   Davies, W. D., "Palestinian and Diaspora Judaism," *Paul and Rabbinic Judaism* (SPCK, 1948), pp. 1–16.

   Fuller, R. H., "Pauline Studies," *The New Testament in Current Study*, pp. 54–69.

   Davies, W. D., *Invitation to the New Testament* (Doubleday, 1969), pp. 254–326.

   Francis, Fred O. and J. Paul Sampley, *Pauline Parallels* (Fortress, 1975), pp. 34–35.

Repetitive Structure in the Biblical Narrative
Reading:
    Numbers 11
    1 Samuel 3, 15
    2 Samuel 13
    Buber, M., "Leitworstil . . . ," *Werke-Zweiter Band: Schriften der Bibel*,
        Vol. 2 (1962), pp. 1111–74.

Doubling and Point of View in the Biblical Narrative
Reading:
    Genesis 37–44
    Esther 1–10
    Fishbane, M., "Composition and Structure in the Jacob Cycle" (Gen.
        25:19–35:22), *Journal of Jewish Studies* 26 (1975), pp. 15–38.
    Scholes, R. and R. Kellogg, "Point of View in Narrative," *The Nature of*
        Narrative, pp. 240–82.

The Poetics of Prayer
Reading:
    Psalms 12,19,122
    Hrushovski, "Hebrew Prosody," *Encyclopaedia Judaica*, Vol. 13, pp.
        1200–1203.
    Fishbane, M., "A Wretched Thing of Shame, A Mere Belly: an Interpre-
        tation of Jeremiah 20:7–12."

Traditions, Sources, and Gospels
Reading:
    Throckmorton, *Gospel Parallels*, pp. 67–71.
    John 6:1–65
    Mk 6:30–56, 8:1–26, 4:1–34 and parallels

The Gospel According to Mark I
Reading:
    Mark 1–16
    Petersen, N. R., *Literary Criticism for New Testament Critics*, pp. 49–80.

The Gospel According to Mark II
Reading:
    Petersen, "Point of View in Narrative," *Semeia* 12 (1978), pp. 97–121.

INSTITUTE READER

Alonso-Schokel, L., "Die stilistische Analyse bei den Propheten,"   Page 1
    Vetus Testamentum Supplement No. 7 (1955), pp. 154–64.

Alonso-Schokel, L., "Erzahlkunst im Buche der Richter,"   7
    Biblica 42 (1961) pp. 143–72

Alter, Robert, "A Literary Approach to the Bible,"   23
    Commentary 60 (Dec., 1975), pp. 70–77

Alter, Robert, "Biblical Narrative,"   31
    Commentary 61 (May, 1976), pp. 61–67

IMPLICATIONS OF SEMIOTIC AND STRUCTURAL RESEARCH FOR THE TEACHING OF THE HUMANITIES

Daniel Patte
Vanderbilt University

At the outset I need to make clear that I do not intend to advocate that semiotic and structuralist theories and methods be taught in undergraduate programs. Rather I want to suggest that these fields of research have much to contribute toward a better understanding of the way in which the Humanities, in general, and the Ancient World, in particular, should be taught in the present cultural situation.

Without trying to give a full definition of semiotics and structuralism by reviewing their development—cf. T. Hawkes as a first general introduction and the bibliography therein[1]—I must nevertheless state most generally what these fields are. In brief, *semiotics* is the research aimed at establishing a general theory of meaning as it occurs (as a "meaning effect") in any type of cultural phenomena. In view of the grandiose scope of this project, it is not surprising to find different and often conflicting semiotic theories, themselves based upon different linguistic theories (since a prime manifestation of meaning is found in linguistic communication). Despite this confusion—comparable to the confusion which reigns in the first stages of any fundamental scientific inquiry—theories which are more and more complete, although still partial, are proposed; for instance, those of U. Eco[2] and of A. J. Greimas.[3] In contrast to semiotics, which can be compared to fundamental scientific research, *structuralism* can be compared to the applications that

---

[1] For a first general introduction to semiotics and structuralism see (in the following order) Terrence Hawkes, *Structuralism and Semiotics* (Los Angeles: University of California Press, Berkeley, 1977); Robert Scholes, *Structuralism in Literature: A Introduction* (New Haven: Yale University Press, 1974); and Maria Corti, *An Introduction to Literary Semiotics* (Bloomington: Indiana University Press, 1978). Each of these books includes excellent bibliographies for further reading.

[2] Umberto Eco, *A Theory of Semiotics* (Bloomington: Indiana University Press, 1976); and Umberto Eco, *The Role of the Reader* (Bloomington: Indiana University Press, 1979).

[3] Greimas's overall theory—which attempts to incorporate critically the many partial theories and ongoing research projects of many scholars in various fields—is presented in A. J. Greimas and Joseph Courtés, *Semiotics and Language: An Encyclopedic Dictionary* (Bloomington: Indiana University Press, 1982).

the technologist makes of the results of this research. Technology can be based upon quite crude scientific views as well as upon more sophisticated ones. Similarly, a structural study is the use of a semiotic theory—whether it merely involves a few principles or a more complex theoretical construct— for the understanding of a given cultural artifact (be it a painting, a building or a text).

Semiotics and structuralism can help us in conceiving how to teach the humanities in three ways.

(1) Certain semioticians have studied the specific nature of "didactic discourses." Their theoretical proposals will help us better understand what takes place in classes on the ancient world and other humanistic fields, and what are the conditions which need to be fulfilled so that our teaching might reach its goal.

(2) One of these conditions is that our teaching be related to our audience—our students as participants in a specific culture. A structural perspective will allow us to suggest what some of the characteristics of this culture are. We need to take these into account when organizing our lectures, courses and programs on the ancient world.

(3) Finally, semiotics and structuralism (together with other fields of theoretical inquiries) can provide us with tools which can help us identify and select the themes and topics we might want to teach according to this model.

As we proceed in this three-part discussion, I will take illustrations and examples from my field—New Testament studies—but, of course, what I will say here applies as well to classical studies and indeed to most humanistic teaching.

I. The Teaching of the Humanities
as a Specific Type of Didactic Discourse

Greimas[4] and Fabbri,[5] as a result of a year-long seminar devoted to this subject, have proposed essential elements of a semiotic definition of didactic discourse which can be our starting point.[6] Most generally speaking, a didactic discourse is a *persuasive* discourse. It aims at having an effect upon the audience. "Didactic discourse is a sub-class of discourses which are characterized by their efficiency and which can be evaluated in terms of it."[7] It is

---

[4] A. J. Greimas, "Pour une semiotique didactique," *Le Bulletin* du Groupe de Recherches Semio-Linguistiques 7, Paris, CNRS, 1979.

[5] Paoli Fabbri, "Champ de manoeuvres didactiques," *Le Bulletin* du Groupe de Recherches Semio-Linguistiques 7, Paris, CNRS, 1979.

[6] For a more complete discussion of the characteristics of didactic discourses, see D. Patte, *Aspects of a Semiotics of Didactic Discourse*, Working Papers 97–98–99, Urbino, Italy: Centro Internazionale di Semiotica e di Linguistica, 1980. See especially pp. 1–20.

[7] A. J. Greimas, "Pour une semiotique didactique," *Le Bulletin* 7, 1979, p. 3, my translation.

thus appropriate to classify didactic discourses according to their effects. We can then distinguish two categories of didactic discourse.

Two Broad Types of Didactic Discourse

(a) The didactic discourses which aim at *causing to do,* including those which aim at causing to learn or to know new data and new information. Learning and knowing are indeed actions which demand the active participation of the addressees. Students are not tape-recorders!

(b) The didactic discourses which aim at *causing to believe*, that is, at causing to appropriate a new vision of life, new values, new convictions.

In fact, these two types are not as far apart as one might think at first. Many didactic discourses (if not most) involve both causing to believe and causing to do. A brief example will help us perceive more concretely essential features of any didactic discourse.

Imagine that you (an enthusiastic fisherman) want to persuade me to go fishing. Since I know nothing about this activity, you will have to cause me to learn a lot of data that I need to know in order to have successful fishing expeditions (how to get the proper fishing gear, how to find the proper location, how to choose and set the proper bait or lure, how to cast it, what to do when a fish bites, etc). Yet giving me all these pieces of information—which could be found in the *Manual of the Good Fisherman*—would not persuade me. These instructions need to be part of your discourse; yet your discourse will be didactic only if it persuades me to learn all these instructions and indeed first persuades me that fishing is an activity in which I might want to get involved.

For this purpose your discourse needs to convince me that fishing is a good activity for me, for instance, by convincing me of the necessity of outdoor activities. And, of course, you will be successful only if you relate this activity to some of the values and categories which govern my present life. (You would be most convincing if you would demonstrate to me that going fishing would help me in my semiotic and structural research because of, say, the relaxing character of this activity!) Now because I want to go fishing, I would be ready and possibly eager to learn all the instructions you intend to impart to me. Yet in order that I might be ready to learn them *from you*, you still need to convince me of the validity (truth) of your instructions. This is what you would do spontaneously by referring to your exploits on various fishing expeditions! It is only if your discourse involves all these elements that you can hope to cause me to learn these instructions and ultimately to cause me to go fishing.

This simple example shows what is involved in any didactic discourse. It is not merely the repetition of the discourse found in the *Manual of the Good Fisherman* (which assumes that the reader is already a devoted fisherman). Rather it involves a recasting of this "discourse of reference" in terms of the categories and values of the addressees. In brief, *a didactic discourse is the re-uttering (the re-telling) of another discourse in terms of a specific audience.*

If we now turn toward what takes place in a college classroom, we can note two very different didactic strategies according to the fields.

(a) In *the sciences and mathematics* the teaching is minimally didactic. In most instances (except for the few courses aimed at students majoring in the Humanities) it is presupposed that the students want to learn. That is, it is assumed that the students are already convinced of the importance of the sciences and math for their future careers in our society. This is a valid assumption in a technological culture. Science is indeed perceived as providing valid (true) views of the reality of everything in our experience and the application of this scientific knowledge is perceived as good (as the only good, "efficient" way to resolve whatever problems are encountered in our society). The students as belonging to this culture (they come from it and will go back to it) already hold these views, values or categories. Didactic discourses in the sciences need not establish or communicate this vision of human experience. They need not cause the students to believe in this vision; they already believe it. The only didactic dimension needed is that which guarantees the validity (truth) of the data (or instructions) that the students have to learn. For the instructor it is enough to establish that he/she is truthworthy, i.e., a good scientist (as is already partially established by the fact that he/she is a faculty member of an institution of higher education), and that the theories proposed are consistent with other scientific knowledge.

(b) In *the Humanities* the situation is quite different. In general terms we can define our vocation as that of teaching our students (or confronting them with) "other" cultures (past or foreign cultures). Ideally this teaching aims at presenting these other cultures in such a way that they might be perceived by the students as plausible visions of human experience and of its goals—so much so that they might truly appear as an alternative to the vision of our culture. In this way humanistic education prepares people for an indispensable leadership role in our society. The ideal "humanists" are no longer accepting passively the vision, values, and goals defined by our culture, but are in a position to compare them with those of other cultures and thus to evaluate them critically. As such, humanists are in a position to function as responsible members and leaders in our culture.

This is how I would describe the ideal goal of humanistic teaching. Unfortunately our teaching, despite notable successes, often fails to reach this goal. Indeed one can speak of the plight of humanistic education.

Before assessing this situation we need to consider the type of didactic discourse necessary in humanistic courses with the above described goal. In contrast with the teaching in the sciences which, in fact, reinforces the students' dependence and faith in the vision of life and reality dominant in our culture, humanistic teaching aims at communicating other visions of life and reality as plausible alternatives to that of our culture. In other words, our humanistic teaching must be a didactic discourse which aims at *causing our students to believe in* the plausibility of these other visions of human experience. It is not unlike religious discourses (sermons, etc.), which also aim at causing to believe. The fundamental difference is that humanistic teaching does not advocate any vision of life as an absolute. Humanistic teaching proposes a *plurality* of cultures as having plausible, coherent visions of life. Yet the didactic strategy found in religious discourses does provide a valid model for humanistic didactic teaching.

An Example of Didactic Discourse

Let us take as an example a well known text—the Parable of the Good Samaritan, Luke 10:30–35—which aims at communicating a new vision of life. This new vision would be comparable to the vision of life found in Homer or Cicero that a classicist might want to communicate to his/her students (a "new" vision from the standpoint of the students). A few remarks[8] will suffice to enable us to perceive the didactic strategy of this text.

For the audience (to be distinguished from the critical biblical scholars) that hears this parable, it is clear that the main theme of this story has to do with compassion—the entire second half is devoted to it—as opposed to violence and indifference—expressed in the first part. In fact, the audience (both the original Jewish audience and the modern Western audience) readily approves the compassionate attitudes and disapproves the violent and indifferent attitudes.

This simple observation enables us to conclude that this part of the text's meaning is *not* new for the audience. The Palestinian Jews of Jesus' audience already held these values as a part of their vision of life (this is clear in the early Jewish literature). If it were the only teaching of this story, hearing it they would not learn anything!

We can also note that the parable introduces personages who represent "thematic roles" that are well known in Jewish Palestine at that time: robbers (evil and violent people), a Priest, a Levite (representing two categories of highly religious and good people), a Samaritan (a hated heretic, good for nothing), and an innkeeper (a person belonging to the business world). These categories of personages are directly recognizable by the audience, because they are categories which belong to the audience's vision of life (or more precisely here, of society). We could say the same thing about the locations mentioned in the text (Jerusalem, Jericho, the road, the inn).

Yet a tension between the audience's expectation (vision) and the story is created by the fact that the good value, compassion, is associated with the evil Samaritan, and a bad value, indifference for a person in need, is associated with the good Priest and Levite. A closer analysis shows that the text is aimed

---

[8] For a complete analysis of this text (as an illustration of the main features of Greimas's semiotic theory), see D. Patte, "Greimas' Model of the Generative Trajectory of Meaning in Discourses," *American Journal of Semiotics* II, 1982.

at transmitting a new vision of the relation between the sacred and the secular. According to this new vision, society and heretics are posited as good (indeed as attuned to the divine). Society, including its business world (despite its dubious nature, since in it one helps others in exchange for money), is good because it provides a valid order for life. The heretics, and more generally the pariahs and impure people who live at the fringe of society, are good because they have practical and realistic attitudes despite (and indeed thanks to) the fact that they live in "disorder" without truly meaningful purpose for their lives. In contrast, the robbers and the religious people are posited as evil. Anti-social people are evil because they belong to an anti-society (an "out of society"). The religious people are evil because they do not truly belong to society, since, in fact, they fully identify themselves with an above society, a sacred realm, a sacred order which gives purposefulness to their lives.

Such are the main features of the new vision communicated by the parable and expressed in many details of its text. For instance, the fact that the Priest and the Levite represent a sacred order which gives purposefulness to their lives is expressed through their clearly oriented journey: they are going down that road. By contrast the Samaritan is said to be "journeying," a non-oriented travel. This expresses what a heretic Samaritan is: a person living without true order and without absolute purpose in life.

Thus, far from being a mere example story—a didactic discourse aimed at causing the audience to do compassionate acts—this parable is first of all a didactic discourse aimed at causing the audience to believe a new vision of life. Its message could be summarized as follows: as long as you do not become a "heretic" by making yours this new vision of life, you cannot truly perform compassionate actions.

The Necessary Features of a Humanistic Didactic Discourse

This example shows the characteristic features that a didactic discourse aimed at communicating a new or different vision of life must have.

(1) Its most apparent organization should *not* be that of the other vision we want to communicate. In other words, our lectures, our courses and our programs should *not* be organized according to the categories of the corpus, the vision of which we want to communicate as a plausible alternative to our contemporary vision of life.

I am aware of the controversial character of this statement. It is going against our most spontaneous way of teaching and of dealing with the corpus which is our field of specialization. Is not the case that we can truly claim to understand a text only when we scrupulously respect its categories and themes and their interrelations in the text? Yes, indeed! This is the approach we need to use in our scholarly research. But there is an essential difference between, on the one hand, us and our graduate students and, on the other hand, the undergraduate students, especially those in our introductory classes. We (and our graduate students) are already convinced that the vision of life found in our corpus (be it Plato's writings or Paul's letters) is a plausible alternative to the contemporary vision of life. We already are "believers." And thus if, when addressing them, we use a scholarly discourse—i.e., a discourse organized according to the categories of the corpus under study—their response will be "so what?" They necessarily will have the same bored attitude as the one I would have if you explain to me in great detail the difference between various lures while, as you have gathered, I have not the slightest inclination to go fishing!

(2) To put it positively, our humanistic teaching—our lectures, our courses, our programs—should be organized according to the categories of our audience—our students. The themes and topics which form the framework of our teaching should be directly recognizable by our students because they are themes and topics which belong to their vision of life (as the thematic roles Priest, Levite, Samaritan were for the Jews). Of course, the themes and topics selected need to be present in our corpus, even though, often, they will not be the central themes therein. But our teaching will aim at showing the specificity of the selected themes and topics of our corpus because of the way in which they are related to other themes in it. This provides the possibility of dealing with the central themes of our corpus even though they had not been selected at first.

For instance, one of the central themes of the New Testament is eschatology. But, because it is not a category of our students' vision of life, it should not be one of the themes around which our teaching is organized. Yet our students can readily recognize themes such as "scripture," "religious community and its organization," "personal religious experience." Thus we should begin by exploring the specific characteristics of these themes in the New Testament. But as we proceed we are soon led to discuss eschatology as an essential factor which allows us to make sense of the specific view of, e.g., "scripture" found in these texts.

(3) Our discussion of the Parable of the Good Samaritan suggests that our humanistic didactic discourse needs to be even more fundamentally organized according to the categories of our audience. Let us keep in mind that the parable owes its overall organization to the values "compassion," "violence," and "indifference" (of the Jewish audience), even though these values do not, in the last analysis, participate in the new vision that the parable aims at communicating. Note that at this point we are not dealing with themes or topics but indeed with fundamental categories (or values) which govern the way of life (all the way of life including the way of thinking) of the audience. In other words, we are dealing with fundamental patterns which characterize a culture.[9]

---

[9] This is what Greimas calls the "fundamental semantics," which, in this case, would characterize a (sociolectal) "semantic universe" (see these entries in A. J. Greimas and Joseph Courtés, *Semiotics and Language: An Encyclopedic Dictionary.*)

This is to say that our humanistic teaching needs to be organized according to the funamental patterns which characterize our contemporary Western culture (the culture to which our students belong). It is here that, too often, our humanistic teaching fails. The failure to organize our teaching according to the fundamental patterns of our present culture is, in my view, the cause of the plight of humanistic education that we deplore. At this point what is at stake is not merely the choice of themes and topics for specific courses or programs, but indeed the very conception of humanistic education in its relationship to the students' culture.

II. *The Plight of Humanistic Education: Toward a Possible Solution*

A candid evaluation of the present situation of humanistic education is the necessary next step in our effort to understand how to conceive our humanistic teaching so that it might successfully fulfill its vocation.

There is no point in my rehearsing the statistics which show the steady decline, over the last two generations, of the Humanities at the expense of the Sciences and the Social Sciences. It is clear that speaking of the plight of humanistic education is not using too strong a language. This situation is, of course, directly related to a change in our society's perception of the place and role of the Humanities. In order to understand fully this change one would need to proceed to an "archaeology" of the concept of "Humanities" in its relationship to those of "culture" and "society" and to study the changes in "epistemes," as Michel Foucault has done on other topics.[10] Obviously, I have not performed this comprehensive structural study. Thus the following remarks certainly need much refinement since they are based on punctual (by contrast to systematic) inquiries. Yet I am confident they express an essential part of the reality of this change in the way in which the Humanities are perceived. Most of what I want to point out is common knowledge in academic circles. I will therefore limit myself to a few general observations.

Past Perceptions of the Humanities and Humanistic Education

In the past, becoming a humanist fulfilled the educational needs of (undergraduate) students because it helped them become members of the elite of society. People with humanistic education were perceived as people able to interpret their culture and thus to function as responsible members and leaders in it. This was the case because the culture was past-oriented. Former cultures (as expressed in the classics) were perceived as *models to be implemented* in the "present" society. The good life (a good society, a good religion, etc.) was a life implementing the standards of this ideal past. Thus former cultures were the necessary *background* of the "present" culture in the sense that it was the *ground* in which any good life is rooted, the *source* of any

---

[10] For instance, see Michel Foucault, *The Birth of the Clinic*, New York: Vintage Books, 1973.

good thing in a culture, the *matrix* which should mold any good culture.

In such a situation the study of the classics, of history, of past religions and philosophies, etc. was directly "relevant" (to use a popular term of the sixties). In other words, humanistic studies addressed directly the existential concern of students. To become learned (scholars) about one feature or another of the past was directly helpful in making sense of the contemporary culture perceived as unfolding according to past patterns. No gap was perceived between the Humanities and the "present" culture, conceived as they were as being in intrinsic continuity with each other. Consequently, teaching the Humanities demanded a minimal didactic discourse as in the case of scientific teaching today. In the sciences one can organize one's teaching according to the categories, themes, topics (and methodology) found in the scientific papers and books of the researchers, because the scientific approaches are in direct continuity with our culture. Similarly, in this past situation, humanistic teaching could be directly organized according to the categories, themes and topics characterizing the classic corpus under study. In other words, teachers could use the same categories as those used and uncovered by the scholars in their research; i.e., the categories of the text. An undergraduate student could be perceived as a "mini-scholar" or as a scholar-in-the-making. In fact, there was no clear distinction between undergraduate, graduate students and scholars except in terms of levels of expertise.

The Present Situation

Whether we like it or not the Humanities are no longer perceived in this way. The advent of the industrial era and its optimistic view of scientific and technological progress, and beyond it, the advent of the technological era, prophesied by Jacques Ellul[11] shortly after World War II, progressively changed, in a fundamental manner, the perception of the nature, place and role of the Humanities. Our culture has fundamentally changed. As a consequence the Humanities are perceived in a fundamentally different way.

Note, for instance, the kind of persons who are viewed as leaders in our society. To be a responsible member of, and leader in, our culture—to be part of the elite—one needs to be knowledgeable about the latest theories and "techniques" (in Ellul's sense of the term), be it in the fundamental sciences, in medical research, in economic and business research, or in any other technical field (including Law). It is on the basis of this scientific and "technical" knowledge that one can hope to address the problems which confront our society. The good life depends upon the the implementation of this knowledge and *not* upon the implementation of past models.

At first the scientific and technical model was only applied to the industrial sphere of our society, while the past-oriented pattern remained the

---

[11] Jacques Ellul, *The Technological Society.* Translated by John Wilkinson. Introduction by Robert K. Merton. New York: Knopf, 1964. First French edition, 1954.

norm in other domains. Yet progressively it was applied to other spheres of human activity—e.g., to the economic and political spheres—up to the point, which I believe we have reached, when the scientific and technical model became the dominant pattern in our culture.

In a situation such as this, the traditional humanistic program became one of the very last vestiges of another age. Let me put it bluntly. In the present cultural situation, which is no longer past-oriented, humanistic studies, focused as they are on the past, represent little else than an antiquarian hobby. Furthermore, the traditional humanistic education described above is perceived as failing to meet the students' educational needs. Indeed how does it prepare students to become responsible members of our society? Everyone knows that it is a scientific or "technical" education which is the necessary prerequisite for a good position in our society.

This is a harsh reality that I state abruptly and somewhat caricaturely because we must be jolted out of our business-as-usual routine. Obviously, for me, this is not a desperate situation. There is a future for the Humanities, and they are indeed much needed in our culture. But is is a serious situation which demands immediate attention and appropriate responses. Happily, many revisions of the curriculum and of ways of teaching are beginning to address the issue. Yet this is often done somewhat haphazardly and tentatively. This is why we need to examine more closely the situation and the way to respond to it.

Alternative Ways of Dealing with the Situation

A first possible way to respond to the plight of the Humanities is to conceive of the goal of our programs as the reestablishment of the traditional humanistic view of our culture. This is what we succeed in doing with the students who enter our graduate programs. We "convert" them. They enter an academic community which becomes a counter-culture. For this, in effect, we transform the image that undergraduate students have of themselves and of their educational needs so that they may be brought to recognize that their "true" educational needs are those pre-supposed by the traditional humanistic programs. By taking this stance, the Humanities are involved in a battle against the prevailing cultural view . . . in a losing battle if we consider the decline in enrollment. Furthermore, note that, as such, humanistic education is no longer playing the role it played in the past: its role was to elucidate what it meant to live in the prevailing (past-oriented) culture, and not to establish that culture. Thus, even in the case of success, the Humanities would have a dubious role. Its role is not to promote one culture or another as an absolute to which the individual has to submit by rejecting the present culture. Rather its role is to give the members of a culture the possibility of having an enlightened attitude *in their culture*. It should free them from blind submission to their culture, but without withdrawing them from it (as would be the case if they were to become bound to another culture, a counter-culture).

The only other alternative is then to accept the challenge of redefining what humanistic education is in terms of the contemporary culture so that it might play its role in it. For this purpose we need to adopt our culture's attitude toward the past, the classic, the foreign, as well as towards the Humanities as a whole. This is a bold move that we hesitate to make because we perceive our culture as anti-humanistic.

The perception is, of course, valid. Yet we have to ask ourselves in what sense our culture is anti-humanistic. The very use I have made of the term "Humanities" in the preceding pages is actually ambiguous. What is being rejected by our culture? Is it "the past, the classic, the foreign"—the subject matter of the Humanities? Or, is it the traditional humanistic programs in that they embody a certain view of *the relation* between the Humanities—the subject matter—and the culture of the humanists? It does not take long to recognize that it is the latter. (And thus from now on I will use the term "Humanities" to designate its subject matter.)

*Changes in the Relation between the Humanities
and the Humanists' Culture*

The relation between the Humanities and the culture of the humanists has not been as stable as we may think. These changes in relation do affect the perception of the subject matter of the Humanities—and especially what is included in the humanistic corpus and what is emphasized in this corpus. But what is most significant is the change in the relational pattern.

Originally the Humanities were limited to the study of Western civilizations, i.e., of civilizations which were historically the source of our culture. The Humanities and the humanists' culture were perceived in terms of a historical continuity, as the source is to the river, as the ground is to the tree which is rooted in it. The term "background" was also used to express this relation, with connotations linked to the preceding analogy understood in a historical perspective. This relation can be visualized as a vertical (historical) relation of continuity.

Subsequently, the study of other civilizations—indeed at first termed "primitive civilizations"—was added to the humanistic corpus, quite possibly because of the romantic view (such as Rousseau's) that the valid model of our culture was to be found in these primitive cultures, which are closer to nature than ours. Thus the study of non-Western civilizations was introduced as a part of the Humanities. This involved a shift in the perception of the relation between the Humanities and the humanists' culture. This relation was no longer primarily characterized by historical continuity, despite the fact that this view was preserved for a while in the designation of these cultures as "primitive." It was rather a relation between "cultural models," i.e., ideal cultures to be imitated, and a culture (the humanists' culture) in which these models were to be implemented. This was still clearly the prevalent view in the 1960s when the Asiatic cultures—their religions, philosophies, arts—were eagerly studied as cultures providing models that should be implemented in our society so as to bring about a "better life" than the life constructed according to Western models. This relation between the Humanities and the Humanists' culture can thus be visualized as a horizontal (without necessary historical dimension) relation between a model and its implementation.

This shift of the relational pattern was, of course, directly related to the culture's perception of itself in terms of certain patterns that we do not need to explore here. But we need to elucidate the dominant pattern which characterizes the contemporary culture so as to be able to envision how the Humanities and our present culture might be related in a positive fashion.

The Dominant Pattern of Our Contemporary Culture

The recent cultural shift can first be perceived in the way in which the key concept of "model" changed meaning. In the preceding era a "model" was something to be implemented or imitated. Indeed, this meaning of the term is still in use. But in the sciences, the social sciences and in a growing number of methodological discussions in other fields (including the Humanities), *a "model" is a theoretical construct accounting for the interrelation of various features of a complex phenomenon.* It is indeed applied to concrete situations, but first of all in order to be verified and refined. Then it is used as a basis for devising "technological" applications. Note that the origin of this "model" lies not in other cultures but indeed in our culture. It is elaborated by scientists or other researchers on the basis of the norms and warrants (the "paradigm" in Kuhn's sense of the term)[12] of our culture.

This concept points to the dominant pattern which characterizes our technological culture: a *systemic* pattern. An event, a phenomenon is perceived as meaningful if, and only if, the various features of this event or phenomenon are perceived as interrelated and as forming a coherent whole—a system which can be represented by a model. This is what has been expressed in semiotic and structuralist metalanguage by the term "synchronic" or "achronic" so as to emphasize the contrast with "diachronic" (involving a historical pattern relating past, present and future). (Yet this should not be taken to mean that a systemic pattern is static; a system can be quite dynamic and can involve processes.)

For instance, one would not dream of resolving the present economic crisis by advocating the application of a successful economic model of the past. The economists emphasize the uniqueness of the present situation. The solution to the present economic crisis will be found when one will have found a way to interrelate the many dimensions of the present economy so that they will interact properly with each other. This demands first constructing a model, an economic theory. When its validity is accepted

---

[12] Thomas Kuhn, *The Structure of Scientific Revolutions*, 2d ed. Chicago: Chicago University Press, 1970.

(whether rightly or wrongly), it is then implemented through the proper legislative and administrative channels. Thus, according to the contemporary perception, our economy is in crisis because it is chaotic, i.e., because it is not a coherent system, and not because it betrays the example which can be found in past situations.

Yet we can also note that the economists and politicians do not ignore the past. Indeed a lot of reflection and discussion of the present economic situation refers to past economic situtations. This is important for our purpose: a humanistic dimension is introduced in these economic discussions. But observe how the past is used. It is not studied with the hope of finding the perfect economic model. Rather past situations are *compared* with the present situation as a way of perceiving what is *different* in the present situation, and thus, as a way of perceiving what requires *new* solutions (new models). In short, the past is used as a necessary *background*, thanks to which the characteristics of the present can appear more clearly.

I have again used the term "background." But now it is conceived as the background of a picture which allows us to see more clearly what is in the foreground, i.e., in the present situation (and no longer as the [back]ground in which the present has its roots).

I believe this suggests how the Humanities could once more play a significant role in our culture. This does involve giving up the view of the Humanities as providing an ideal model to be implemented so as to have a "good life." But it can provide a background over against which one can perceive the contemporary culture in a critical light. If the Humanities could function in this way, they would once again fulfill their vocation. Indeed they would be perceived as having "relevance" in our culture.

But this will take place if, and only if, the humanistic programs are no longer shaped by bygone cultural patterns—the vertical pattern of historical continuity or the horizontal pattern of models to be implemented. Our humanistic teaching (our lectures, our courses, our curricula) needs to be shaped by the systemic pattern which characterizes the contemporary culture.

A Culture Governed by a Systemic Pattern

This last statement presupposes that the shift to a culture dominated by a technological, systemic pattern has indeed taken place. This is not denying the fact that there are vestiges of the previous cultural eras—such as (unfortunately!) many of our humanistic programs. But in my view, after many years of resistance against this shift, our society finally adopted, in the mid-1970s, the systemic pattern as its dominant pattern. I dare to date this final shift at that time because it is in these years that two of the traditional last bastions of a culture fell and submitted to the new dominant pattern. I want to allude to the museums and to the conservative religions.

Earlier in this century the major pattern characterizing museum exhibitions involved the presentation of the various artifacts (painting, sculpture, etc.) in different rooms so as to present separately the historical development of painting, or sculpture, etc. In the mid-1970s this type of exhibition gave way to systemic expositions: all the artifacts of a given period are gathered together so as to allow the visitors to perceive their interrelations in a culture.[13]

Similarly, as late as the early 1970s, one of the mottos of conservative Christian churches was "Returning to New Testament Christianity." It was a matter of implementing the ideal model of Christianity found at its source. But since the mid-1970s this motto is apparently no longer operative. It is rarely heard any longer. It has been replaced by the motto "Good News for Modern Man" (to use the title of a Bible much used in these circles). Furthermore, the quality of the individual believer's religious life came to be evaluated more and more in terms of its coherence. The primary question became: How is the religious experience proper related to the other aspects of one's life? How is the religious community organized? How is the religious community related to the secular and political dimensions of our society? While social and political involvement of Christians can take place following other patterns (e.g., the Social Gospel movement clearly followed a historical pattern), I would submit that the so-called New Right or Moral Majority is directly related to the adoption of a systemic pattern for perceiving one's religion. Of course, the Bible, Scripture, still plays a central role for these conservative Christian churches, but not as a historical document. It functions rather as a contemporary document—Good News for Modern Man—whose meaning is directly apprehended in terms of its relation to other aspects of the life of the Christian community in the present.

From these two examples—and without speaking of all the areas of our society which are clearly dominated by technology—I cannot but conclude that we are currently in a culture whose dominant pattern is systemic. It is from such a culture that our students are coming and it is to it that they will return. And thus if we want them to be truly confronted by the vision of life of ancient civilizations, indeed if we want them to rediscover the central place of history in an enlightened perception of human experience, our humanistic teaching needs to be organized according to the systemic pattern of their technological culture. Otherwise, either we fail to communicate with them, or we convert them to a counter-culture and in the process betray the vocation of humanistic education.

III. Implementing These Theoretical Reflections in Our Teaching

As Jesus organized his discourse according to the categories "compassion, violence and indifference" of his Jewish audience in order to communicate

---

[13] This is according to the preliminary findings of a Ph.D. dissertation being written at the University of Toronto under the direction of Professor Paul Bouissac.

to the Jews a new vision of life, we need to organize our humanistic teaching according to the systemic categories of our students who belong to a technological culture. But how could we do it?

Since as a teacher you strive to respond to the needs of your students, there is a good chance you are already doing it in at least some parts of your teaching. Thus what I will now propose will not be totally new to you, especially if you have taught interdisciplinary or comparative courses. The necessary reorientation of humanistic teaching has already begun. But it is urgent that we carry out this reorientation much beyond its present stage. And for this it was necessary for us to gain first an overall perspective of the situation, which the preceding pages have attempted to sketch.

The difficulty with such overall perspectives is their imprecision. What is a systemic pattern? What are systemic categories? Concrete examples would help! But I hesitate to give you concrete examples. For indeed my goal is not to give you some pedagogical recipes with guaranteed successful results. Such recipes do not exist! In order to give back to the Humanities their due place in higher education and, ultimately, in our culture as a whole, what is required is nothing other than a bold and fundamental rethinking of the teaching of the Humanities. In other words, the Humanities will have a future only insofar as we accept the challenge to engage in a fundamental research upon which our teaching will be based, rather than attempting to address the problem of humanistic teaching in a piecemeal fashion.

In addition to the customary and necessary research through which we acquire a thorough knowledge of the corpus and of the cultural era which is our field of specialization, we need to proceed to another type of research—a systemic research. We need to learn to conceive the texts (or other cultural artifacts) that we study in a systemic way so that we might be able to present them from this perspective in our teaching.

Comparative and Interdisciplinary Teaching
as Valid Humanistic Teaching in the Present Cultural Situation

The nature of this necessary research can be understood by considering what we are doing in this part of our teaching which is already successful because it uses the students' categories. I want to refer to our comparative courses (and to our interdisciplinary teaching, which is itself often comparative in character). How do we proceed when we want to compare different periods of history, different civilizations, different texts? We choose certain themes or topics which these civilizations or texts have in common: e.g., the place and role of women in society, the conception of the city, of war, or of ethics. But how are these themes defined? So that a true comparison might take place, we have no alternative but to start from a general, indeed theoretical, definition which can encompass all the specific manifestations found in the various corpora that we will compare in terms of this theme. But on what basis are these general and theoretical definitions established? We might want to say that they are established on the basis of our study of the texts we want to compare. Even when this is the ideal that we are pursuing, after some candid introspection we would have to confess that our preconceptions played an important role in the establishment of this definition. This could be expected in the creative process, which consists of abstracting a general definition from a series of different concrete manifestations. And, of course, often we proceed on the basis of an intuitive and implicit definition!

I am not condemning the role of our preconceptions or preunderstandings. I applaud it! Indeed, it is thanks to it that our comparative teaching is successful and valid humanistic teaching! This is the case because our preconceptions reflect *our* cultural milieu, and thus also the systemic pattern which characterizes the present culture. These preconceptions play a legitimate role as long as they are used to establish the general definition of a theme, so that we might be in a position to elucidate the *specific* ways in which this theme is manifested in the various texts. Indeed, they help us discern the specificity of a text or a civilization (rather than hiding this specificity as is the case when we subconsciously project them on a text that we are reading by itself).

Comparative and interdisciplinary teaching has proved to be quite successful. And this is not an artificial success (this is not fad teaching). In fact, we can say that it is indeed a valid response to the educational needs of students in our present cultural situation. It uses categories of our contemporary culture for the main organization of the teaching, and as such it is able to communicate effectively to the students certain parts of the vision of life found in other cultures.

Application of the Principles Used in Comparative Teaching
to Non-Comparative Teaching

Obviously, a humanistic program cannot be exclusively made up of comparative and interdisciplinary courses. Besides the practical problems that it would create, such a program would fail to present to the students any comprehensive past vision of life which could be perceived as a plausible alternative to our culture's vision of life. But the principles at work in comparative teaching can also be used to teach about a single text or about a single civilization. Let us review them.

First, and most generally, we need to teach a single humanistic text "comparatively" so as to satisfy our cultural view of the relation between the Humanities and our culture. Remember that in our culture the past (as well as the foreign) is readily accepted as a background over against which the characteristics of the present can be perceived. This is another comparative relation. Thus our teaching should be such as *to allow for this comparison* with the present cultural situation. Let me emphasize it: this does *not* mean that our courses should make references to the present situation. All that is needed is that the humanistic corpus be presented in such a way that it might function as background for our present culture. For this the only thing required is that our teaching be organized according to contemporary categories.

Second, we need to start by choosing in this corpus certain "themes" upon which we shall focus the study. Yet I wrote themes between quotation marks because, when the study is devoted to a single text, we may end up dealing with certain of its features or certain of the dimensions of its meaning. The choice of these "themes" may be quite subjective, following the instructor's interest, yet it has to satisfy two conditions: (1) the "themes" need to be features of the text (and not projected upon it); (2) they need to be recognizable by the students because they correspond to something relatively easily identifiable in our culture.

Third, and most importantly, we then need to formulate a theoretical definition of this theme such that this definition may be used for the study of this theme in any number of texts from various cultures. This is where the fundamental research mentioned above needs to take place. It is essential at this point to acknowledge without reservation that we will formulate a modern definition of this theme. In the process we will make explicit preconceptions we might have. Since this theoretical definition will be general, it will be designed in such a way as to allow us to elucidate the specific way in which this theme is manifested in the text. Let me repeat it, this procedure has the effect of reducing the risk of projecting our preconceptions upon the text.

But how should we proceed in this search for a theoretical definition of a theme? Of course, by taking advantage of the ongoing theoretical research in the various fields (including the social sciences). Thus if the chosen theme concerns the hermeneutical principles at work in the text, of course one needs to turn toward the philosophers for help in defining it. If the theme is related to sociology, or anthropology, or psychology or political sciences, of course one looks for help in these fields. If one wants to deal with the view of history, one needs to consider the various theories about history elaborated by the historians. In the case of a religious phenomenon, one turns toward the research on the phenomenon of religion (phenomenology of religion, etc.). In the case of literary genre or other literary features, one needs to turn to the literary critics. And so on and so forth. Now, of course, one will find conflicting theories about the same phenomenon. One can then choose the one which appears to be the most helpful for the study of the text at hand. After all, this is exactly what is done in the sciences. For instance, there are several conflicting theories of electricity, and the scientists use one or the other according to the application they want to make. Thus the choice of theory in case of conflicting theories can be quite pragmatic.

Yet not all theories are valid. That is, only certain theoretical definitions of a given theme can be the basis for successful teaching in the contemporary situation. These theoretical definitions have to use categories of our audience: students who belong to a systemic, technological culture. The definitions which involve these categories are, in fact, quite easy to recognize. Remember the concept of "model" which characterizes our culture: a model is a theoretical construct accounting for the interrelation of various features of a phenomenon which is then verified and progressively refined. The definitions of the themes need to be models, in this sense of the term. One can thus identify relatively easily the type of research which provides us with definitions attuned to our culture and to our pedagogical needs. These are all the research projects that use a hypothetico-deductive approach, i.e., an approach according to which a hypothesis (a tentative model) is posited and then tested through its application on specific manifestations of the phenomenon. Then it is either rejected or, if partially satisfactory, it is revised, and then tested again, etc. In contrast, the definition of a theme or phenomenon arrived at by means of empirical research does not correspond to the dominant categories of our culture because it presupposes that we would have direct access to the outside reality, and thus ultimately that meaningful reality is not a construct—while for our technological culture the only truly meaningful reality is a construct. The same could be said about "dogmatic definitions," derived from a dogma (a theology, a philosophy) viewed as an absolute. In such a case a definition is no longer viewed as a construct but as a direct representation of reality (to which the "dogma" gives us access).

In each field one can find scholars using hypothetico-deductive approaches. Yet in the case of the many "themes" having to do with one or another dimension of meaning (in a text or in most other cultural artifacts), as well as with one or another dimension of the phenomenon of communication—that is, with many "themes" studied in various fields—semiotics strives to provide definitions which are based on a resolutely hypothetico-deductive research. Such is the case, at any rate, of the semioticians (A. J. Greimas, U. Eco) who are proposing semiotic theories (by contrast with a number of "empirical semioticians"). This is why I believe that semiotics has a very important role to play in helping us find the appropriate approach for teaching the Humanities.

As a result of this theoretical research, we find ourselves with the definitions of the "themes" we have selected. The next step, still a part of our research, involves developing an analytical method for the study of these themes in texts (or other artifacts). If the definition is complete enough—as in the case of themes defined in semiotics—it describes the interrelation of a number of formal features (empty slots). One can then study the specific way in which a text invests this model—the way in which the empty slots are filled. In other words, the definition allows us to read the text with special attention for certain features which belong to the theme.

At last we are then ready to teach, that is to present the results of this research to our students and to invite them to participate in it at a limited level. Unfortunately, it is not as easy to teach in this way as it could be, for the simple reason that in most instances no adequate textbook is available (most of the existing textbooks follow patterns related to former cultural eras). Many systemic textbooks need to be written. Furthermore, when we teach in this way we have to expect "reactions" from our students. Indeed, we present other cultures to them in such a way that they can be perceived as plausible alternatives to our culture. This means, of course, that we challenge their view of our culture as an absolute, and consequently we challenge their identity. We can thus expect defensive, reactionary attitudes. This actually shows that our teaching is reaching its goal. Yet despite the difficulty and the amount of work necessary, making the effort to hold a didactic discourse that truly addresses our audience is quite rewarding although it might not always be pleasing to the students.

Allow me to conclude with a brief concrete example (at this point, one hopes it will not be construed as a recipe). I want to refer to a course in New Testament that I am teaching at Vanderbilt University. There is no need to emphasize that traditional introductions to the New Testament use constantly a pattern of historical continuity (which includes the emphasis on the author and the development of his/her thought on the basis of received traditions).[14] Thus the question was: What kind of systemic theme should I choose? Since this is a course in religious studies, I chose "faith," which I was able to define, thanks to Greimas's semiotic theory, as a "system of convictions."[15] The problem is, of course, that students do not spontaneously recognize this concept, even though they do perceive religion in a systemic way. Thus I begin with a topic which concerns them: Scripture. What does it mean that the New Testament is perceived as Scripture by the Christians? I then show them that various churches have different answers to this question because they relate Scripture to different aspects of their religious experience. With this example—a natural one since we are dealing with a text that is viewed as Scripture by the Christians—the students readily grasp the concept of *system* of convictions. In the process I have also established that the "structures of religious authority" often display the characteristic pattern of a given system of convictions. We thus proceed to study the various structures of authority in the different New Testament texts. Then we can move into a comparative study of the various types of faith found in the New Testament and its (Jewish and Hellenistic) "background." Despite the obvious historical connections, this is not what is stressed. Rather each faith system is described independently and then they are compared as systems.

[14] See my discussion of the characteristic patterns of "historical exegesis" in D. Patte, *What Is Structural Exegesis?* (Philadelphia: Fortress Press, 1975) Chapter I.

[15] On the concept of "faith as system of convictions" defined on the basis of Greimas's theory, see D. Patte, *Paul's Faith and the Power of the Gospel: A Structural Introduction to His Letters* (Philadelphia: Fortress Press, 1982) Chapter I.

In the process the students are confronted with faith systems quite different from those they are acquainted with in contemporary society. Some of these systems not only have eschatological convictions but also historical perspective! What are the results? As is clear from the discussion groups, the students are able to relate, on specific issues, the New Testament texts to their own (or other people's) faith in a critical way. And they study much more enthusiastically by comparison with the time when I was teaching the course in a traditional way. By the end of a second semester, focused exclusively on two types of faith (e.g., Paul and the Pharisees), it was clear that they could truly see the contemporary religious scene over against the background of these New Testament and early Rabbinic texts (a last paper gave them the opportunity to do so if they chose). I was quite positively surprised at the remarkable way in which they were able to relate to the New Testament aspects of the contemporary religious scene which were apparently very far removed from the texts. And yet, let me emphasize it, during the entire course I devoted all my lectures to the "description" of this theme—faith as system of convictions—as it is found in the New Testament and focused all the discussions on the close reading of texts showing them how to study in them what characterizes the faith of the author. In other words, I dealt exactly with the same corpus: the New Testament and its historical background. Thanks to a didactic discourse which used the students' categories—indeed this discourse about the New Testament was not organized according to New Testament categories but according to systemic, technological categories—the students have entered into dialogue with this text and its vision of life, so much so that, at least some of them, have discovered it as a plausible alternative to their modern vision of life. Indeed for them it is a new vision of life! It includes, as one of its essential characteristics, a historical perspective!

The use of a contemporary systemic model for an aspect of the phenomenon of religion allows the students to read this text of another culture in such a way that it begins to become a "background" over against which they can perceive in a critical light a similar aspect of our contemporary cultural experience. But obviously one course is not enough. Such teaching will be truly effective only if the entire humanistic program is reoriented in similar ways. And as is clear, I believe that nothing less than the future of the Humanities depends upon such a reorientation.

POST-BIBLICAL JUDAISM
AND THE TEACHING OF THE HUMANITIES

Gordon Tucker
The Jewish Theological Seminary of America

I

The appearance in the college humanities curriculum of periods of Jewish history, other than the periods of political autonomy (i.e., pre-70 C.E. and post-1948 C.E.), is a relatively recent phenomenon, and still not very widespread. The reasons for that neglect, which undoubtedly extend back to another century and another continent, need not concern us here. What is to be noted, however, is that it has needlessly deprived humanities educators of resources which can have unusually broad pedagogic applications, even for those who do not teach ancient or religious studies *per se*. Illustration of this proposition is the purpose of this essay.

We will be dealing here with the varieties of Judaism which coexisted (not always peacefully) in Palestine just prior to the opening of the Christian era, and the eventual predomination of rabbinic Judaism in the Talmudic period. Since the roots of this polychrome religious and intellectual landscape stretch back through most of the Second Temple period, we shall focus on the Jewish world of Palestine (and some parts of the Diaspora, especially Babylonia) from the early fourth century B.C.E. (the Alexandrian conquest) through the early sixth century C.E. (the completion of the vast majority of the Babylonian Talmud). The subject thus defined will be referred to below as "post-biblical Judaism."

The consideration and understanding of any period of cultural and religious history evidently requires a command of the raw historical data, i.e. places, names, dates, events, etc. But having staked out an interval of nearly a milennium on the time line, we would lose sight of the significant "deep structure" of the period (to borrow a term from another discipline) were we to focus on all of these details. Since the concern here is to unpack some of the most interesting cultural and intellectual developments hidden in that deep structure, the following skeletal outline of some of the major historical benchmarks will suffice for our purpose. More comprehensive treatments of historical minutiae can be found in works cited in the bibliographical appendix to this essay.

516 B.C.E.	Second Temple is built in Jerusalem by returning exiles from Babylonia
458 B.C.E.	Ezra's arrival in Jerusalem from Babylonia
445 B.C.E.	Nehemia's first mission to Jerusalem
444 B.C.E.	On New Year Day, the Torah is publicly read and interpreted to the general populace
332 B.C.E.	Alexander's conquest of the Persian empire
200 B.C.E.	Antiochus III conquers Syria and Palestine, wresting them from the Ptolemies
175 B.C.E.	Antiochus IV (Epiphanes) begins his reign
165/164 B.C.E.	Revolt against corruption and Hellenization by the Maccabees under Judah succeeds in reconquering and rededicating the Temple; institution of the post-biblical festival of Hanukkah
134–76 B.C.E.	Reigns of Maccabean kings John Hyrcanus and Alexander Jannaeus
63 B.C.E.	Pompey enters Jerusalem after arbitrating dispute for throne between Hyrcanus and Aristobulus, and Jewish autonomy in Palestine comes to an end
37 B.C.E.	Herod the Great claims the throne in Jerusalem
4 B.C.E.	Death of Herod; tripartite division of Palestine and direct Roman administration
30 C.E.	Approximate date of Jesus' crucifixion
66–70 C.E.	Jewish revolt brought on by Roman misrule and Jewish messianic expectations; destruction of Temple
73 C.E.	Fall of Masada, one of the last pockets of resistance
115–117 C.E.	Widespread Jewish revolts, soundly suppressed, in Cyrenaica, Alexandria, and Cyprus
132–135 C.E.	Revolt of Bar Kosiba and his followers in southern Palestine; following its collapse, Jerusalem becomes a pagan city and the rabbinic movement moves to the Galilee
200 C.E.	After several decades of development and consolidation of legal traditions in various rabbinic schools, an authoritative Mishnah is compiled by Rabbi Judah the Prince
After 200 C.E.	Bifurcation of rabbinic movement, as Mishnah and competing legal traditions are studied in Palestinian and Babylonian academies. Palestinian talmudic activity generally completed by end of fourth century

| 500 C.E. | Date by which most of the Babylonian Talmud has been produced |

II

Post-biblical Judaism was the subject of a Humanities Institute located at The Jewish Theological Seminary of America in the summers of 1978 and 1979. Under its aegis, thirty-nine college professors from departments of history, religion, philosophy, literature, and classics participated in a collaborative effort to study this period in ways which would enable them to enrich and augment their own course offerings. The ideas as organized and presented in this essay are products of that collaboration, and especially of the scholarship and insights of the Institute faculty: Professors David Weiss Halivni (Director), David Wolf Silverman, Shaye J.D. Cohen, Yochanan Muffs, Joseph Lukinsky, and this writer.

The notion that familiarity with post-biblical Judaism could provide fresh resources even for humanities educators not ordinarily concerned with history of religion was one that did not at first occur to the founders of the Institute. Originally, the motivation was much simpler and more direct; to provide teachers of undergraduates with the tools necessary to restore to the curriculum a neglected period of history which represented a synthesis of Hellenic, Israelite, and other Near Eastern traditions, and had thus contributed a great deal to the world of late antiquity and to later periods as well. However, as applications began to arrive from such unexpected quarters as departments of English literature and colleges of law, it became clear that even the brief description of what we intended to do had touched responsive chords in representatives of an extraordinarily wide range of disciplines. The planning for the Institute accordingly began to take new directions, and the faculty ultimately defined the enterprise as one of distilling out of the mass of historical data a number of themes and institutional developments which have important connections to and relationships with counterparts in other historical contexts. Thus, for example, it was decided that it was necessary to go beyond a treatment of rabbinic exegesis on its own terms, to a consideration of how that might be related to, or echoed in, a setting as seemingly far removed as judicial debates on interpretation of the United States Constitution.

Conceived in this way, the Institute was able to make two distinct and gratifying sorts of contributions. On the one hand, it provided direct enrichment to courses in early Christianity, the Hellenistic Age in the Near East, ancient philosophy, surveys of western civilization, and others. As we had assumed from the inception of the project, the period to which we confined our attention is one with inherent interest, and which stands as a complete object of study in its own right. This was reflected in the new course units which many participants created and then taught. On the other hand, the most innovative uses of the material were accomplished by those who chose instead to treat the particular historical context of post-biblical Judaism (i.e. places, times, personalities) as a kind of "hardware" which supported what was of greatest significance, to wit, the ideas, struggles, institutions, literary genres, and forms of social development which could be discerned in the historical grid. Those who adopted this approach focused on those features of post-biblical Judaism which can be recognized in variant forms in other places and times, on the evidently sound assumption that such contrasts and comparisons which traverse many cultural and temporal boundaries have important pedagogic power, and tend to promote a heightened appreciation for the significance of humanistic studies generally.

A highly suggestive article by Hans Jonas entitled "Jewish and Christian Elements in Philosophy: Their Share in the Emergence of the Modern Mind"[1] provides an excellent illustration of this approach. The stated aim of that article is to consider the shadow cast by some of the doctrines created by the monotheistic faiths, especially the "transplantation" of Jewish and Christian ideas concerning creation, will, voluntarism, and contingency to the field of secular philosophical thought. In the author's own words:

> . . . certain ideas, motifs and choices of revealed religion pass over, open or concealed, into the patrimony of philosophy itself and—eventually dissociated from their origin in revelation and its authority—become genuine parts of the modified philosophical landscape. . . .
> . . . I am speaking of the legitimate continuation, in the medium of philosophy, of existential insights and emphases whose original locus was the world of faith, but whose validity and vitality extend beyond the reaches of faith. . . . In this sense of an assimilation which may be transforming enough to make us speak of a secularization of originally religious thought, one can meaningfully look for Jewish or Christian elements in a philosophy that need not therefore be a Jewish or Christian philosophy, or indeed a religious philosophy at all.

Or, as one of the participants was fond of observing: Mark Twain noted that although history doesn't repeat itself, it does rhyme. That perspective revealed itself in new and augmented syllabi which generalized features of post-biblical Judaism such as allegorical exegesis, sectarian religious competition, and individualism. The remainder of this essay will sketch some of these features of the post-biblical Jewish landscape and suggest ways of utilizing them in the teaching of a range of course in the humanities.

One additional note before proceeding to specifics: the foregoing discussion implies that in an important sense, this essay, and to a large extent the Institute itself, is not about post-biblical Judaism alone. Or, to be more precise, it implies that there is nothing particulary special about post-biblical Judaism other than the fact that it yields a nice crop of cultural and intellectual produce. Other periods of Jewish history, and certainly of general history,

[1] H. Jonas, *Philosophical Essays* (Englewood Cliffs: Prentice Hall, 1974).

might have done as well as models and may yet do so in future Institutes. It is that characteristic, in the opinion of this member of the Institute faculty, which made it truly a *humanities* institute. And if this brief essay sends no one rushing out to read Philo or the Talmud, but gives impetus to the utilization of other historical periods in similar ways, it will have achieved its real purpose.

III

It is time to put some of what I have called the "deep structure" of Post-Biblical Judaism on display. I shall attend to four major themes; others could have been chosen as well, and those readers who choose to utilize the appended bibliography to gain greater familiarity with the period may well identify others with greater potential for contributing to their own interests and teaching fields. What these four have in common is that they are all quite prominent artifacts of our period, and at the same time have general significance which is evident. The themes are:

(1) From Temple to Synagogue
(2) Implications of Monotheism - Religious Absolutism
(3) Learning and Education
(4) Hermeneutics

From Temple to Synagogue

The title of this first theme refers to the fact that a comparison of Judaism at the beginning of our period with what was called Judaism at its end would present some serious problems of recognition and identification. The "before and after" stills would not obviously be of the same religion at all. The most direct and straightforward way to express this is to say that Judaism was transformed during Second Temple times and into the rabbinic period from a cultic system to a religon which vested authority of a new sort in a clergy of a new sort, i.e. rabbis. Ignoring for the moment the question of what happened in between and why, the following table gives a more immediate sense of the most notable changes from 500 B.C.E. to 500 C.E. (in fact, much of the transition took far less than a milennium, although exact data in this area for parts of the period under consideration are simply not available):

	Cultic Judaism	*Rabbinic Judaism*
Central Institution	Temple	Synagogue and school
Form of Religious Expression	Sacrifice and laws of ritual purity	Prayer, and observance of much expanded law
Religious Authorities	Priests, prophets (in earliest period)	Rabbis, texts
Locus of Authority	Centralized	Decentralized

Attention to this particular theme in Post-Biblical Judaism thus provides a starting block from which emanate several different tracks. The "before and after" images which were referred to above can motivate, for example, an investigation within the historical framework of Post-Biblical Judaism of how and why this transition was accomplished. Such an investigation would have to take note of several things, among them the following: (a) the origins and nature of the synagogue, as presented to us by archaeological and literary evidence; (b) the fact that the synagogue, particularly outside of Palestine, significantly predates the destruction of the Second Temple in 70 C.E., and thus cannot be construed simplistically as an institution created as a Temple replacement; (c) foreshadowings of the transition in the Bible itself (e.g. Solomon's prayer of dedication in I Kings 8, in which the Temple is principally presented as a house of prayer); (d) the diversity of synagogue practices and the beliefs represented in them; and (e) the career of Ezra and his emphasis on public subjugation to the written law (referred to in the brief chronology given above) as a transition from prophecy and priesthood to a new order. This in itself would expose students to a very critical process in the history of western religion.

However, as the table given above shows, the transition from Temple to synagogue can also be seen more abstractly as a move from community and nation to individual. The synagogue's most striking departure from the Temple is that unlike the latter, which was the province of a privileged priestly class which effected atonement and other religious states vicariously, the synagogue was a place of *individual* participation in acts of piety accessible to all (at least in principle). The new clergy was, correspondingly, open to all (again, in principle) in ways in which the priesthood and the prophetic calling could not, by their very natures, be. The post-biblical move from Temple to synagogue can therefore be taken beyond its original setting and referred to by classicists, for example, as a parallel or variant of similar trends in the Greco-Roman world towards individualism. One example: W. S. Ferguson, in his essay "The Leading Ideas of the New Period" in *The Cambridge Ancient History*, volume VII, discusses that growing individualism and suggests ways of explaining it on the basis of political and social developments. A course unit which takes up that issue can clearly use the parallel in the Jewish world represented by this theme, and the political and social data of *that* world (see the appended bibliography) to confirm, refine, and generally heighten understanding of conclusions reached with students about the Greco-Roman world. Another fruitful avenue of approach could be taken by teachers of early Church history. The innovations of the synagogue could be mapped into and contrasted with features of the early Church: indeed, such a consideration could give students a great deal of vital information about and insight into Jewish–Christian relations and Jewish–Christian–Gentile relations in an extremely graphic and—to most students—novel way.

As a final suggestion, one might consider how the emphasis on individualism reflected in the table can function as a model or paradigm for many other instances of the preeminence of the individual in either popular thought or philosophy. Working behind the scenes in the Temple to synagogue transition seems to be a recognition of the individual soul (and thus *individual*, as opposed to *corporate*, immortality). The significance of this philosophical notion is especially independent of historical context. It can be used to further the intelligibility of Philo, to examine other contemporaneous phenomena such as the move, in the Hellenistic world, from the primacy of the city-state to the growth of mystery cults with their appeal to the special status of the individual. But it can also illuminate much later, secular systems of philosophical thought; this is particularly true of those aspects of Western philosophy which, as Jonas observes in the article cited earlier, emphasize will over necessity, or the particular over the universal. The possibilities certainly do not end here, but an attempt to list all the permutations of this first theme which would be valuable to teachers in diverse fields would prevent us from moving on the the next of the four themes.

Implications of Monotheism—Religious Absolutism

This theme subsumes a number of components, including conversion, proselytization, intolerance, martyrdom and the proliferation of sectarian communities. In order to appreciate its generalizable significance, it is necessary to understand first how all of these component phenomena are related and why they are lumped together under this particular rubric.

The Babylonian exile had been weathered in large part because of a notion that was rather revolutionary in the ancient world—that of a universal God, one who had not been defeated when His city was sacked, but who had rather temporarily exposed his close but sinful people to exile and suffering. Those who took advantage of Cyrus's decree and returned to Jerusalem brought back that idea of one universal deity sovereign over all, and the concept grew progressively more characteristic of Jewish thought, becoming a predominant theme in the latest biblical writings of the post-exilic centuries. In contrast to the attitude reflected throughout most of the Bible, post-biblical Judaism began to make exclusive claims to religious validity and truth. Idolatry was no longer to be a legitimate form of worship for the Gentile.

One of the first implications of this exclusivity is the institution of conversion (absent in biblical Judaism), for it simply will not do to claim access to the "one true church" and yet bar access to others. Indeed, one who knows that he has the only effective program for salvation is morally bound to share the secret willingly with those who sincerely wish to have it. (Conversion, it should also be noted, is related to the theme of individualism as well, for it presupposes a notion that a decision of individual conscience can override the national and ethnic identity of the person making the decision to convert).

This is how Bickerman sums up the point just made, in *From Ezra to the Last of the Maccabees* (p. 20):

> . . . the pagans made no efforts to convert a stranger but, for the same reason, excluded him from their own religion. Everybody was a true believer, in the opinion of the heathen, if he worshipped his ancestral gods. Thus, each city was exclusive and intolerant within its walls, but recognized the other gods outside. On the other hand, knowing that the Lord is the One True God, the Jews naturally proselytized among the heathen and admitted the converted to the universal religion. And for that same reason they were intolerant of those outside the congregation and rejected the folly of idolatry.

Paradoxically, openness (to conversion) and intolerance would seem to go hand in hand. The offensive religious practices of the pagan were balanced by the mitigating factor of tolerance and acceptance of other beliefs; the purity and moral elegance of monotheism had to bear the burden of intolerance and rejection of alternatives. When exclusivity reaches its logical conclusion, openness to conversion gives way to even more active measures. Thus, the Maccabees indulged in high-handed, enforced proselytization of peoples in conquered territories. And not suprisingly, we begin to get intolerance between Jews and Gentiles, in both directions, expressed in literature (see the appended bibliography for some references to early anti-semitic literature).

One more paradoxical implication of the claim to exclusive truth is the development, not of one unified solid bloc of the faithful, but rather of distinctly defined sectarian communities. It is, in fact, a consequence of the habit of making such absolute religious claims that deviations, even if slight, require separation and distinction, so as to avoid contamination by what are seen as heretical beliefs or practices. So it is not surprising that in the late Second Temple period, one of great relgious zeal and absolutism, sects make a prominent appearance on the Jewish stage. Sects defined themselves by their distinctiveness and purity in the realm of theology, and often by their social standing and political activity as well. But the primary yardstick of separation and distinction was the code of behavior, the *halakhah*, which they espoused and on which they would not compromise. Claims to exclusive religious truth often require that a sect either triumph or fall by the wayside. Middle ground does not fit the milieu of absolutism.

Several phenomena have thus been explained as originating in the post-biblical Jewish world from one overarching religious trend in post-exilic times. The shadows of those phenomena were in fact cast much further. It is, for example, quite obvious how and why Christianity acquired its own particular forms of proselytization, intolerance, and martyrdom (the ultimate commitment to the one truth). A consideration of the development of all these features in their native Jewish environment is evidently invaluable for the teacher of Church history and Church–synagogue relations. Indeed, it is quite plausible to view Christianity itself as originally a Jewish sect; it certainly meets the criterion of distinctiveness in theology as well as in *halakhah* (see, for example, the discussion recorded in Acts 15.13–29), and it referred to itself as the true Israel, the custodian of the valid and purified tradition. There is scarcely a better way to present to students a vivid and plausible explanation for why Christianity developed in ways which were to make tragic conflict with the non-Christian world inevitable than to acquaint them first with the roots of sectarianism and intolerance and their sprouting during the career of post-biblical Judaism.

Finally, revealing a close and complex relationship between intolerance, with its negative valence, and the yearning for a pure universal truth, with its positive connotation, can have great instructional value. It is quite clear that the light shed in this way on the *general* phenomenon of intolerance— as the darker side of a commitment to a perceived universal truth—can open up new ways of treating that phenomenon in a wide range of settings, from the martyrdom of Socrates to the abjuration of Galileo.

Learning and Education

The article by Judah Goldin appended to this essay is intended to give some indication of the various roles of the academy in rabbinic Judaism, and of the ethical dimension that study and intellectual achievement came to acquire.[2] Because learning reached a level of esteem in rabbinic Judaism

---

[2] (N.B. This article, as it originally appeared, had several citations in Hebrew characters which have either been eliminated or transliterated here. More important, the extensive and scholarly footnotes have been reduced in the interest of space, to the minimum necessary for the purposes of this volume. Those readers who intend to follow up on points or arguments made by Goldin, either in their teaching or research, are both cautioned and advised that those notes contain an impressive and indispensable trove of scholarly material which they *must* consult in the original.)

which is not nearly so apparent in the Bible, it is often assumed that this emphasis represents a Greek import which interacted with existing Jewish values. That view does not do justice to the movement which is already discernible in early Second Temple times (and even earlier) toward the eventual rabbinic ideal. Deuteronomy, for example, does stress the education of children, and in chapter 31 actually prescribes a public reading of Scripture to every man, woman, and child. Although prescribed as only a septennial ritual, it is nevertheless an important idea, as we shall presently see.

It was mentioned earlier that an actual (not just prescribed) public ritual of scriptural reading is reported in Nehemia chapter 8. The law, the text there tells us, was read to the people at the Water Gate, and was interpeted to them. This extremely important event was not just a ritual, but rather a concrete dramatization of a shift of religious paradigm.

As late as the prophet Malachi, the priest was portrayed as the custodian of wisdom, and it was to him that one had to repair for instruction in God's word. It is no great wonder that the priests kept their esoteric knowledge to themselves and dispensed it sparingly; not simply a matter of their privilege of birth, their religious monopoly had to do with *power* as well. Quite simply, the giving up of the custodianship of religious doctrine is the yielding of power and control over that body of doctrine. Once it is out in the public domain, it is no longer possible to control its use; if it is a sacred text we are dealing with, public access will make control and authority over its interpretation increasingly difficult. It is thus quite clear that the publication (in the literal sense) of the Pentateuch in the time of Ezra and Nehemia had to have enormous religious, social, and political ramifications. And yet, with the end of prophecy at hand, and the need for a focus of loyalty among the returning exiles, that step was all but inevitable. It is difficult to imagine, however, that the event of New Year Day 444 B.C.E. could have taken place without other groundwork, e.g., the beginnings of a general democratization of religious structure, which is none other than the already identified movement, just beginning at that time, from Temple to synagogue!

In any event, the publication of the Torah meant that the law was now the property of the entire people, who could in principle, and should ideally, participate in its study. God's will was no longer heard through the words of the prophet, but rather through a *text*. And in order for that text to be a thorough and edifying guide for life, it had to be studied and interpreted. So Midrash (literally, "seeking out") eventually became not just an exegetical device, but a constant, and indispensable part of Jewish religious activity. The most salient feature of this theme, however, is the way in which it illuminates the complicated relationship between authority and public, the power inherent in the right of interpretation, how such power is wielded, and the conditions under which it must be yielded. These matters are among those most commonly encountered in the study of virtually every culture and historical period.

The growing preoccupation of Judaism with study and education in Second Temple and rabbinic times produced a number of other important developments with enduring significance for the Western world. Only two will be mentioned here: The first is the institution of a system of compulsory universal education for children. The effect of this revolutionary system can be grasped from the words of Josephus (*Against Apion*), even allowing for some stretching of the truth:

> Indeed, most men, so far from living in accordance with their own laws, hardly know what they are. Only when they have done wrong do they learn from others that they have transgressed the law. Even those of them who hold the highest and most important offices admit their ignorance; for they employ professional legal experts as assessors and leave them in charge of the administration of affairs. But, should anyone of our nation be questioned about the laws, he would repeat them all more readily than his own name. The result, then, of our thorough grounding in the laws from the first dawn of intelligence is that we have them, as it were, engraven on our souls.[3]

Finally, the translation of the Torah into Greek, begun in the third century B.C.E., was an indispensable step towards the opening up of a tradition for the Greek speaking Jews of the Hellenistic world. This willingness to translate sacred scripture out of the sacred tongue, a phenomenon related to the emphasis on public education, contributed enormously to the ability of Judaism to survive and to its ability (and especially that of Christianity) to project its religious message far beyond its own community.

Hermeneutics

If the Torah was to serve as the religious authority for the people, then it would be necessary to have an active, operative oral law. The oral traditions, which no doubt coexisted with written Scripture for some time, had several functions to fulfil:

(a) the resolution of contradictions in the written law;
(b) the definition of terms in the written law or the filling in of missing details (e.g. defining what constitutes "work" for purposes of Sabbath law);
(c) the legitimizing through scriptural exegesis of old usages not explicitly sanctioned in the written law (e.g. the disqualification of women from legal testimony); and
(d) the creation of new standards and norms to meet new circumstances.

To preserve order and control over this process, exegesis was generally confined to certain standard forms; however, these were neither rigid nor recognized in identical forms by all rabbinic schools. Some academies allowed forms of inference which were not deemed valid by others. Nevertheless, the

---

[3] Gerson D. Cohen, "The Talmudic Age," in *Great Ages and Ideas of the Jewish People* (ed. Schwartz; Random House, 1956) p. 188.

idea of a fixed, written text which was made fluid through the use of exegetical rules was one which satisfied the dual desiderata of an authoritative text and an adaptive tradition. This has had reverberations ever since in the development of Christianity and Islam, Western political history, and—as will be alluded to below—even in philosophy of language and hermeneutics.

For the sake of concreteness, consider one use of an exegetical rule used for the fourth function of new legislation. As reported in the Babylonian Talmud, Tractate *Pesahim* 66, Hillel the Elder resolved a pressing question about whether the Paschal sacrifice, prescribed for the 14th day of Nissan, should be offered even if that day falls on the Sabbath, by appealing (in part) to an *a fortiori* argument. Hillel noted that the penalty for neglecting the Paschal sacrifice without good cause is extremely dire (on a par with neglecting circumcision, for example), while the penalty for similar neglect of the daily offering is not nearly so serious. So he set up the following table:

	Penalty for neglect	Overrides Sabbath
Daily Offering	Minor	Yes (known independently from an *explicit* text)
Paschal Offering	Major	?

Inspection of this table thus immediately yielded the reasonable result that the Paschal offering must override the Sabbath. The ruling, based on the quasi-logical (it is *not* deductively valid!) reasoning, was accepted as authoritative in practice.

Yet another use of exegesis was its application in non-legal contexts to reinterpret Scripture to fit theological positions not necessarily consonant with the original biblical intention. This much more free-form use of exegesis was a dominant feature of the New Testament and both Jewish and Christian religious writings to the present day. One example of this: Exodus 34 presents a list of the attributes of God, among which appears the following: "yet He does not remit all punishment, but visits the iniquity of fathers upon children and children's children upon the third and fourth generations." In the context of the biblical notion that sin and impurity constitute debts which must be repaid, this makes perfect sense. However, in an age for which repentance and the possibility of clearing the slate were axiomatic, this presents a theological embarrassment. The solution: a first century rabbi rereads the Hebrew ("Nakeh lo Yenakeh") as "He remits and He does not remit," i.e. God forgives those who repent, but for those who do not repent, retribution can continue. Crimes against Hebrew grammar were not deemed to be as serious as getting the wrong theological message from Scripture!

Now this last example brings up the question of how much violence can be done to the plain meaning of the text, and herein lies the most far-reaching implication of rabbinic exegetical activity. It is perhaps best epitomized in the quite well-known Talmudic story (Tractate *Baba Mezia* 59b) of the first century rabbis who had a dispute over a matter of ritual law. One rabbi, finding himself outvoted in the academy, but convinced of the correctness of his view, appealed successively to logic and then miracles of nature to prove his point. Despite his ability to call forth several impressive natural wonders at will, the majority remained determined in their view and found the miraculous events interesting but irrelevant to the legal point. So the final trump card was played: an appeal to Heaven. And when a heavenly voice explicitly corroborated the minority view, Rabbi Joshua, representing the majority, arose and declared (citing a Scriptual verse in a non literal way!) that the Torah was not the concern of heaven, but rather only of the human academy, where the majority must rule (by the Torah's very prescription!). This story, which ends with an acknowledgment by God that He had been bested at His own game, reveals a great deal about the rabbis' view of their own enterprise.

One of the questions which commonly arises in discussions of hermeneutics (and literary analysis as well) is what counts as evidence for the meaning of a text. Here, as in many other places, the rabbis tell us directly that the intent of the author (in this case, the Author!), even if it could be discovered, has no veto over the use of the text. If the concept, which had its genesis back in the time of Ezra, that the text was now to function as oracle is taken seriously, no more modest conclusion could be drawn. Indeed, one might say that in the rabbinic view, meaning in the Torah was not to be *discovered* as much as it was to be *invented* and reinvented. To be sure, there were some constraints, of logic and tradition, upon interpretation, but within those loose constraints, the biblical text meant what the rabbis said it meant. There are significant affinities between this stance and many modern theories of meaning, particularly Bultmann's notion that meaning is the end result of a participatory *relationship* between the text and the one to whom the text is now speaking.

The troubling questions of relativism and unpredictability which obviously arise from this position have been part of rabbinic Judaism ever since, even as they arise in many diverse contexts far removed from the rabbinic world. Theories of law in virtually all societies struggle with much the same problem. But the fact that the rabbinic program is fraught with possible pitfalls and dangers does not erase the fact that it was and has been an extraordinarily successful way of dealing with the problems of religious authority, adaptation of traditional forms, and continuity with the past. Even a modest amount of study of the rabbis' methodology, their successes, and their failures, can contribute a great deal to considerations of all of these problems, and related ones, in a host of humanistic disciplines.

IV

What has been said above was intended to illustrate, through use of a mere sampling of examples, ways in which teachers looking for fresh material and novel, engaging perspectives can find succor in disciplines to which they would normally not think of turning. Further uses of the post-biblical Jewish material focused on here are limited only by the educator's creativity and willingness to experiment. In order to bolster this invitation to the reader to innovate in this way, several items are now appended:

(1) An article by Judah Goldin referred to in the essay. (Originally published in *Traditio*, vol. 21 (1965), Fordham University Press; reprinted in Dimitrovsky (ed.), *Exploring the Talmud*, Ktav, New York: 1976).

(2) Three syllabi developed at the Humanities Institute mentioned earlier; one on Hellenistic Judaism, one on ancient medicine, using biblical and post-biblical materials, and one on the Epistles of Paul.

(3) A bibliographical guide reprinted from Jacob Neusner's *Invitation to the Talmud* (Harper & Row, New York: 1973). It contains essential references to primary sources available in English.

(4) A bibliography of books and articles especially suited for undergraduates, broken down by the themes discussed in this essay.

In addition, films, kinescopes, and tapes of broadcast materials on certain topics can often be useful alternatives to lectures and readings. Information on availability can be obtained from:

National Center for Jewish Film
Brandeis University
Waltham, Massachusetts

Jewish Media Service
New York, New York

National Jewish Archive of Broadcasting
c/o The Jewish Museum
New York, New York

A PHILOSOPHICAL SESSION
IN A TANNAITE ACADEMY*

Judah Goldin

Commenting on the verse[1] which reports the devastation of Jerusalem by Nabuzaradan, that "he burnt the house of the Lord, and the king's house; and all the houses of Jerusalem, even every great man's house,"[2] the Midrash[3] makes the following remark:

> And to what does the clause *every great man's house* refer? That's the academy (*bet midrash*) of Rabban Johanan ben Zakkai. And why is it called *bet gadol* [literally, the house of the great one]? Because there the *shebah* (*shevah*) of the Holy One, blessed be He, was rehearsed, related, recited.

—the verb used is *teni*, which means not only to recite but to study and to teach. To translate *shebah* by the neutral word "praise," is to miss the real intent of the statement. *Shebah* in the present sentence, as in a great many others in talmudic-midrashic literature, is clearly δόξα; and one of the traditional commentators on our midrashic passage has already correctly explained it: in Johanan ben Zakkai's academy they were engaged in the Creation and Merkabah (Chariot) speculations.[4] The parallel passage in the Palestinian Talmud[5] bears him out. Here we do not read *shebah*, but *gedulot*, the Magnificence, and the citation of II Regum 8.4 as proof-text ("nara mihi omnia *magnalia*" etc.; LXX: πάντα τὰ μεγάλα,)[6] makes the meaning perfectly clear. As G. Scholem wrote long ago in another connection,[7] "The term employed:

---

* From *Traditio*, vol. 21 (1965), reprinted in Dimitrovsky, ed., *Exploring the Talmud* (N.Y.: Ktav, 1976).

[1] II Reg. 25.8 f.; cf. Jer. 52.13.

[2] This translation is, of course, in accordance with MT; cf. the translation of the Jewish Publication Society.

[3] *Lamentations Rabba*, Petiha 12, ed. Buber 12.

[4] On *shebah* = *doxa*, cf. also S. Lieberman in G. G. Scholem, *Jewish Gnosticism, Merkabah Mysticism, and Talmudic Tradition* (New York, 1960) 123.

[5] J. Megillah 3.1.

[6] Is this perhaps what lies behind "magnalia DeL" of Acts 2:11 also, at least in part? Cf. the commentary by K. Lake and H. J. Cadbury in F. Jackson and K. Lake, *Beginnings of Christianity* IV (London, 1933) 20.

[7] *Major Trends in Jewish Mysticism* (Jerusalem, 1941) 65 (paperback ed. New York, 1961, p. 66).

shivho shel hakadosh barukh hu, signifies not only praise of God—in this context that would be without any meaning—but glory, δόξα, *shevah* being the equivalent of the Aramaic word for glory, *shuvha*. The reference, in short, is not to God's praise but to the vision of His glory."

Our Midrash, in other words, testifies that in the academy of Johanan ben Zakkai there were sessions devoted to speculations on the theme of visions of God's glory. And in fact this should not surprise us, for it is in keeping with what talmudic literature tells us elsewhere about an exchange between the great sage and his favorite disciple, Eleazar ben 'Arak—how on one occasion, when Eleazar discoursed brilliantly on the Merkabah theme, Johanan could not resist praising him in most superlative terms. "He rose and kissed him on his head and exclaimed: Blessed be the Lord, God of Israel, who gave such a descendant to our father Abraham," and so on and so forth.

We shall shortly examine more closely this well-known encounter of Johanan and Eleazar ben 'Arak. I have referred to it at this point, however, because along with our midrashic passage it may serve to suggest something about the nature of the curriculum (if I may be permitted such a term) in Johanan's academy. That is to say: it is already evident that in this famous academy not only were there sessions devoted to the study and devlopment of Halakah, Law, as talmudic literature abundantly demonstrates, but there were also sessions devoted to esoteric lore, the kind of speculation that one customarily associates only with mystics and gnostics, and supposedly shunned by the talmudic Rabbis. As Scholem proved in some of his most recent publications,[8] so-called gnostic themes can be traced back to the "normative" rabbinic thought of the second century A.D., and even late first century. I hope in the near future to prove that already *early* in the first half of the first century, Pharisaic teachers were aware of theurgic practices, of which at least one sage did not approve, outspokenly. The point is, talmudic sources evidently reveal that in the academy of Johanan ben Zakkai there was more than preoccupation with the Law. This there is no need to belabor. But I would like to suggest that in addition to Halakic studies, in addition to general Haggadic (non-legal) sessions, in addition to concerns with esoteric lore, there were also sessions devoted to the consideration of philosophical questions.

Needless to say, it is not always easy to draw a sharp line between esoteric statements that involve one in metaphysics, and philosophical expositions. But when I speak of philosophical questions in the present study, I have in mind the exploration of ethical problems in the idiom which had become characteristic of Hellenistic philosophical circles, particularly after the period

---

[8] See especially the work referred to in n. 4 *supra*, and cf. the review by M. Smith in *Journal of Biblical Literature* 80 (1961) 190f.

of classical Greek philosophy. As scholars have universally observed, in the Hellenistic period, more and more, ethics came to be central in the preoccupation of philosophers.[9] This does not mean that there was no interest in the other branches of philosophy—physics, or rhetoric, or metaphysics. But as A. D. Nock put it,[10] to quote one historian out of many, ". . . in the Hellenistic age the philosophic centre of interest became primarily ethical."

It is with this therefore that we are here concerned when we speak of philosophical questions. But one more preliminary observation before we proceed to analysis of the talmudic texts: I do not seek to blur distinctions, to make of the vineyard of Jamnia an epicurean garden with Hebrew Florilegi, to equate a talmudic epigram lifted out of context with some Greek sentence also uprooted from its natural habitat. The rabbis were not Platos in Hebrew disguise, nor were they students (much less disciples) of Plato. On the other hand, however, especially after the detailed researches of E. Bickerman, Hans Lewy, and S. Lieberman,[11] it is impossible to deny that in the tents of Shem quite a number of Japhet, Hellenistic influences took up residence. That being the case, one may not a priori dismiss the possibility that in a tannaite academy there should be sessions devoted to philosophical problems. Some texts at least suggest otherwise; let us look at them, without more ado. And we shall begin with Johanan ben Zakkai's *favorite* disciple, Eleazar ben 'Arak.[12]

To him, chapter II of Pirqe 'Abot[13] attributes the following saying: "Be diligent in the study of the Torah, and know how to answer an Epicurean. Know in whose presence thou art toiling; and faithful is thy taskmaster to pay thee the reward of thy labor." A typical rabbinic view, one is tempted to say: there is emphasis on the study of Torah, there is opposition to epicureanism, there is affirmation of the doctrine of reward. No doubt. The difficulty is this however: what *exactly* did Eleazar ben 'Arak say? Already in 'Abot de-Rabbi Natan (*Fathers According to Rabbi Nathan*, hereafter ARN),[14] when Eleazar is quoted, the last clause, "to pay thee the reward of

[9] See, for example, E. Zeller, *Outlines of the History of Greek Philosophy* (New York, 1911) 208: ". . . in the systems of Hellenistic philosophy ethics and social theory occupy the most prominent positions. . . ."

[10] *Conversion* (London, 1933) 114.

[11] Merely by way of example (for very many details are scattered throughout the rich and numerous studies of these men) the following may be listed: by E. J. Bickerman, *Der Gott der Makkabäer* (Berlin, 1937); *The Maccabees* (New York, 1947); "La chaine de la tradition pharisienne," *Revue biblique* 59 (1952), 44ff.; "The Maxim of Antigonus of Socho," *Harvard Theological Review* 44 (1951) 153ff.; by Hans Lewy, the collection of essays in *'Olamot Nifgashim* [Heb.] (Jerusalem, 1960); by S. Lieberman, *Greek in Jewish Palestine* (New York, 1942) and *Hellenism in Jewish Palestine* (New York, 1962).

[12] See Pirqe 'Abot (hereafter PA) 2.8-9; and cf. J. Goldin, *Fathers According to Rabbi Nathan* (New Haven, 1955) 74 and n. 13 *ad loc.*

[13] PA 2.14.

[14] p. 66.

thy labor," is omitted, and there is good reason to believe that this clause
came to be attached to Eleazar's maxim as a result of its similarity to part of
Rabbi Tarfon's maxim cited immediately thereafter in the same chapter of
Pirqe 'Abot.[15] Not only that, but in Pirqe 'Abot Eleazar's term for God
appears as "thy taskmaster," *ba'al melakteka*, whereas in ARN the term used
is "author of the covenant with thee, thy Confederate," *ba'al beritka*.
Perhaps these are small matters. But more serious is the following: An
examination of each of the maxims by Johanan ben Zakkai's disciples cited
in the second chapter of Pirqe 'Abot reveals that each is made up of three
sentences—this it their basic design and stylistic character. On the other
hand, if you analyze Eleazar's saying, you discover not three, but four
sentences, even if the clause about reward is omitted; thus: (1) Be diligent in
the study of Torah; (2) Know how to answer an Epicurean; (3) Know in
whose presence thou art toiling; (4) Faithful is thy taskmaster. ARN is of no
help in this regard; actually it complicates matters all the more, for in
addition to these sentences it adds still another, to wit, "Let not one word of
the Torah escape thee."

Textual difficulties of this sort can prevent us from ever getting at the
substance of an author's statement. But in the present instance we are rather
fortunate in having a reading preserved by a large number of Genizah manuscripts in the Cambridge University Library. Here we find the following
version of Eleazar's saying—and note that it is indeed composed of three,
rather than four, sentences: "Be diligent to learn how to answer an Epicurean, know in whose presence thou art toiling, and faithful is thy *ba'al
berit*." Not a word, in short, about the study of Torah. And this is unques-
tionably the correct reading. The expression *lilmod Torah*, to learn or study
Torah, is so fixed a stereotype and cliché in rabbinic literature, that one can
easily see how Eleazar's saying came to be garbled. Be diligent to study?
Surely, said some later transmitter or copyist, Eleazar had in mind studying
Torah. No wonder the editor of ARN decided to improve even on this, and
added, "Let not one word of the Torah escape thee."

Since, however, we are interested in what Eleazar said, and not in what
later teachers thought he said, we had best focus on his own words, which
are, to repeat, "Be diligent to learn how to answer an Epicurean, know in
whose presence thou art toiling, and faithful is thy taskmaster" (or, thy *ba'al
berit*). If we focus on these words we cannot, I believe, fail to recognize that
a kind of anti-epicurean polemic is before us, some as-it-were Stoic (I
emphasize as-it-were) remark. I insist: this is not to say that Eleazar is a
former member of a Stoic school. All that is intended thus far is to call
attention to the fact that if we hear what Eleazar is saying, we shall discern
that he is *urging* us to learn how to refute an Epicurean (note his idiom: "be
diligent to learn to refute," *hewe shaqud lilmod le-hashib*), that he exhorts

15 2.15–16; cf. ARN (both versions) 84.

us to remember that our toils in this world do not go unattended, and that there is one to whom we are subject and He is trustworthy, dependable.

One notion we had best dispose of at the outset, and that is, that talmudic sources use the term *epiqurus* indiscriminately to suggest any kind of heretic or unbeliever. Despite widespread impression to the contrary, the term occurs in the Mishnah only in the Pirqe 'Abot passage we have cited and once more, also in an old Mishnah,[16] which incidentally describes the points of difference on dogmatic issues between Pharisees and Sadducees. "The following have no share in the *'olam ha-ba'*, the World to come (or, Age to come): He who says, there will be no resurrection, Torah was not revealed, and Epiqurus" i.e., an Epicurean—note especially that the text reads, (an) Epiqurus, not *the* Epicurean. Except for these two places the word does not appear anywhere else in the Mishnah—all other appearances of the term in the Mishnah, as one may learn even by consulting Kasovsky's Concordance,[17] are untrustworthy. In the Mishnah, then, the word has not yet been worn thin by frequent usage. All of which is simply meant to underscore, that it is wisest not to water down Eleazar's remark, and if he said an Epicurean, he meant just that. Very likely he had not non-Jewish, but Jewish Epicureans in mind. But he very likely did have in mind such Jews as had become epicurean more or less in outlook, not just any heretic at all.

To be sure, by the latter half of the second century, as would appear from Lucian's "Alexander the False Prophet," the term Epicurean seems to have become a dirty word, one can frighten audiences with it although they might not know what the term meant really, somewhat like the word "communist" in some circles today. But that Eleazar was using Epicurean in a slovenly name-calling manner is most unlikely. Observe, he does not say, Beware (*hewe zahir*) of an Epiqurus—an idiom so congenial to Pirqe 'Abot. What he says is, Be *shaqud*, diligent, *lilmod*, to study, to learn, *le-hashib*, to reply, to refute. He is speaking of serious refutation of the Epicurean, and like a Stoic insists that there is a trustworthy God before whom we engage in our toiling.[18]

We are now in a position, I believe, to understand part of the story of Rabban Johanan's enthusiasm over his disciple's brilliant Merkabah discourse. The talmudic sources relate that when Eleazar finished speaking, his master not only kissed him and exclaimed "Blessed be the Lord, God of Israel, who gave such a descendant to our father Abraham," but went on as follows:

---

[16] *Sanhedrin* 10.1, and for the correct reading and the implications thereof cf. J. Goldin in Proceedings, *American Academy for Jewish Research* 27 (1958) 40, and notes *ad loc.*

[17] C. Y. Kasovsky, *Thesaurus Mishnae* [Heb.] (Jeruslaem, 1956) I 261.

[18] Cf. R. D. Hicks, *Stoic and Epicurean* (New York, 1910) 304: "The Epicureans were never tired of arguing against the conception of God as either Creator or Providence. . . . On these points their chief antagonists were the Stoics. . . ."

> There are some who teach, interpret (doresh) becomingly, but do not
> practice, do not carry out, becomingly; there are some who practice what is
> becoming, but do not teach becomingly. But Eleazar ben 'Arak teaches
> becomingly and practices becomingly. How fortunate you are, O father
> Abaraham. . . .

"Practices what he preaches," na'eh doresh we-na'eh meqayyem, has
become so familiar an expression in Hebrew, that occasionally one imagines
that it occurs frequently in the classical sources. The fact is, it occurs only in
one other context. When, it is reported, the bachelor Ben 'Azzai held forth on
one occasion, on the importance of the first biblical commandment, to be
fruitful and to multiply, his colleague Eleazar ben Azariah rejoined stingingly:

> Things are well said when they come from the mouths of those who put
> them to practice, na'im debarim ke-she-hen yots'in mi-pi 'osehen. There are
> some who teach becomingly and practice becomingly. Ben 'Azzai teaches
> becomingly but does not practice becomingly.

Or as we might put it, he talks a good line. Now, in this context Eleazar's
rejoinder is perfectly intelligible. But what can that remark mean in the
story of Eleazar ben 'Arak's Merkabah discourse in the presence of Johanan
ben Zakkai? What practice, ill or otherwise, would be at issue? That when
Johanan warned him that esoteric subjects are not discussed in public,
Eleazar assented? As the texts read, it is no wonder commentators have had
difficulty with that sentence. What meaning can na'eh meqayyem have
here, even if na'eh doresh does apply to a brilliant discourse?

It is a Hellenistic source which furnishes the answer to this question.
Diogenes Laertius says that when the Athenians honored Zeno, the founder
of the Stoic school, among other things this is what they said of him:[19]

> . . . Zeno of Citium . . . has for many years been . . . exhorting to virtue
> and temperance those of the youth who come to him to be taught, directing
> them to what is best, affording to all in his own conduct a pattern for imita-
> tion in perfect consistency with his teaching. (παράδειγμα τὸν ἴδιον βίον
> ἐκθεὶς ἅπασιν ἀκόλουθον ὄντα τοῖς λόγοις οἷς διελέγετο).

And so, "practices what he preaches" is a topos, a way of
complimenting pure and simple. And since I wrote the paragraph above,
S. Lieberman has graciously sent me in private communication, two or three
additional examples, one of them by the way from Plutarch (Moralia 1033
seq.), in which Stoics are criticized for not living, conducting themselves, as
they themselves teach. One cannot help therefore recalling what Lucian
writes of the philosophers in his Menippus:[20] τοὺς γὰρ αὐτοὺς τούτους
εὕρισκον ἐπιτηρῶν ἐναντιώτατα τοῖς αὐτῶν λόγοις ἐπιτηδεύοντας.

It may be no more than a coincidence that Eleazar ben 'Arak should be

---

[19] Diog. Laert. 7.10–11 (ed. Hicks in Loeb Classics, II 121, whose translation I am using).
[20] Men. 5 (in Loeb Classics, IV 82).

praised by his teacher as the founder of the Stoics was praised. And I certainly do not intend to press this too hard. Let us therefore get on with our sources. We read:[21] When Johanan ben Zakkai's son died, his five famous disciples came to comfort him. Each one made the earnest effort, Eliezer ben Hyrqanos, Joshua ben Hananiah, Jose the Priest, Simeon ben Nathanel, and Eleazar ben 'Arak. But all of them, except the last, failed. As Johanan put it to each one in turn, as each finished his little homily, "Is it not enough that I grieve over my own, that you remind me of the grief of others?" But when Eleazar appeared, the outcome was different. As soon as he appeared, Johanan knew he would be comforted, and in fact he was. And here is what Eleazar had said and what proved to be the genuine consolation:

> I shall tell thee a parable. to what may this be likened? To a man with whom the king deposited some object. Every single day the man would weep and cry out, saying: "Woe unto me! When shall I be quit of this trust in peace?" Thou too, master, thou hadst a son: he studied the Torah, the Prophets, the Holy Writings, he studied Mishnah, Halakah, and Haggadah, and he departed from the world without sin. And thou shouldst be comforted when thou hast returned thy trust unimpaired.

Now, this notion of the soul of one's beloved held in trust is not unknown in rabbinic sources; it is especially familiar in the anecdote of the death of Rabbi Me'ir's sons. It occurs also in non-rabbinic sources,[22] and I would like to cite a relevant passage from Philo (de Abrahamo 44)[23] who in praising Abraham says:

> . . . I will speak of one [merit] which concerns the death of his wife, in which his conduct should not be passed over in silence. When he had lost his life-long partner . . . when sorrow was making itself ready to wrestle with his soul, he grappled with it, as in the arena, and prevailed. He gave strength and high courage to the natural antagonist of passion, reason, which he had taken as his counsellor throughout his life and now particularly was determined to obey. . . . The advice was that he should not grieve over-bitterly as at an utterly new and unheard-of misfortune, nor yet assume an indifference as though nothing painful had occurred, but choose the mean rather than the extremes and aim at moderation of feeling, not resent that nature should be paid the debt which is its due, but quietly and gently lighten the blow.
>
> The testimonies for this are to be found in the holy books. . . . They show that after weeping for a little over the corpse he quickly rose up from it, holding further mourning to be out of keeping with wisdom, which taught him that death is not the extinction of the soul but its separation and detachment from the body and its return to the place from whence it came; and it came, as was shown in the story of creation, from God. *And, as no reasonable person would chafe at repaying a debt or deposit* (χρέος ἢ πυρακαταθήκην) *to him who had proffered it, so too he must not fret when nature took back her own, but accept the inevitable with equanimity.*

---

[21] ARN 58f.

[22] See for example Sapientia 15.8, 16, and especially Josephus, Wars 3.8.5.

[23] I am using Colson's translation (Loeb Classics, VI 125ff.).

The passage, as is clear, reverberates with Stoic echoes. "Never say about anything," Epictetus tells us,[24] "'I have lost it,' but only 'I have given it back.' Is your child dead? It has been given back (ἀπεδόθη). Is your wife dead? She has been given back." Interesting enough, when Tarn comes to summarize Stoic teaching, even he chooses as one of its distinctive emphases, "the Stoic will not grieve for his son's death."[25]

Once again perhaps it may be wise to repeat the note of caution already struck. It does not *necessarily* follow from all we have thus far explored, that without the Stoics the talmudic fathers could not have arrived at the idea of the soul as a deposit—though I must say, even Ps. 30.6 (MT 31.6), "In manus tuns commendo spiritum meum," does not *altogether* suggest the idea to the tannaite midrash, the *Mekilta*, which cites the verse as prooftext for the statement that "all souls are in the hand of Him by whose utterance the world came into being." In the companion midrash, *Mekilta of R. Simeon*, the idea is not even given the benefit of this prooftext: the verse isn't even cited at all! Be that as it may, even a novice knows that it is fake scholarship to declare that there is necessary dependence simply because one finds similarity of ideas. But, firstly, similarity should be recognized if it exists, even if there may be no dependence. Secondly, however, there is a detail that must be introduced in this connection.

Josephus cannot be depended on either when he protests *pro vita sua* or—and it is this which concerns us here—when he describes sects in Jewish Palestine as though they were Greek schools of thought. This has been underscored so frequently by so many scholars that it would be childish to ignore their remarks. And yet, even if we grant that it is grotesque to look upon Pharisees, Sadducees, and Essenes as though they were imitation Greek schools, perhaps we may learn something from the particular form of absurdity of which the author is guilty. It is instructive that, when Josephus describes the Pharisees, of all schools, he chooses the Stoics to compare them with: "the Pharisees, a sect having points of resemblance to that which the Greeks call the Stoic school."[26] The statement is not to be dismissed cavalierly: observe how carefully he has expressed himself, "a sect having points of resemblance," ἤ παραπλήσιός ἐστι. That Josephus is capable of giving an accurate characterization of a Greek school, we know from his observations on the Epicureans:[27]

> It therefore seems to me, in view of the things foretold by Daniel, that they are very far from holding a true opinion who declare that God takes no thought for human affairs. For it were the case that *the world goes by some*

[24] *Encheiridion* 11, ed. W. A. Oldfather (Loeb Classics II, 491.)

[25] *Hellenistic Civilization* (London, 1936) 299. In *Republic* 10, 603, Plato also says that the good man will not mourn excessively over the loss of his son; but though he gives several reasons for this, he does not speak of the soul as a deposit or trust.

[26] *Vita* 2, end, ed. Thackeray 7.

[27] *Antiquities* 10, end, ed. R. Marcus (Loeb Classics VI, 313.)

automatism (εἰ συνέβαινεν αὐτοματισμῷ τινι τὸν κόσμον διάγειν), we should
not have seen all these things happen in accordance with his prophecy.

Josephus may be stretching a point, and more than a point, when he feels he
has to. But he is undoubtedly registering something real about the Pharisees—they *were* affected by a Stoic climate; and as Tarn has written:[28]
"The philosophy of the Hellenistic world was the Stoic; all else was
secondary." Jewish Palestine was not immune to this.

Such at least is the climate of notions around Eleazar ben 'Arak,
Johanan ben Zakkai's favorite disciple of whom the text says: "Happy the
disciple whose master praises him and testifies to his gifts!" And if we keep
this climate in mind we shall understand a famous block of passages in *Pirqe
'Abot* (hereafter PA), often cited, but perhaps not sufficiently appreciated.

When the second chapter of PA resumes the chain of tradition which is
the basic scheme of the first chapter, it quite properly introduces Johanan
ben Zakkai with the customary formula. "Rabban Johanan ben Zakkai took
over from Hillel and Shammai." Then, as is the practice of PA, it quotes his
saying. Since the editor is eager to show that the chain of tradition, whose
first link was forged with Moses at Sinai, was not broken even after Johanan
ben Zakkai—though in his day the Temple had been destroyed—he proceeds to introduce the five famous disciples of Johanan, and to quote *their*
sayings. But as everyone knows, this introduction is not quite like all the
previous introductions. Before the editor quotes these men, he first informs
us how Johanan used to describe them.[29] Even after that he does not quote
the disciples; before the editor gets down to their sentences he introduces a
long conversation piece, a section recording an exchange between Johanan
and his disciples.[30] Only after all this does he transmit their sayings. Nothing
like this, description or conversation, occurs anywhere else in PA.

The insertion of a description of the disciples is easily explainable. Since
the editor is eager to assert that despite the national, the political and institutional disaster, the destruction of the Jerusalem Temple, the Pharisaic chain
of tradition remained unbroken, we can appreciate why he feels he ought to
report the master's own testimony regarding the stature of his disciples.
There were no ordinary disciples, no run of the mill sages. Eliezer ben
Hyrqanos was "a plastered cistern which loses not a drop. Joshua—Happy is
she who gave birth to him. Jose—A saint. Simeon ben Nathanel—Fears sin.
Eleazar ben 'Arak—Ever flowing stream." I wish I could understand specifically each of these compliments—they are obviously intended to suggest
something extraordinary; and perhaps to have called Eliezer ben Hyrqanos
"a plastered cistern which loses not a drop," was more or less what Zeno

[28] *Op. cit.* 290. And regarding semitic influences on Stoic thought, cf. Rostovtzoff, *Social and
Economic History of the Hellenistic World* (Oxford, 1981) 1426 n. 232.
[29] PS 2.8.
[30] 2.9.

meant when he compared his successor Cleanthes "to hard waxen tablets which are difficult to write upon, but retain the characters written upon them."[31] But, as I say, while it is not the practice of PA otherwise to include such data regarding the other sages, in the case of the five disciples of Johanan the motive is understandable. But why, after he has introduced them so handsomely, does not the editor begin to quote them, as he does with all other sages? Why before quoting their sayings does he insert the long conversation, especially in a treatise where no other give-and-take is presented, halakic *or* haggadic? And since this is not the only question raised by the long passage, perhaps it would be wise to quote it, so that we may see vividly what the problems are:[32]

> Rabban Johanan said to them: Go forth and see which is the right way to which a man should cleave.
>> Rabbi Eliezer replied: A liberal eye.
>> Rabbi Joshua replied: A good companion.
>> Rabbi Jose replied: A good neighbor.
>> Rabbi Simeon replied: Foresight.
>> Rabbi Eleazar replied: Goodheartedness.
> Said Rabban Johanan ben Zakkai to them: I prefer the answer of Eleazar ben 'Arak, for in his words your words are included.
> Rabban Johanan said to them: Go forth and see which is the evil way which a man should shun.
>> Rabbi Eliezer replied: A grudging eye.
>> Rabbi Joshua replied: An evil companion.
>> Rabbi Jose replied: An evil neighbor.
>> Rabbi Simeon replied: Borrowing and not repaying; for he that borrows from man is as one who borrows from God, blessed be He, as it is said, "The wicked man borrows and does not repay, but the just man shows mercy and gives." (Ps. 36.21; MT 37.21)
>> Rabbi Eleazar replied: Meanheartedness.
> Said Rabban Johanan to them: I prefer the answer of Eleazar ben 'Arak, for in his words your words are included.

There it is, a conversation (as I said) unlike anything else in PA, and only after it has been reported, are we offered the sayings of these sages. As one reads it, not only must he ask, what in the world is it doing here, but he cannot escape at least two other questions. First, what are these men talking about? True, their master had asked them about the right way, or course, to which a person ought to cling, and they had offered their replies. But is it not fantastic that these men, the best disciples Johanan ben Zakkai had— Johanan ben Zakkai who had been quoted a paragraph or so before as the author of the saying, "If thou hast wrought much in the study of Torah take no credit to thyself, for to this end wast thou created," and as ARN added,

---

[31]   Diogenes Laertius 7.37 (II, 149).
[32]   PA 2.9; for the translation cf J. Goldin, *Living Talmud: the Wisdom of the Fathers* (Chicago, 1958) 99.

"for men (*haberiyot*) were created only on condition that they study Torah"—is it not fantastic that, when the best disciples of such a master, leading sages in Israel, are asked about the right course to which a man should cleave, not even one of them suggests in his answer something connected with Torah? Jewish sages without a word about the Torah? Second, what is the meaning of asking first about the right way and then about the evil way, and then the answers which are simply the negation of the former affirmations? What have I learned from the second conversation that I did not already learn from the first one?

That the ancients already found this passage something of a serious problem is evident from the way it is preserved in ARN.[33] To give only a couple of examples: In PA Johanan had asked, which is the right way to which a man should cleave. In ARN, his question appears as, "Which is the good way to which a man should cleave, *so that through it he might enter the world to come*? . . . Which is the evil way which a man should shun, *so that he might enter the world to come*?" In other words, "the world to come" has suddenly made an entrance. Or again: In PA, to the first question Rabbi Jose has replied, "A good neighbor," and to the second question, "An evil neighbor." In ARN on the other hand, he seems to have grown a little more garrulous in his answers. To the first question he replies, "A good neighbor, a good impulse (*yetzer tob*), and a good wife"; to the second, "An evil neighbor, an evil impulse, and an evil wife." These are not the only variants; study of the parallel passages will reveal interesting variants in Eleazar ben 'Arak's answer too.

The answers of the disciples are far from clear, but if we wish to capture something of the meaning of this exchange between Johanan and his disciples, it is terribly important to listen to his question with utmost attention. Johanan did not ask a trivial question, nor did he express himself carelessly. He asked about the way to which a man should "cleave," *dabaq*. Properly to feel the force of this verb *dabaq*, one might compare Johanan's question with the almost identical—*almost* but not entirely—question later raised by Judah the Prince, the redactor of the Mishnah, also quoted in the second chapter of PA—indeed he is the first sage cited there. Judah asks: "Which is the right course that a man ought to *choose* (*she-yabor*) for himself?" But Johanan speaks not just of choice, but of *cleaving*. That the Hebrew sources take the verb *dabaq*, cleave, very seriously, can be demonstrated by a number of texts. The biblical verse (Deut. 11:22) exhorts, "to love the Lord your God, to walk in all His ways, and to cleave (προσκολλᾶσθαι) unto him (*adhaerentes et*)." At which the tannaite midrash, the *Sifre*, exclaims: "But how is it possible for a human being to ascend on high and cleave to the Fire?" Even in Scripture the verb *dabaq* has a fervor to it; here is Jeremiah (13.11) expressing himself: "For as the girdle cleaveth (*yidbaq ha-'ezor*, κολλᾶται) to the loins of a man, so have

I caused to cleave unto Me (hidbaqti 'elai, ἐκόλλησα) the whole house of Israel and the whole house of Judah, saith the Lord." (*Sicut enim adhaeret lumbare ad lumbos viri, sic ailutinavi mihi omnem domum Juda, dicit Dominus.*) That the Midrash is fully sensitive to this verse can be seen in the Tanhuma comment on Lev. 19:2: "Be ye holy! Why? For I am holy, for it is said, 'As the girdle cleaveth to the loins of a man,' etc." "Let him kiss me with the kisses of his mouth" (*Osculetur me osculo oris sui*), says the poet of Canticles (Cant. 1:1, MT 1:2); and the Midrash in its homiletical pun explains, "*Let Him kiss me*, let Him cause me to cleave to Him (*yishaqeni, yadbqeni*)."

So long as we are lingering over the word *dabaq*, "cleave," I hope it is not out of place to call attention to one more point, especially for the benefit of Hebraists. According to our sources, both PA and ARN, the question Johanan asked was: What is the way (or, course) to which a man should cleave? In other words, he is speaking of *cleaving to a way*. But though *dabaq* is not a rare word in Scripture, nowhere does such an expression occur—and not only in Scripture, but at least for the time being, in none of the documents from the Dead Sea. A man cleaves to his wife,[34] the tongue cleaves to the roof of the mouth,[35] one cleaves to the truth and good deeds and the testimonies of the Lord,[36] curses cleave to a man,[37] and Ps. 62:9 (MT 63:9) offers even "My soul cleaveth unto Thee" (*Adhaesit anima mea post te*), literally, after thee, (cf. LXX 62.9, ἐκολλήθη ἡ ψυχή μου ὀπίσω σου); as we have seen, there are those who cleave to the Lord (cf. Deut. 4.4; LXX, Ὑμεῖς ὐὲ οἱ προσκείμενοι [ἱ] κυρίῳ, *Vos aulem adhaeretis Domino Deo vestri*). But nowhere else will one find this combination *dabaq bederekh*— nowhere else, that is, except in a statement of old exegetes whom the tannaite sources call *Doreshe Reshumot* or *Doreshe Haggadot*. Lauterbach once called *them* the Allegorical Interpreters. Be that as it may, the exegesis of these anonymous teachers is of a figurative-speculative kind. And it is in one of their comments, preserved in the tannaite *Sifre* that the following occurs: "If it is your wish to recognize (acknowledge?) Him at whose utterance the world came into being, study Haggadah—for thus you come to recognize God and cleave to His ways."

The term *dabaq* then is no ordinary term, and it was no ordinary question Johanan asked, and the give-and-take with his disciples was no ordinary conversation. The idiom reveals a certain intensiveness, a certain *fervor*, and this is the telling thing. It is the idiom which suddenly summons up remembrances of a mood and a tone of voice which were current in Hellenist circles. As Nock wrote three decades ago:[38]

---

[34] Cf. Gen. 2.24.

[35] Ps. 136:6 (MT 137:6).

[36] *Dead Sea Scrolls* II 2: *Manual of Discipline*, ed. M. Burrows (New Haven, 1951) Plate I, line 5; *Thanksgiving Scroll*, ed, J. Licht (Jerusalem, 1957) 202; Ps. 118:31 (MT 119:31).

[37] *Dead Sea Scrolls* II, Plate II, lines 15f.; *Zadokite Documents*, ed. C. Rabin (Oxford, 1958) 5.

[38] Conversion 181. And see also H. I. Marrou, *History of Education in Antiquity* (New York,

. . . this idea [that devotion to philosophy would make a difference in a man's life] was not thought of as a matter of purely intellectual conviction. The philosopher commonly said *not* "Follow my arguments one by one, check and control them to the best of your ability; truth should be dearer than Plato to you," but "Look at this picture which I paint, and can you resist its attractions? Can you refuse a hearing to the legitimate rhetoric which I address to you in the name of virtue?" Even Epicurus says in an argument, "Do not be deceived, men, or led astray: do not fall. There is no natural fellowship between reasonable beings. *Believe me*, those who express the other view deceive you and argue you out of what is right." Epictetus, II, 19, 34 also employs the same appeal, *Believe me*, and counters opponents by arguments which appeal to the heart and not to the head. Inside the schools, at least inside the academic school, there was an atmosphere of hard thinking, of which something survives in the various commentaries on Aristotle. Yet even in the schools this was overcast by tradition and loyalty. . . . The philosophy which addressed itself to the world at large was a dogmatic philosophy seeking to save souls.

This is the mood of our PA passage, and this is the mood of Johanan's question, which I believe can almost be rendered in the words from Diogenes Laertius, τί πράττων ἄριστα βιώσεται.[39] It was then a philosophical question Johanan asked; and first he asked which is the right way, and then which is the evil way. In other words, what is he doing? He formulates his question first in the positive, then in the negative, one way and its opposite. And when his disciples replied, as we saw, they did the same thing (to Simeon's answer we shall get shortly), one way and its opposite: liberal eye, grudging eye; good companion, evil companion; good neighbor, evil neighbor; goodheartedness, meanheartedness.

It will now be instructive to review the summary of Stoic teaching drawn up by Diogenes Laertius[40] (of which Hicks says, by the way, "the summary of Stoic doctrine in Book VII (39–160) is comprehensive and trustworthy"):

Amongst *the virtues* (τῶν δ'ἀρετῶν) some are primary, some are subordinate to these. The following are the primary: wisdom, courage, justice, temperance. Particular virtues are magnanimity, continence, endurance, presence of mind, good counsel.

Similarly, *of vices* (τῶν κακιῶν) some are primary, others subordinate: e.g., folly, cowardice, injustice, profligacy are accounted primary; but incontinence, stupidity, ill-advisedness subordinate. Further, many hold that *the vices* are forms of ignorance of those things whereof the *corresponding virtues* are the knowledge. . . .

Another particular definition *of good* which they give is "the natural perfection of a rational being *qua* rational." To this answers virtue and, as being partakes in virtue, virtuous acts and good men; also its supervening accessories, joy and gladness and the like. So *with evils*: either they are vices,

1956) 206.

[39] 7.2 (Loeb Classics II, 110).

[40] 7.92 ff (II, 199ff., Hicks's translation).

folly, cowardice, injustice, and the like; or things which partake of vice, including vicious acts and wicked persons as well as their accompaniments, despair, moroseness, and the like.

Again, *some goods* (τῶν ἀγαθῶν) are goods of the mind, and others external, which some are neither mental nor external. The former include the virtues and virtuous acts; external goods are such as having a good country or a good friend, and the prosperity of such. Whereas to be good and happy oneself is of the class of goods neither mental nor external. Similarly of *things evil* (τῶν κακῶν) some are mental evils, namely, vices and vicious actions; others are outward evils, as to have a foolish country or a foolish friend and the unhappiness of such; other evils again are neither mental nor outward, e.g., to be yourself bad and unhappy.

Again, *goods* (τῶν ἀγαθῶν) are either of the nature of ends or they are the means to these ends, or they are at the same time ends and means. A friend and the advantages derived from him are means to good, whereas confidence, high-spirit, liberty, delight, gladness, freedom from pain, and every virtuous act are of the nature of ends.

The virtues (they say) are goods of the nature at once of ends and of means. On the one hand, in so far as they cause happiness they are means, and on the other hand, insofar as they make it complete, and so are themselves part of it, they are ends. Similarly *of evils* (τῶν κακῶν) some are of the nature of ends and some of means, while others are at once both means and ends. Your enemy and the harm he does you are means; consternation, abasement, slavery, gloom, despair, excess of grief, and every vicious action are of the nature of ends. Vices are evil both as ends and as means, since insofar as they cause misery they are means, but insofar as they make it complete, so that they become part of it, they are ends. . . .

. . . *Of the beautiful* (τοῦ καλοῦ) there are (they say) four species, namely, what is just, courageous, orderly and wise. . . . Similarly there are four species *of the base or ugly* (τοῦ αἰσχροῦ), namely, what is unjust, cowardly, disorderly, and unwise. . . .

Goods ('Αγαθά) comprise the virtues of prudence, justice, courage, temperance, and the rest; while the opposites of these are *evils* (κακά), namely, folly, injustice, and the rest. . . . *To benefit* (ὠφελεῖν) is to set in motion or sustain in accordance with virtue; whereas *to harm* (βλάπτειν) is to set in motion or sustain in accordance with vice. . . .

. . . Things of the *preferred class* (προηγμένα) are those which have positive value, e.g. amongst mental qualities, natural ability, skill, moral improvement, and the like; among bodily qualities, life, health, strength, good condition, soundness of organs, beauty, and so forth; and in the sphere of external things, wealth, fame, noble birth, and the like. To the class of *things "rejected"* (ἀποπροηγμένα) belong, of mental qualities, lack of ability, want of skill, and the like; among bodily qualities, death, disease, weakness, being out of condition, mutilation, ugliness, and the like; in the sphere of external things, poverty, ignominy, low birth, and so forth. . . .

Again, *of things preferred* some are preferred for their own sake, some for the sake of something else, and others again both for their own sake and for the sake of something else. . . . And similarly with the class of *things rejected* under the contrary heads. . . .

Befitting acts (καθήκοντα) are all those which reason prevails with us to do; and this is the case with honoring one's parents, brothers and country, and intercourse with friends. *Unbefitting, or contrary to duty* (τὸ καθῆκον) are all acts that reason deprecates, e.g. to neglect one's parents, to be indifferent to one's brothers, not to agree with friends, to disregard the interests of one's country, and so forth. . . .

Surely, this is enough, more than enough. The summary of Stoic ethics has manifestly been drawn up along a certain line, first the positive, then the negative, first in terms of the good and then immediately thereafter in terms of the evil. I am in no position to say whether this pattern or idiom is unique to the Stoics, especially when I recall some sections in the *Republic*, for example;[41] and I would indeed be grateful to classicists if they could inform me whether such a style is characteristic of study and discussion in Hellenistic schools generally. But it is impressive, is it not, that only in Diogenes' summary of *Stoic* teaching, and in no other summary of his (including the long presentation of Epicurean teaching),[42] is this style so distinct. Whatever else one may wish to conclude, this at least seems to me legitimate—that in Stoic circles defining and discussing were carried on in this style, first the one term, and then its opposite.

And this is precisely the form of the give-and-take between Johanan and his disciples, first the good course, and then the evil course. It is a philosophical *façon de parler* Johanan is using. And since it was a philosophical question he had asked, as we saw earlier in our analysis of the idiom of his question, his disciples answered him in the philosophical way, first in the positive, then the negative. Since it was a philosophical question, his disciples answered in characteristic philosophical terms—and that is why not one of them even bothered to refer to Torah. And since it was an important session, though nothing like it occurs elsewhere in the treatise, the editor of PA preserved the record of it, put it down right after he had recounted the praises of the disciples—but before he cites their sayings. It is as though the editor were asserting: You see, not only did their master Johanan testify to the greatness of these men, but here is a transcript of a very significant session conducted in their academy. Only after all this does the editor begin to cite them—and significantly enough, these sayings are introduced by the very formula he had used in introducing the Men of the Great Assembly, the first spokesmen of the Oral Torah: "and they said three things."

One more point, and then we shall arrive at the conclusion. We noted that the disciples had replied to Johanan's questions first positively, and then negatively: "Liberal eye, grudging eye; good companion, evil companion; good neighbor, evil neighbor; goodheartedness, meanheartedness." So the answers of four of the disciples. But what of the reply by Simeon ben Nathanel? To the first question, what is the good course, he had replied,

---

[41] Cf. 3.400; 4.442–43; and compare especially 8–9 with the earlier books. See also Diogenes on Plato, 3.103ff. (II, 367f.).

[42] ". . . Book X is made up largely of extracts from the writings of Epicurus, by far the most precious thing preserved in this collection of odds and ends" (Hicks in his Introduction, p. xx).

"Foresight"; to the second question, what is the evil course, he had replied, "Borrowing and not repaying." Many a commentator has insisted, and probably correctly, that since the other four replies were in the fixed form of Johanan's question, of positive and negative, the same must no doubt be true of Simeon's reply. This stands to reason. But one thing we cannot fail to recognize:

> But speaking of this very thing, justice, are we to affirm thus without qualification that it is truth-telling and *paying back what one has received* from anyone . . . ? I mean, for example, . . . if one took over weapons from a friend who was in his right mind and then the lender should go mad and demand them back, that we ought not to return them in that case and that he who did so return them would not be acting justly. . . . Then this is not the definition of justice: to tell the truth and return what one has received.
>
> "Nay, but it is, Socrates," said Polemarchus breaking in, "if indeed we are to put any faith in Simonides" . . .
>
> "Tell me, then, . . . what is it that you affirm that Simonides says, and rightly says about justice." "That it is just," he replied, "to render to each his due (ὅτι . . . τὸ τὰ ὀφειλόμενα ἑκάστῳ ἀποδιδόναι δίκαιόν ἐστι). In saying this I think he speaks well."
>
> "I must admit," said I, "that it is not easy to disbelieve Simonides. For he is a wise and inspired man. . . ."[43]

To be sure, Socrates is being ironic, but Simonides' definition was, as we know, the current and generally accepted one. As Shorey remarks in his note: "Owing to the rarity of banks 'reddere depositum' was throughout antiquity the typical instance of just conduct." And see also what Shorey cites as regards Stoic terminology.[44]

At least therefore in one of his answers, Simeon is echoing the kind of opinion that one overheard in the schools of the larger world outside the rabbinic academy. And perhaps "foresight" is, as some commentators suggest, the opposite of *reddere depositum*.

What does all this add up to? In a sense, not very much. We certainly have no evidence that the Palestinian Jewish sages read Plato or Zeno, much less studied them. But one result seems to me inescapable: living in the Hellenistic-Roman world the Tannaim could not remain unaffected by that world. It is not simply a matter of loan words; it is something much more profound. Not only did the Palestinian sages appropriate the terminology for some hermeneutic rules from the Hellenistic rhetors,[45] but inside the *bet ha-midrash*, the rabbinic academy, apparently one did take up from time to time philosophical questions, and one did attempt to answer these questions in the current philosophical idiom. Study of the Law of course remained

---

[43] Plato, *Republic* 1, 331D–E, ed. P. Shorey (Loeb Classics I, 20f.); cf. Diogenes Laertius 3.83 (1, 35f).

[44] P. 22 note a.

[45] See on this the important researches of S. Lieberman, *Hellenism in Jewish Palestine* 28–114.

paramount. But along with such activity went an awareness, at least in the School of Johanan ben Zakkai, of the subject and style popular in intellectual circles generally.

One thing should not mislead us. The fact that in a number of stories the *philosophos* is bested in his encounter with the rabbi, indicates nothing more than a typically recurring popular attitude: anything they can do, we can do better. This is not anti-philosophy as such; indeed, there is in such stories a distinct acknowledgment that among the Gentiles the wisest are the philosophers; but of course the *hakam* is superior since he is a master of the Torah. Such stories are in spirit and intent like those anecdotes in the first chapter of the Midrash on Lamentations where an Athenian, in other words, one universally reputed to be particularly clever, is outwitted by Jerusalemites, and even by youngsters of Jerusalem. In no way do such stories demonstrate that philosophy, and the current manner of discussing what was generally regarded as philosophical questions, were repugnant to the talmudic sages and therefore were excluded from the rabbinic academy. Whether professional philosophers would have been impressed by the level or range of philosophical discussion inside the rabbinic academy is beside the point: it would be like asking what a Kant would think of various courses offered by many collegiate departments of philosophy. No one is suggesting that the talmudic sages were technical philosophers. But the popular terms and ethical themes of dominant Hellenistic philosophical speculations were not alien at least to the circle around Johanan ben Zakkai. He and his disciples did not shun either the subject or the style.[46] Their place of meeting was of course the *bet ha-midrash*, but inside it they found the spaciousness for the study of scripture and the study of Mishnah, the dialectic of law and the contemplation of mystic lore, the engagement with the dogmas of Revelation and the deliberations of philosophy.

[46] That the give-and-take recorded in PA 2.9 took place before Johanan withdrew to Jamnia is clear from an analysis of the sources; see also G. Alon, *Studies in Jewish History* [Heb.] 1 (Tel Aviv, 1957) 26ff.

A SURVEY OF HELLENISTIC
JEWISH THOUGHT: A SYLLABUS

Theodore M. Klein

The purpose of this course is to introduce students to the richness and variety of the Hellenistic period in Jewish thought. The class begins with a general historical overview of the period and with an introduction to the standard bibliographies (First and Second Weeks). The curriculum for the Third and Fourth Weeks is designed to focus the student's attention on the Talmudic age in particular. At this point, annotated bibliographies of Jewish thought and literature are introduced.

The student is now ready for a comparative study of the Hellenistic age in which the Hebrew, Greek, and Roman traditions blend, interact and clash; having acquired some historical knowledge of the periods of peace, as well as of the Maccabean period, the Alexandrian riots, and the wars with the Romans, the student can now appreciate Hellenistic cosmopolitanism and also the underlying ideological and cultural tensions of the age. Spartian's *Life of Hadrian* (supplemented by Marguerite Yourcenar's *Memoirs of Hadrian*) and Louis Finkelstein's *Akiba*, will present the sharpest possible contrast between the Graeco-Roman and Rabbinic weltanschammgen. On the other hand, the *Pirkei Avot*, read together with selected passages from Epictetus's *Encheiridion* and Marcus Aurelius's *Meditations* (supplemented perhaps by J. M. Rist's *Stoic Philosophy* [Cambridge: Cambridge University Press, 1969]) will reveal many similarities and parallels between the two cultural traditions (Fifth and Sixth Weeks).

The most obvious indicator of tension in an age of cultural uniformity and diversity is, of course, the emergence of sectarianism. The Seventh and Eighth Weeks are accordingly devoted to a study of the Essenes, the Pharisees, the Sadducees, and the Jewish Gnostics. Messianism and the Jewish Apocalyptic is stressed during the Ninth and Tenth Weeks, which also deal with the literary genres of the apocryphon and the pseudepigraphon. The impact of these literary forms on the Graeco-Roman world are clearly discernible in the traditions of the Sibylline Oracles and in the paradoxography of Phlegon of Tralles, not to mention the *Alexandra* of Lycophron, and well-known works such as Vergil's *Fourth Eclogue* and the Sixth Book of the *Aeneid*.

Philo, of course, remains the best example of the rapprochement of the

Hebraic and Greek traditions; he is carefully studied in the Eleventh and Twelfth Weeks of class (the *De Officio Mundi*, the *De Migratione Abrahami*, and the *De Confusione Linguarum* are especially recommended).

A consideration of the *Mishnah* and *Gemara* during the Thirteenth and Fourteenth Weeks should include sizeable portions from the "Abodah Zarah" or the "Treatise on Idolatry." The picture of the Jews' cultural exclusiveness, which arises from these pages of the Talmud, can profitably be contrasted with the works of Saul Lieberman. The rest of this unit is devoted to the Rabbinic world-view. At least one of Kadushin's books should be read. Schechter, who is intense and protreptic, is nicely complemented by readings from the leisurely and sedate volumes of Moore.

During the last week the class addresses itself to a consideration of Josephus. The Penguin translation of *The Jewish War* (supplemented by brief readings from Thackeray's translation of the *Antiquities*) takes the student back to the very first unit of the course and provides a good summary of the tensions and the complexities of the period.

FIRST AND SECOND WEEKS: A GENERAL HISTORICAL OVERVIEW

Michael Avi-Yonah, *The Jews of Palestine: A Political History from the Bar-Kochba War to the Arab Conquest* (New York: Schocken Books, 1976).

H. H. Ben Sasson, *A History of the Jewish People* (Cambridge: Harvard University Press, 1976), pp. 185–382.

Elias J. Bickerman, "The Historical Foundations of Post-Biblical Judaism," in *The Jews: Their History, Culture and Religion* I, ed. Louis Finkelstein (New York: Schocken Books, 1970), 72–118, II (1971).

——————————, *From Ezra to the Last of the Maccabees* (New York: Schocken Books, 1962).

W. S. Ferguson, "The Leading Ideas of the New Period," in *The Cambridge Ancient History* (Cambridge: University of Cambridge Press, 1954), VII, 1–40.

Michael Grant, *The Jews in the Roman World* (New York: Scribner, 1973).

Jean Juster, *Les Juifs dans l'empire romain: leur condition économique et sociale* (Paris: P. Geuthner, 1914) 2 vols.

Harry Joshua Leon, *The Jews of Ancient Rome* (Philadelphia: The Jewish Publication Society, 1960).

Ralph Marcus, "The Hellenistic Age," in *Great Ages and Ideas of the Jewish People*, ed. Leo Walder Schwarz (New York: Modern Library, 1956), pp. 95–139.

Emil Schürer, *The History of the Jewish People in the Age of Jesus Christ* (175 B.C.–A.D. 135), rev. and ed. Geza Vermes and Fergus Miller (Edinburgh: T. and T. Clark, 1973), vol. I (vol. II in preparation).

E. Mary Smallwood, *The Jews under Roman Rule from Pompey to Diocle-tian* (Leiden: Brill, 1976).

Morton Smith, "Palestine Judaism in the First Century," in *Israel: Its Role in Civilization*, ed. Moshe David (New York: Harper and Brothers, 1956), pp. 67–81.

—————————, *Palestine Politics and Parties that Shaped the Old Testament* (New York: Columbia University Press, 1971).

Victor I. Tcherikover, *Hellenistic Civilization and the Jews* (New York: Ath-eneum, 1977).

—————————, and Menahem Stern, *Corpus Papyrorum Judaicarum* (Cambridge: Harvard University Press, 1957–1964), 4 vols.

Bibliographies:

Gerhard Delling, *Bibliographie zür judisch-hellenistischen und intertes-tamentarischen Literatur 1900–1970* (Berlin: Akademie-Verlag, 1969).

Ralph Marcus, "A Selected Bibliography (1920–1945) of the Jews in Hellenistic and Roman Periods 1946–1770," *Proceedings of the American Academy for Jewish Research*, 16 (1946–1947), 97–181.

U. Rappaport, "Bibliography of the Works on Jewish History in the Hellenistic and Roman Periods 1946–1770," *Mehqarin betoledot am yisrael ve' erez yisrael*, 2 (1972), 247–321.

General Reference:

Samuel Safrai and Menahem Stern, *The Jewish People in the First Century: Compendia Rerum Judaicarum ad Novum Testamentum* (Assen: Van Gorcum, 1974–1976), 2 vols.

THIRD AND FOURTH WEEKS: THE TALMUDIC AGE

Richard Bavier, "Judaism in New Testament Times," in *A Study of Judaism: Bibliographical Essays* (New York: Ktav, 1972), pp. 9–34.

Gershom Cohen, "The Talmudic Age," in *Great Ages and Ideas*, pp. 142–212.

Judah Goldin, "The Period of the Talmud (135 B.C.E.–1035 C.E.)" in *The Jews: Their History*, I, pp. 119–89.

—————————, "Judaism," in *A Reader's Guide to the Great Religions*, ed. Charles J. Adams (New York: The Free Press, 1965), pp. 191–228.

FIFTH AND SIXTH WEEKS: WORLD OF IDEAS
AMONG THE HEBREWS, GREEKS AND ROMANS

Ben Zion Waxholder, *Eupolemus: A Study of Judaeo-Greek Literature* (Cin-cinnati: Hebrew Union College Press, 1974).

Norman Bentwich, "The Graeco-Roman View of the Jews," in *Understanding the Talmud*, ed. Alan Corre (New York: Ktav, 1975).

Anthony Birley, *Lives of the Later Caesars*, (Harmondsworth, England: 1978), especially "Hadrian," pp. 57–87.

David Daube, "Rabbinic Methods of Interpretation and Hellenistic Rhetoric," *Hebrew Union College Annual*, 19 (1949), 239–64.

Israel I. Efros, "Israel and Greece," in *Ancient Jewish Philosophy* (New York: Block, 1964), pp. 141–53.

Louis Finkelstein, *Akiba: Scholar, Saint and Martyr* (New York: Atheneum, 1970).

Henry A. Fischel, "Studies in Cynicism and the Near East: The Transformation of a Chria," in *Religions in Antiquity*, ed. Jacob Neusner (Leiden: Brill, 1968), pp. 372–411.

——————————, *Essays in Greco-Roman and Related Talmudic Literature* (New York: Ktav, 1977).

——————————, *Rabbinic Literature and Greco-Roman Philosophy: A Study of Epicurea and Rhetorica in Early Midrashic Writings* (Leiden: Brill, 1973).

John C. Gager, *Moses in Greco-Roman Paganism*, Society of Biblical Literature Monographs (Nashville: Abington Press, 1972).

Judah Goldin, "A Philosophical Session in a Tannaite Academy," in *Exploring the Talmud*, ed. Hayim Zalman Dimitrovsky (New York: Ktav, 1976), pp. 357–77.

Erwin Ramsdell Goodenough, *Jewish Symbols in the Greco-Roman Period* (New York: Pantheon Books, 1953 et seq.), 13 vols.

——————————, *By Light, Light* (New Haven: Yale University Press, 1935).

Jonathan A. Goldstein, *Apocrypha: I Maccabees*, The Anchor Bible (New York: Doubleday, 1976).

Moses Hadas, *Apocryphal Books: 3 & 4 Maccabees* (New York: Harper, 1953).

——————————, *Hellenistic Culture: Fusion and Diffusion* (New York: Columbia University Press, 1959).

Martin Hengel, *Judaism and Hellenism: Studies in their Encounter in Palestine during the Early Hellenistic Period* (Philadelphia: Fortress, 1974).

Saul Lieberman, *Greek in Jewish Palestine: Studies in the Life and Manners of Jewish Palestine in the II–IV Centuries* C.E. (New York: The Jewish Theological Seminary of America, 1942).

——————————, *Hellenism in Jewish Palestine* (New York: The Jewish Theological Seminary of America, 1962).

—————————, "The Martyrs of Caesarea," *Annuaire de l'institute de philologie et d'histoire orientales et slaves*, 7 (1939–1944), 395–446.

—————————, "How Much Greek in Jewish Palestine?" in *Texts and Studies* (New York: Ktav, 1974), pp. 216–20.

Jacob Neusner, *Christianity, Judaism and Other Greco-Roman Cults: Studies for Morton Smith* (Leiden: Brill, 1975), III and IV.

Morton Smith, "Goodenough's Jewish Symbols in Retrospect," *Journal of Biblical Literature*, 86 (1967), 53–68.

Menahem Stern, *Greek and Latin Authors on Jews and Judaism* (Jerusalem: Academy of Sciences and Humanities, 1974).

Marguerite Yourcenar, *The Memoirs of Hadrian* (New York: Farrar, Straus and Young, 1954).

SEVENTH AND EIGHTH WEEKS: JEWISH SECTARIANISM

The Essenes:

André Dupont-Sommer, *The Essene Writings from Qumran*, trans. Geza Vermes (Gloucester, Mass.: Peter Smith, 1973).

Joseph A. Fitzmyer, S. J., *The Dead Sea Scrolls: Major Publications and Tools for Study*, Sources for Biblical Study VIII (Missoula, Mont.: Scholars Press, 1977).

Theodor H. Gaster, *The Dead Sea Scrolls* (Garden City, New York: Anchor Books, 1976).

Chaim Rabin, *Qumran Studies* (New York: Schocken Books, 1975).

Geza Vermes, *The Dead Sea Scrolls in English* (Harmondsworth, England: Penguin, 1975).

The Pharisees and Sadducees:

Leo Baeck, *The Pharisees* (New York: Schocken Books, 1947).

Louis Finkelstein, *The Pharisees: The Sociological Background of Their Faith* (New York: Jewish Publication Society of America, 1962).

Robert Travers Herford, *The Pharisees* (London: George Allen and Unwin, 1924).

Jean Le Moyne, "Pharisiens," in *Dictionnaire de la Bible*, Supplement 7 (Paris: Letouzey & Ané, 1966), 1022–115.

—————————, *Les Sadducéens* (Paris: Lecoffre, 1972).

Ralph Marcus, "Pharisees, Essenes and Gnostics," *Journal of Biblical Literature* 73 (1954), 157–61.

_____, "Pharisees in the Light of Modern Scholarship," *Journal of Religion*, 32 (1952), 153–64.

Jacob Neusner, *From Politics to Piety: Pharisaic Judaism in New Testament Times* (Englewood Cliffs, New Jersey: Prentice Hall, 1972).

_____, *Rabbinic Traditions about the Pharisees Before Seventy* (Leiden: Brill, 1971).

_____, *Early Rabbinic Judaism: Historical Studies in Religion, Literature and Art* (Leiden: Brill, 1975).

The Gnostics:

Robert M. Grant, *Gnosticism and Early Christianity* (New York: Columbia University Press, 1959).

Hans Jonas, *Gnostic Religion: The Message of an Alien God and the Beginning of Christianity* (Boston: Beacon Press, 1958).

James M. Robinson, *The Nag Hammadi Library* (New York: Harper and Row, 1977).

Gershom Scholem, *Jewish Gnosticism: Merkabah Mysticism and Talmudic Tradition* (New York: Jewish Theological Seminary of America, 1960).

_____, *Major Trends in Jewish Mysticism* (New York: Schocken Books, 1954).

NINTH AND TENTH WEEKS:
THE APOCRYPHA, PSEUDEPIGRAPHA AND APOCALYPTIC

Apocrypha, Revised Standard Version of the Old Testament (New York: Thomas Nelson and Sons, 1952).

C. K. Barrett, *The New Testament Backgrounds: Selected Documents* (New York: Harper, 1961).

Elias J. Bickerman, *Four Strange Books of the Bible: Jonah, Daniel, Koheleth, Esther* (New York: Schocken Books, 1968), especially pp. 3–138.

Joshua Block, *On the Apocalyptic in Judaism* (Philadelphia: Dropsie College, 1952).

F. C. Burkitt, *Jewish and Christian Apocalypses* (London: Publications for the British Academy, 1914).

The Apocrypha and Pseudepigrapha of the Old Testament in English, ed. R. H. Charles (Oxford: Oxford University Press, 1976).

James H. Charlesworth, *The Pseudepigrapha and Modern Research* (Missoula, Mont.: Scholars Press, 1976).

The Shorter Books of the Apocrypha, ed. J. C. Dancy (Cambridge: Cambridge University Press, 1972).

Erwin Ramdell Goodenough, "Literal Mystery in Hellenistic Judaism," *Quantulacumque*, November, 1937.

R. Travers Herford, *Talmud and Apocrypha* (New York: Ktav, 1971).

Yehezkel Kaufmann, "Apokalyptik," in *Encyclopaedia Judaica*, 2 (Berlin: Verlag Eschkol, 1928), 1142–61.

Naphtali Lewis and Meyer Reinhold, *Roman Civilization: Selected Readings* (New York: Columbia University Press, 1951), pp. 140–43, 474–75, 375–78 (on the Sibylline Oracles and Phlegon of Tralles respectively).

Lycophron, *Alexandra in Callimachus, Lycophron, Aratus*, trans. A. W. Mair and G. R. Mair (Cambridge: Harvard University Press, 1960), The Loeb Classical Library.

Robert Pfeiffer, *History of New Testament Times with an Introduction to the Apocrypha* (New York: Harper and Row, 1947).

David Syme Russell, *The Method and Message of Jewish Apocalyptic 200 B.C.E. –100 C.E.* (London: SCM Press, 1964).

ELEVENTH AND TWELFTH WEEKS: PHILO

Louis H. Feldman, *Bibliography of Philo and Josephus (1937–1962)* (New York: Yeshiva University, 1963).

Erwin Ramsdell Goodenough, *Introduction to Philo Judaeus* (New Haven: Yale University Press, 1938).

——————, *The Politics of Philo Judaeus with a General Bibliography* (New Haven: Yale University Press, 1938).

Samuel Sandmel, *Philo's Place in Judaism: A Study of Conceptions of Abraham in Jewish Literature* (New York: Ktav, 1971).

Harry A. Wolfson, *Philo* (Cambridge: Harvard University Press, 1947).

——————, *The Philosphy of the Church Fathers* (Cambridge: Harvard University Press, 1965).

——————, *From Philo to Spinoza* (New York: Behrman House, 1977).

THIRTEENTH AND FOURTEENTH WEEKS:
THE TALMUD AND THE RABBINIC WORLD

The Mishnah, trans. Herbert Danby (Oxford: Oxford University Press, 1974).

Mishnayoth, trans. Philip Blackman (New York: The Judaica Press, 1965), 4 vols.

The Babylonian Talmud (London: Soncino Press, 1961), 18 vols., esp. "Abodah Zarah," trans. A. Mischon and A. Cohen, 1–366.

Le Talmud de Jerusaleum, trans. Moise Schwab (Paris: Editions G. P. Maisoneuve, 1960).

Gemara: The Fathers According to Rabbi Nathan, trans. Judah Goldin (New Haven: Yale University Press, 1955).

Abraham Cohen, *Everyman's Talmud* (New York: E. P. Dutton, 1949).

Judah Goldin, *The Living Talmud* (New York: Mentor, 1957).

Claude Joseph Montefiore and Herbert Loewe, *A Rabbinic Anthology* (New York: Schocken Books, 1974).

Louis I. Newman and Samuel Spitz, *The Talmudic Anthology: Tales and Teachings of the Rabbis* (New York: Behrman House, 1945).

Adin Steinsaltz, *The Essential Talmud* (New York: Bantam, 1976).

Introductions:

Alan Corre, *Understanding the Talmud* (New York: Ktav, 1975).

Hayim Zalman Dimitrovsky, *Exploring Talmud* (New York: Ktav, 1976).

Moses Mielziner, *Introduction to the Talmud* (New York: Block, 1968).

Hermann L. Strack, *Introduction to the Talmud and Midrash* (New York: Atheneum, 1978).

John T. Townsend, "Rabbinic Sources," in *The Study of Judaism*, pp. 35–80.

A SYLLABUS FOR A COURSE UNIT
ON BIBLICAL–TALMUDIC MEDICINE
FOR A COURSE ON ANCIENT MEDICINE

Stephen Newmyer

I offered my course on Ancient Medicine for the first time in the Spring semester, 1978, to a class of undergraduates in humanities, nursing, pharmacy, and the natural sciences. The course, which I will repeat in the Fall semester, 1979, supplemented by a new unit on Jewish medicine in the Biblical and Talmudic periods, is a chronological survey of the theories and practices of medicine among the ancient nations culminating in a detailed investigation of medical practice among the Greeks and Romans. The course material began with an attempt to form some judgement on the nature and range of medical knowledge among primitive nations. Conclusions on this subject are heavily dependent upon analogies with present-day primitive societies. I encouraged the students to imagine to themselves how primitive man discovered medical knowledge. Observation of the selfhealing measures taken by animals (licking wounds, chewing grass for its laxative qualities, and so forth) must have figured heavily in this stage of medical history. No doubt it was at this stage that man first came to associate sickness and recovery with the action of beneficent and, more often, malevolent spirits and deities. From this point on, ancient medicine, with few but vital exceptions, became a function of religious belief. Developing ways of placating angry divinities and exorcising spirits of sickness were man's first groping steps in the direction of restorative medicine, while the use of amulets and charms were man's first attempts at prophylactic medicine.

The question of medical knowledge among the Egyptians deserves careful attention in a course on Ancient Medicine. Scholars are becoming increasingly aware of the high state of medical science in ancient Egypt, especially from examination of mummies. This study has led to a greater understanding of the diseases from which the ancient Egyptians suffered, in particular liver flukes and tooth decay. Yet despite the surprising degree of supervision exercised over the practitioners of medicine in the ancient Near East, the discipline could not develop into a science until medicine became free of its connection with the priesthood, with the generally conservative orientation of the religious establishment which hindered the development of those techniques which we consider essential to modern medical research.

As a result of this influence, dissection was almost unknown in ancient medical practice except for a brief appearance in the liberal intellectual climate of Alexandria.

My course culminated in an extensive consideration of Greek and Roman medicine, with special attention to Hippocrates and the school of Cos and Galen and his work in Rome. We saw that here, for the first time in the history of medicine, the discipline found the favorable intellectual climate combining rationalism and curiosity about the working of the human body that fostered the development of the science of medicine.

As the semester progressed, it became increasingly clear to me that ancient medicine did not end with the fall of the Roman Empire, but continued through the Middle Ages. I therefore devoted a number of lectures to medicine in the early Medieval period with emphasis on the role played by the physicians of the Middle Ages in the transmission of Greek medical knowledge and theory. In my investigation of Arab medicine in the Middle Ages, I became aware of the part played by the Jews in the spread and preservation of classical medical knowledge, and I became acquainted to some degree with Jewish medicine, both in Biblical times and in the post-Biblical period, which led me to develop a unit on Biblical–Talmudic Medicine to supplement my course during my study at the Jewish Theological Seminary of America as a Fellow of the Institute for the Teaching of the Post-Biblical Foundations of Western Civilization in Summer 1978.

The materials of the course as I taught it in Spring 1978 were organized according to nation:

I.   General Introduction: Some Basic Assumptions of Ancient Medicine

  A. Spirits
  B. Theory of Humors
  C. Environment and Health
  D. Disease and Death

II.   Egypt

  A. Egyptian Medical Texts and Problems of Knowledge
  B. Religion and Medicine: Priests and Lay Doctors
  C. Mummification and its Contribution to Medical Knowledge
  D. Egyptian Medical Science

III.   Assyria

  A. Possession and Demonism
  B. Pharmacology

IV.   Greece

  A. Rationality in Medicine: Advantages and Drawbacks
  B. Pre-Hippocratean Greek Medicine
  C. Hippocrates

      1. Humors
      2. Theory of Nature
      3. Therapeutics
      4. Influence of Environment on Disease
      5. Disease and Diagnosis
    D. Thucydides and the Plague at Athens
    E. Plato: The *Timaeus* and Psychology
    F. Aristotle and Theophrastus
    G. Alexandrian Medicine: Erasistratus, Herophilus, and Pathology

V.   Rome

    A. Greek Medicine in Rome
    B. Asclepiades and Atomistic Medicine
    C. Methodists and Pneumatists
    D. Cornelius Celsus
    E. Rufus of Ephesus as a Precursor of Galen
    F. Galen
      1. Theory of Organisms
      2. Teleology in Medicine
      3. The Four Humors
      4. Neurology, Hematology, Anatomy

VI. The Position of the Doctor in Ancient Society

The bibliographical resources available to the student of ancient medicine are rich. Some of the more important works include:

Allbutt, T. C. *Greek Medicine in Rome*. London, 1921.
    Although somewhat diffuse, this classic work includes much valuable information on the development of Greek medical theory in Rome. The material on Asclepiades and Galen is particularly worthwhile.

Brock, Arthur, ed. *Greek Medicine*. New York, 1972.
    Brock's work is an anthology of Greek medical treatises in English, including works by the Hippocratic School, Thucydides, Plato, Aristotle, Rufus and Galen, and is especially suited for use as a textbook in Ancient Medicine.

Castiglioni, Arturo. *A History of Medicine*, trans. and ed. by E. B. Krumbhaar. New York, 1948.
    Perhaps the standard work in the field of medical history, Castiglioni's study is remarkable for its enthusiasm for and appreciation of the achievements of ancient medical science.

Dawson, Warren. *The Beginnings: Egypt and Assyria*. New York, 1964.
    Contains a valuable discussion of the contents of the Egyptian medical papyri.

Ghalioungui, Paul. *Magic and Medical Science in Ancient Egypt*. London, 1963.
    Contains chapters on magic, priestly medicine in ancient Egypt, the medical papyri, Egyptian investigations on anatomy and physiology, surgery, and the position of the doctor in ancient Egyptian society.

Hippocratic Writings, ed. and trans. by G. E. R. Lloyd. Harmondsworth, 1978.
This Penguin paperback fills a need for an inexpensive and readily available selection of the writings attributed to Hippocrates and his school and makes an excellent textbook for a course in Ancient Medicine.

Levine, Edwin Butron. *Hippocrates*. New York, 1971.
This clearly-written volume, in the Twayne's World Authors Series, offers chapters on the life of Hippocrates and treatments of the several branches of medical science in which the Hippocratic school excelled.

Mead, Kate Campbell. *A History of Women in Medicine from the Earliest Times to the Beginning of the Nineteenth Century*. Haddam, Connecticut, 1938.
Although somewhat sketchy on women in ancient medicine, this work is valuable for the information it provides on the prominent place of female doctors and teachers of medicine in medieval Italy.

Phillips, Eustace D. *Greek Medicine*. London, 1973.
An exhaustive treatment of the subject covering medical pronouncements in the Pre-Socratic philosophers and providing a thorough discussion of the contents of all major treatises in the Hippocratic Corpus.

Sarton, George. *Galen of Pergamon*. Lawrence, Kansas, 1954.
By one of the most promonent scholars of ancient science, this little volume offers much interesting material on both the strange personality and influential theories of Galen, the most important ancient doctor after Hippocrates.

Scarborough, John. *Roman Medicine*. Ithaca, New York, 1969.
More selective that its companion volume by Phillips cited above, this book concentrates on the place of medicine in Roman popular estimation and its position in society. Especially interesting is the chapter on the Roman achievement in hygiene and camp medicine.

A unit on Jewish medicine in the Biblical and Talmudic periods should prove a welcome addition to a course on Ancient Medicine. Primary source reading for this unit should include those sections of Leviticus which deal with purification and isolation (Chapters 11–15), those sections of Numbers treating these same topics (Chapter 5:1–3), and those chapters of Deuteronomy which cover dietary laws (Chapter 14:3–21) and deal with military sanitation (Chapter 23:9–14). For the Rabbinic view of medicine, many parts of the Talmud are useful. Masechta Hulin, dealing with the sacrifice of animals and containing a great deal of material on anatomy and physiology, masechta Yebamoth, on female illnesses and uncleanness, and the masechtoth of Seder Hulin, dealing with uncleanness, are essential texts.

A unit on Biblical–Talmudic medicine is essential to a historical survey of the history of medicine in antiquity because of the extraordinary insights which the Jews had about medicine, particularly in the areas of infection and preventive medicine. A discussion of Jewish medicine must begin with a consideration of monotheism, a respect in which the Jews differed from other ancient nations and which had profound implications from a medical point of view. The questions of infection, uncleanness, and diet will form the core of my lectures on Biblical medicine, for these constitute the most important contributions to medicine made by the Jews. Talmudic medicine offers innumerable significant insights which differ from Greek medicine and are often superior to even the best of Greek medicine. The emphasis in my Talmudic section of the unit will close with an examination of medical ethics in the Talmud.

Students will need help in dealing with the intricacies of the Talmud, and I plan an introductory lecture to cover the form and contents of the Talmud with emphasis on typical rabbinic techniques of reasoning and argumentation, which allowed the Rabbis to see the validity of both sides of an issue in the moral-ethical questions that arise in medicine. The same Talmudic dialectic which operates in purely theological matters obtains equally in medical matters. Students need, moreover, to understand that the Talmud is essentially a legal and not a medical document and that therefore medical lore in it, however revolutionary and insightful it may be, is nevertheless incidental.

My lectures for the new unit will follow this outline:

I. Biblical Medicine

    A. Monotheism and Its Implications for Medical Theory: the Absence of Magic in Jewish Medicine
    B. Hygienic Law and Its Influence on the Theory of Infection
    C. The Medical Implications of the Sabbath Day

Assigned reading: Leviticus 11–15; Numbers 5:1–3; Deuteronomy 14.3–21.

II. Talmudic Medicine

    A. General Introduction
      1. The Form and Purpose of the Talmud

Assigned reading: Moses Mielziner, *Introduction to the Talmud, With a New Bibliography, 1925–1967*, by Alexander Guttman. New York, 1968, pp. 1–15.

      2. Incorporation of Medical Lore into the Talmud
      3. The Rabbis as Practicing Physicians
    B. Rabbinic Law as the Basis for Talmudic Medical Investigations
    C. Specific Medical Researches and Opinions of the Rabbis: Medical Discoveries of the Talmudic Scholars and their Relation to the Medical Discoveries of Classical Antiquity
      1. Anatomy and Physiology
        a. Rabbinic Dissection of a Woman Executed by the Romans

Assigned reading: Bekoroth 45a

        b. Rabbinic Embryology on the Shape of a 6-Week Embryo

Assigned reading: Nida 25a

    2. Physiology
       a. The Place of the Brain in the Bodily Functions of the Human Being

Assigned reading: Yebamoth 9a

    3. Etiology
       a. Sickness as a Punishment for Sin

Assigned reading: Sabbath 32b

       b. Repentence as a Cure for Illness

Assigned reading: Taanith 21b

       c. Rabbinic Recognition of Inheritance of Illness

Assigned reading: Yebamoth 64b

       d. Rabbinic Conception of Infection

Assigned reading: Berachoth 25a

    4. Pathology
       a. The Invention of the Science of Pathology by the Rabbis in their Concept of Structural Alternation of Tissue as the Sign of Pathology, an Advance over Greek Pathology
       b. Rabbinic Pathology in the Service of Dietary Law

Assigned reading: Hulin 42b

    5. Diagnosis
    6. Prognosis
       a. The Superiority of Rabbinic Diagnosis over Greek in Some Respects
       b. Prognosis in the Case of Water on the Lungs

Assigned reading: Taanith 5a

       c. Splenectomy

Assigned reading: Sanhedrin 21b

    7. Hygiene and Preventive Medicine
       a. Cleanliness as Necessary to Health

Assigned reading: Erubin 65a

       b. Rabbinic Concept of Nutrition as Necessary to Health

Assigned reading: Erubin 83b

       c. Rabbinic Eugenics
          1. The Ban on Marrying into Families with Epileptic Members

Assigned reading: Yebamoth 64b

> 2. The Ban on Marriage between Very Short and Very Tall Persons

Assigned reading: Berachoth 45b

> 8. Treatment
>   a. Rabbinic Concept of Homeopathy

Assigned reading: Sabbath 41a

> 9. Obstetrics
>   a. Difficulties of Labor and Priority of the Mother's Life over That of the Child until the Child Has Appeared

Assigned reading: Oholoth vii. 6

> b. Caesarian Section and the Legal Rights of the Caesarian Child

Assigned reading: Niddah 40a–41a

> D. Medical Ethics of the Talmudic Rabbis
>   1. Talmudic and Later Jewish Attitudes Toward the Practice of Medicine and the Work of the Physician: Medicine Should not be Practiced *versus* a Belief in the Admissibility of its Practice

Assigned reading: Berachoth 60a

> E. The Influence of Talmudic Medicine on the Course of Medical History
>   1 Talmudic Medicine not Influential because not Studied by non-Jews and Incorporated into a Legal Text only Incidentally Concerned with Medicine
>   2. Some Opposition to Talmudic Medicine among Later Jews
>   3. The Rabbis as Practicing Physicians
>   4. The Rabbis as Possible Teachers of the Church Fathers

III. Medicine Among the Jewish Sects in Antiquity

> The Essenes

Assigned reading: Flavius Josephus, *The Jewish Wars*, II. 136 and 148–49 on the study of medical substances by the Essenes and their strange sanitary habits; G. Vermes, ed. *The Dead Sea Scrolls in English*, Baltimore, 1965, 111–14. The Damascus Rule on purification and dietary regulations of the Essenic community.

IV. The Jews as a Transmission Factor in the Middle Ages

> A. The Preservation of Greek Medicine by the Jews
> B. Translation of Greek Medical Works into Arabic by the Jews

My unit on Jewish medicine is based, in good Rabbinic fashion, upon close study of primary texts. As an example of how such a unit might be handled, we may take the question of medical ethics of the Rabbis (Section II.D of the outline). The text of Berachoth 60a is an example of characteristically Rabbinic dialectic dealing with the position of the physician in society. While in general Biblical and post-Biblical Judaism held the physician in high repute, there was some contrary feeling. As the centuries passed into the Medieval period, the medical lore of the Talmudic Rabbis came increasingly to be doubted and even rejected as harmful. In the masechta Berachoth, that is, "Benedictions," sections 60a, Rabbis Acha and Abaye debate the value of the physician. The question at issue is: should the practice of medicine be an occupation of man? A student should read the text aloud. Attention should be focused on the Rabbinic manner of reasoning, in which a Biblical text, namely Exodus 21:19, is examined carefully for its possible bearing on the issue. No solution is reached, as is common in Talmudic debates. Examination of the passage teaches how truth is sought by dialectical reasoning and how frequently the debate ends with no solution, leaving the reader to draw his own conclusions.

As in the study of medicine in Greece and Rome, the student is faced with an embarrassment of riches in approaching the subject of Jewish medicine in antiquity. The following works can serve as a core reading for preparation of a unit on Jewish medicine:

I. Abrahams, ed. *The Legacy of Israel*. Oxford, 1927.
Contains material on the Jews as transmittors of knowledge.

Carmoly, Eliakim. *History of the Jewish Physicians*. Baltimore, n.d.
Biographical in nature, this work contains a brief section of Moses and short considerations of medical lore in the Prophets and the Essenes.

Castiglioni, Arturo. "The Contribution of the Jews to Medicine," in *The Jews: Their Role in Civilization*, ed. by Louis Finkelstein. New York, 1974, 184–215.
Minimizes the original contribution of the Jews to medicine and emphasizes their role as intermediaries between Greece and the Arabs. Their chief original contributions are seen as the emphasis on sanitation and their monotheism.

Friedenwald, Harry. *Jewish Luminaries in Medical History*. New York, 1967.

—————. *The Jews and Medicine*. Baltimore, 1944.
A collection of the author's essays on the role of the Jews in the history of medicine.

Goodhill, Victor. *Maimonides: Medical Relevance for 1970*. Los Angeles, 1970.

Harris, H. H. and J. N. "Pulmonary Pathology in the Talmud," *Ann. Med. Hist.*, VIII (1936), 553–57.

Jacobovits, Immanuel. *Jewish Medical Ethics: A Comparative and Historical Study of the Jewish Religious Attitudes to Medicine and its Practice.* New York, 1959.

Kagan, Solomon R. "Etiology, Pathology and Prognosis According to Ancient Hebrew Literature," *New England Journal of Medicine*, CCII (1930), 355.

_____. *Jewish Medicine.* Boston, 1952.
A full treatment with complete documentation from the Bible and Talmud on Jewish sanitation, dietetics, etiology, pathology, and pharmacy.

Leibowitz, Joshua. *Some Aspects of Biblical and Talmudic Medicine.* Israel, 1969.
A published version of a lecture, the book is sketchy and selective, but contains interesting treatments of sexual matters, obstetrics, neurology, and forensic medicine in the Talmud with documentation.

Preuss, Julius. *Biblish-talmudische Medizin: Beiträge zur Geschichte der Heilkunde und der Kultur Uberhaupt.* Berlin, 1921.
The fundamental work on the subject of Biblical and Talmudic medicine, containing exhaustive treatment of all aspects of medicine, healing, and disease as these appear in the Biblical and Rabbinic literature. The work is highly factual and makes little attempt to interpret the place of medicine in Jewish culture or to assess the contribution of the Jews to medicine.

Snowman, J. *A Short History of Talmudic Medicine.* New York, 1974 (reprint of edition of 1935).
A systematic treatment of Talmudic anatomy, physiology, etiology, gynaecology, surgery, embryology, and obstetrics somewhat weakened by complete absence of references to the location in the Talmud of the passages discussed in the work.

With increasing attention being given to the question of the advances made by the ancient nations in medical science, a course on Ancient Medicine such as I have outlined makes a welcome and unusual addition to the undergraduate Classics curriculum. Source material, both primary and secondary, is readily available to aid the instructor in the preparation of the course, and the wide range of interests to which a course in Ancient Medicine can appeal assures a gratifying enrollment.

THE LETTERS OF PAUL:
A PRELIMINARY SYLLABUS

Thomas M. Finn

Course Description

A study of the letters of Paul of Tarsus in their social, cultural and religious setting. Special attention is paid to the issues which occasioned the letters, the impact of Greco-Roman Hellenism and Synagogue Judaism, and the distinctive traits of developing Pauline Christianity.

Course Rationale

The letters of Paul, seven of which are the earliest extant Christian records, are invaluable windows which open onto a variety of Christian communities in Asia Minor, Greece and Rome. They permit one to enter the environment of the communities to which they are addressed, to feel the currents which shape and propel them, to grasp the problems which divide them, and to share something of their social, intellectual and religious life. But the access they provide is not easy. The letters are largely personal, *ad hoc* rather than systematic, spontaneous responses rather than developed treatments. In addition, each has an intended audience, urban in composition, whose world of experience and discourse is conditioned by time, place, and complex cultural setting. To put the matter briefly, the letters of Paul are neither self-evident nor self-explanatory.

The goal of this course is, none the less, to read the letters on their own terms and in their proper contexts. To accomplish this one must become conscious not only of form and content but also of concrete circumstances and of social, intellectual and religious situation (*Sitz im Leben*). Perspective is needed.

The communities of Pauline allegiance emerge at the point of confluence of two powerful cultural streams in the Roman empire, Judaism and Hellenism. Immersed in the confluence and impelled by both currents, though not always and not equally, the Pauline churches surface with distinctive traits. To read the letters aright, one must have recourse to the lenses of first-century Synagogue Judaism and Greco-Roman Hellenism.

It is possible, for instance, to read Paul's First letter to the Corinthians as a spirited reply to two reports, one oral and one written, to troubling issues of attitude and conduct. The issues may prove obscure and the reasoning and tone of his reply abrupt. But if one interposes the lens of emerging Rabbinic Judaism, Paul's function as a Rabbi and his letter as a series of Rabbinic *responsa* add perspective which clarifies form, content and tone. Further, when one realizes that the problems reported and the questions posed are those of Gentiles attempting to live as Hellenized Jewish Christians in a turbulent Romanized Greek city, added perspective is introduced—the confluence of two cultures, Judaism and Hellenism. In the process, both are modified, neither is excluded, and the distinctive traits of Pauline Christianity come into view.

Perspective which allows the reader to take into account form, content, concrete circumstances, and cultural context allows the letters to be three-dimensional. The result is living documents about live issues among flesh and blood people. The method this course will employ is to read the letters of Paul in the perspective of their Jewish and Greco-Roman social, intellectual and religious setting.

Course Units

Presumed in the following description is the need to bring to bear the consensus findings of Pauline scholarship on questions of chronology, author-ship, time, place, and concrete circumstances. Each unit envisions three presentations, the forms of which will vary: lecture, textual dialogue, debate based on the text, and group inquiry with an eye to the methods of the Tannaitic academy and the philosophical schools. In addition to the letters, the reading assignments, where possible and appropriate, will deal with primary sources in translation. They are intended to provide background and perspective. The maximum assignment will be 100 pages per unit together with a short (two-page, double-spaced) paper of inquiry. Several questions for inquiry will be proposed and allowance made for individual initiative in posing a question.

Unit 1   Christianity as a Jewish Sect

The intent of this unit is to present the principal varieties of first-century Judaism: Sadducees, Pharisees, Essenes, Christians. The method will be from specific to general. The focal point is the textual description of the schism between the Johannine community and Synagogue Judaism. The causes of this specific break will be explored together with its consequences and a working definition of sect proposed. The work will then move on to the Qumran sect and then to a profile of the Sadducees and the Pharisees.

Reading assignments will include: Gospel According to John, Josephus, *Jewish Wars* (2,8,2–14); *Jewish Antiquities* (13,10,5–6); selections from Jacob Neusner, *The Life of Johannan ben Zakkai.*

Unit 2   First-Century Judaism, Postbiblical Foundations

The intent of this unit is to present: (1) a chronological account of the major periods and events in Palestine from Babylonian exile to Hadrianic interdict; (2) the centrality and constitution of Tanach and the process of biblical canonization; (3) the dynamics of covenant and commandment; (4) the genesis and function of oral Torah; and (5) the synagogue as communal center of prayer and study.

Reading assignments will include: Nehemiah 8–10; Judah Goldin, *The Living Torah*, excellent introduction.

Unit 3 Diaspora Judaism

The intent of this unit is to construct a working profile of Diaspora Judaism by using Alexandrian Judaism as a case study and then to present in context: (1) Tarsus and Paul, and (2) Hellenistic Judaism and Hellenistic Jewish Christianity.

Reading assignments will include: Philo, *On Moses II*; Acts of the Apostles; Paul's autobiographical record in Gal, 1–2 Cor, Phil, Rom.

Unit 4 Thessalonian Apocalyptics

The intent of this unit is to: (1) present a profile of the apocalyptic movement from Daniel through Mk; (2) explore the apocalyptic movement of 1 Thess and its concrete impact; (3) study resurgent apocalyptic in 2 Thess; and (4) review the apocalyptic ambience of earliest Christianity.

Reading assignments will include: selections from Dan, Enoch, Pss of Solomon, the Assumption of Moses, Mk 13 and a reconstruction of the Q source.

Unit 5 Galatians: Gentiles and the Torah

The intent of this unit is to: (1) explore Paul's concept of the nature and function of Torah as he articulates it in Gal; (2) its nature and function among the Tannaim; (3) and to compare and contrast.

Reading assignments will include: selections of Edward Sanders, *Paul and Palestinian Judaism* and selections from *The Mishnah* and *Gemara* (tentatively, *Yoma*).

Unit 6 Romans: Christ and Torah

The intent of this unit is to reconstruct Paul's gospel of justification, explore his characteristic terms (hamartia, nomos, pistis/dikaiosune, hilasterion, apolutrosis), and present the tannaitic view of salvation/redemption in the context of covenant and commandment, reward and punishment, charity and ethics.

Reading assignments will include: additional selections from Sanders and selections from Philip Goodman, *The Yom Kippur Anthology*.

Unit 7 Corinthian Correspondence: A Rabbi's Responses

The intent of this unit is to reconstruct a profile of Hellenistic religious enthusiasms as evidenced in Corinth and then to present Paul's first letter to the Corinthians as rabbinic responsa to problems posed by daily Christian life in Corinth.

The reading assignments will include: Judah Goldin, "Introduction," in *The Living Talmud*, and *Mishnah* selections indicating the religious function, methodology and authoritative character of the Rabbis.

Unit 8   Philippians and the Pre-Existent Christ

The intent of this unit is to: (1) explore wisdom literature; (2) relate it to the Middle Platonic world; and (3) place in Jewish and Hellenistic perspective the redacted hymn to the Pre-existent Christ in Phil 2.

The assigned readings will include: five parallel hymns (Heb, Col, Eph, Jn, and 1 Pet), selections from Proverbs, the Nicene Creed, and selections from Samuel Sandmel, *Philo of Alexandria*.

Units 9–13

With the exception of 2 Thess, the letters so far discussed are indisputably Pauline. There remain Col, Eph, Heb, 1–2 Tim and Tit, letters considered post-70 C.E. and of second and third generation Pauline origin. Eph can be usefully approached from the standpoint of the dialectic: synagogue, ecclesia, versus Israel. Col affords the opportunity of studying incipient Gnosticism as the conflict at Colossae. Heb, which is Pauline only by attribution of an extremely ambivalent tradition, is best illuminated as a Jewish Christian response to the trauma of the Temple destroyed. Shekinah, Temple and liturgy are recapitulated in the risen in rough analogy with the way in which Temple, sacrifice and priesthood are functionally absorbed by Torah, synagogue and rabbinic sages.

Although Eph and Col are treated as deutero-Pauline, the Pastorals (1–2 Tim, Tit) are clearly third-generation Paul and reflect the need to: (1) legitimate authority within the Pauline circle of churches, and (2) harness Paul to the needs of the later first and early second centuries of the common era. This is the approach of the twelfth unit. The final unit will comprise an overview of Pauline Christianity in the perspective of the encounter between Greco-Roman Hellenism and Synagogue Judaism.

BIBLIOGRAPHICAL SUPPLEMENT[*]
"Go, Study"

Jacob Neusner

Two sorts of further study may be undertaken. First, you may wish to examine other specimens of Talmudic literature. Second, you certainly will want to consider how the Talmud and related rabbinic collections have been used for the study of the history of Judaism and of the Jewish people in late antiquity. The answer is found in the systematic scholarly reconstructions, based upon Talmudic sources, of that history. I shall first of all propose some next steps in the study, in English, of Mishnah and Talmud, then provide an introductory bibliography through which the reader may find counsel for further studies.

Further Texts

Certainly, the next Talmudic text should be *Avot* (The Fathers), in the translation and commentary of Judah Goldin, *The Living Talmud* (N.Y., 1957: Mentor, New American Library). Along with *Avot* should go its *Gemara, The Fathers According to Rabbi Nathan* (New Haven, 1955: Yale University Press), translated by Judah Goldin. These two texts do not exhibit the sort of closely reasoned argument we have examined. But they do provide a comprehensive account of the religious and intellectual ideals of the Talmudic rabbis, in Goldin's masterly translation of the Talmudic language and idiom.

Further tractates of Mishnah to be studied in English might well include the whole of *Berakhot* (Blessings), Chapter One of *Peäh* (Gleanings), all of *Bikkurim* (First Fruits), Chapter Ten of *Pesahim* (Passover), Chapter Eight of *Yoma* (The Day of Atonement), Chapter Nine of *Sotah* (The Suspected Adulteress), Chapter Six of *Gittin* (Divorces), Chapter One of *Bava Qamma* (The First Gate; civil damages), Chapter Ten of *Sanhedrin* (on those who have a portion in the world to come), Chapter Three of *Avodah Zarah* (Idolatry), all of *Tamid* (The Daily Whole-Offering), Chapter Twenty-four of *Kelim* (Vessels Susceptible of Receiving Uncleanness), Chapter Two, paragraphs 2–7, of *Tohorot* (Cleannesses), Chapter Four of *Yadaim* (Unclean

---

[*]Reprinted from Jacob Neusner's *The Way of Torah*

Hands). These chapters illustrate both the varieties of legal topics and themes, and some of the types of literary forms used for the formulation of Mishnaic law. The best translation of the Mishnah is in the Soncino Talmud (cited below), because the notes are copious and helpful.

A felicitous translation of a complete, and not too difficult, tractate is Henry Malter, *The Treatise Ta'anit of the Babylonian Talmud* (Philadelphia, 1928: Jewish Publication Society). The reader who wishes to study an entire tractate on his own, in English, may start here.

Jewish History and Religion in Talmudic Times

The place to begin is with Judah Goldin, "The Talmudic Period," in Louis Finkelstein, ed., *The Jews: Their History, Culture, and Religion* (Philadelphia, 1960: Jewish Publication Society); and Gerson D. Cohen, "The Talmudic Age," in Leo Schwarz, ed., *Great Ages and Ideas of the Jewish People* (N.Y., 1956: Random House). The essays by Menahem Sern, "The Hasmonean Revolt and Its Place in the History of Jewish Society and Religion," E. E. Urbach, "The Talmudic Sage—Character and Authority," and S. Safrai, "Elementary Education, Its Religious and Social Significance in the Talmudic Period," in *Journal of World History* XI, 1–2, 1968; *Social Life and Social Values of the Jewish People,* are concise and informative.

For an introductory account of the religious history of Babylonian Jewry in Talmudic times, this writer's *There We Sat Down. Talmudic Judaism in the Making* (Nashville, 1972: Abingdon) is available. An analysis of the sources on pre-70 Pharisaic Judaism and an effort to construct a critical account are in his *From Politics to Plenty: The Emergence of Pharisaic Judaism* (Englewood Cliffs, 1973: Prentice-Hall). His Haskell Lectures for 1972–1973 closely relate to the legal materials reviewed in this book. They are published as *The Idea of Purity in Ancient Judaism* (Leiden, 1973: E. J. Brill).

After reading the suggested essays and introductions, you will have formed your own inquiries. To find out how to pursue them, you will want to consult bibliographical guides, the best of which is Judah Goldin, "Judaism," in Charles J. Adams, ed., *A Reader's Guide to the Great Religions* (N.Y., 1965: The Free Press), pp. 191–222. Goldin gives a careful and responsible account of the scholarly literature before 1960. He surveys the state of knowledge and is the most judicious and sage master of the subject.

The Study of Judaism, Bibliographical Essays (N.Y., 1972: for Anti-Defamation League of B'nai B'rith) contains two papers of importance for our topic, Richard Bavier, "Judaism in New Testament Times," and John T. Townsend, "Rabbinic Sources." The former is a guide, by a student, for beginners in the study of ancient Judaism. The latter is an extraordinary account of the manuscripts, printed editions, translations of the Scriptures into Aramaic (Targumim), the Mishnah, Tosefta, Palestinian and Babylonian Talmuds, extra-canonical tractates, and the like. Townsend's bibliography is, for its subject, without peer.

Moses Mileziner, *Introduction to the Talmud*, with a new bibliography, 1925–1967, by Alexander Guttman (N.Y., 1968: Block), contains helpful lists of books arranged according to various topics.

The Mishnah in English

Herbert Danby, *The Mishnah, Translated from the Hebrew with Introduction and Brief Explanatory Notes* (London, 1933: Oxford University Press) is a painstaking and, on the whole, accurate version. The notes do not offer much help to the beginner. Danby's translation of *The Code of Maimonides, Book Ten, The Book of Cleanness* (New Haven, 1954: Yale University Press. Yale Judaica Series, Vol. VIII) also should be mentioned. Maimonides presents the Talmudic purity laws with unparalleled thoroughness and clarity. The task of translation was challenging because of the complexity of the laws; it occupied Danby for more than five years.

Somewhat fuller notes and a good translation of the Mishnah, along with the Hebrew text, are provided by Philip Blackman, *Mishnayoll* (N.Y., 1965, Third Edition: The Judaica Press, Vols. I–VI). Knowledge of Hebrew is advantageous in using this translation, all the more so the commentary.

The Talmud in English

The Palestinian Talmud has never been translated into English. A French translation, Moise Schwab, *Le Talmud de Jerusalem* (Paris, 1871–1889, reprinted 1960: Editions G.-P. Maisonneuve), is in no way satisfactory.

A complete and reliable English translation of the Babylonian Talmud was executed in Britain under the general editorship of Isidoro Epstein and published by the Soncino Press, London, between 1935 and 1948 in thirty-five volumes. An eighteen-volume edition was issued in 1961. The translation is accompanied by brief and helpful notes. Some volumes of a bilingual edition have appeared. I wonder whether a person not already familiar with Hebrew and Aramaic and without a Talmudic text before him will fully follow the excellent work of the Soncino translators, for, being close to the original, it also is somewhat concise and preserves the Talmud's exceptional terseness. Often, too, the thrust of argument will not be wholly clear. But one may make considerable progress with the Soncino Talmud, a work of painstaking care and admirable intelligence.

An English translation, with extensive commentary, of selected chapters of the Talmud under the general editorship of A. Ehrman is being issued in fascicles by El-Am-Hoza as Leor Israel (Jerusalem and Tel Aviv, beginning in 1965) and the National Academy for Adult Jewish Studies of the United Synagogue of America (N.Y.). The commentary includes three parts. First come "realia," explanations, frequently not very scholarly, of the practical laws. These explanations are written in a pseudocritical spirit and exhibit a strong homiletical interest. Second, biographical notes are supplied, consisting of compilations of Talmudic allusions to various authorities mentioned in the text. The main commentary, third, is a wordy and prolix paraphrase and expansion of the translation of the Mishnah and *Gemara*. At some other points a commentary on the practical law is supplied.

A sixteen-page fascicle may cover a single folio-page of the Talmud; so far, there are twenty-five fascicles for tractate Blessings (Berakhot), reaching folio 17b; twenty fascicles of tractate on Betrothals (*Qiddushin*), for twenty-eight folios; and twenty fascicles for two chapters of *Bava Mesi'a'* (the Middle Gate, civil law), covering folios 33b through 57b. I think the English reader will find it difficult to use this "popular" translation, because he will need a score card to dope out the four English sections on a given page. The actual Talmud on a page is brief and truncated. One has to keep in balance a whole mass of information—the translation of the Talmud, various notes strung out along the sides; an extended, not particularly illuminating commentary, which is full of Hebrew words and therefore not entirely helpful to the English reader. And each section of a page will continue on the next, without regard to where the other columns of type have left off, so one may end up reading three or four pages at once, going back and forth. In the balance, the Soncino Talmud is much preferable.

B. Elizur-Epstein, *A Chapter of the Talmud* (Jerusalem, 1963) translates the ninth chapter of Bava Mesi'a' with brief explanatory comments. The work seems competent, especially helpful for those who already know some Aramaic and Hebrew.

Anthologies

Three anthologies of Talmudic materials arranged according to topics such as the law, divine mercy, hope and faith, and the like, may be mentioned. The best is C. G. Montefiore and H. Loewe. *A Rabbinic Anthology* (Cleveland and New York, 1963: Meridian Books, World; and Philadelphia: Jewish Publication Society of America). This indeed is the finest anthology of materials pertinent to the study of Judaism of any period. Montefiore and Loewe do not merely collect and arrange interesting passages; they comment on them, cross-reference and rework them. The reader has a pair of reliable, urbane guides through thoughtfully selected and lucidly presented materials.

The other anthologies are A. Cohen, *Everyman's Talmud* (N.Y., 1949: E. P. Dutton), and Louis I. Newman with Samuel Spitz, *The Talmudic Anthology, Tales and Teachings of the Rabbis, A Collection of Parables, Folk-Tales, Fables, Aphorisms, Epigrams, Sayings, Anecdotes, Proverbs, and Exegetical Interpretations* (N.Y., 1945: Behrman House). Cohen strings together allusions to Talmudic and related texts; but the texts are not fully translated. Newman's compendium of "tales and teachings" is arranged to serve preachers looking for stunning sayings. It will not meet any other purpose.

Talmudic Lore

A magnificent compilation of Talmudic and later legends, both Jewish and Christian, about biblical history and biography is presented by Louis Ginzberg, *The Legends of the Jews* (Philadelphia, 1947: Jewish Publication Society, Vols. I–VIII). Ginzberg paraphrases the stories and arranges them according to the order of the biblical narrative. The stories are not distinguished as to their approximate time of origin, who told them, the texts in which they occur, and the like, so the collection as a whole is of limited historical utility. But the notes, in Vols. V–VI, are thorough and contain numerous important points. A one-volume summary is Louis Ginzberg, *Legends of the Bible* (Philadelphia, 1956: Jewish Publication Society) with a brilliant introduction by Shalom Spiegel, the master of Jewish lore. Spiegel's introduction constitutes an illuminating explanation for Jewish folklore and legend. A still better specimen of Talmudic and later folklore is Shalom Spiegel, *The Last Trial, On the Legends and Lore of the Command to Abraham to Offer Isaac As a Sacrifice: The Akedah. Translated from the Hebrew with an Introduction by Judah Goldin* (N.Y., 1967: Pantheon Books). Spiegel carries the biblical story through Talmudic and medieval times in a wide-ranging and highly literate account.

Talmudic Methodology

Little is available in English to delineate the method of Talmudic logic and the traits of the Talmud as literature. In general, Talmudists tend to neglect systematic presentation of such matters as the structure of Talmudic discussions and the formulation of arguments. An essay in these questions, admittedly not a complete guide but an important beginning, is Louis Jacobs, *Studies in Talmudic Logic and Methodology* (London, 1961: Vallentine, Mitchell). It is a sophisticated account of four logical and six literary questions, a model for further research.

Midrash

Midrash, from the root *darash*, "to seek," comprises the Talmudic interpretation of biblical literature. Midrashic literature dating from Talmudic and medieval times has been translated in the following works (among others): *Mekilta de Rabbi Ishmael*, by J. Z. Lauterbach (Philadelphia, 1933: Jewish Publication Society, Vols. I–III); *Midrash Sifre on Numbers*, by P. P. Levertoff (London and N.Y., 1926: Macmillan); *Midrash Rabbah, translated into English with Notes, Glossary, and Indices*, under the editorship of H. Freedman and Maurice Simon (London, 1939: The Soncino Press, Vols. I–X); *The Song at the Sea, being a Commentary on a Commentary in Two Parts*, by Judah Goldin (New Haven, 1971: Yale University Press), covering tractate Shirta of Mekhilta; *The Midrash on Psalms*, by W. G. Braude (New Haven, 1959: Yale University Press, Vols. I–II); *Pesikta Rabbati, Discourses for Feasts, Fasts, and Special Sabbaths*, by W. G. Braude (New Haven, 1968: Yale University Press, Vols. I–II); and the same translator's *Pesikta deRav Kahana* is underway.

History

E. Schürer, *History of the Jewish People in the Time of Jesus Christ* (Edinburgh, 1886–1890: T. & T. Clark), will reappear shortly in a revised and updated edition by Geza Vermes and Fergus Millar. It remains the standard account of Palestinian Jewry down to 70. We have in English no satisfactory history of that community from 70 to the end of its corporate existence in 425. For the Jews in the Roman Empire, the definitive account is Jean Juster, *Les juifs dans l'empire romain* (Paris, 1914; Vols. I–II). There is nothing like it in English. For Babylonian Jewry, one may find helpful this writer's *History of the Jews in Babylonia* (Leiden: E. J. Brill). I. *The Parthian Period* (1970, Second Edition); II. *The Early Sasanian Period* (1966); III. *From Shapur I to Shapur II* (1968); IV. *The Age of Shapur II* (1969); and V. *Later Sasanian Times* (1970). A supplementary study is *Aphrahat and Judaism, The Christian-Jewish Argument in Fourth-Century Iran* (Leiden, 1971: E. J. Brill).

On the Pharisees before 70, you may consult this writer's *The Rabbinic Traditions about the Pharisees before 70* (Leiden, 1971: E. J. Brill). I. *The Masters*; II. *The Houses*; III. *Conclusions*; this work is summarized in *From Politics to Piety.*

Talmudic Religion

Morton Smith, the great historian of religions in late antiquity, writes, "A gift for systematic theology . . . is a great handicap in the study of rabbinic literature." The reason is that systematic theology requires the imposition of an artificial construct, such as "the rabbis" or "the rabbinic mind," upon sayings and stories which derive from a great many discrete and unsystematic authorities, living in various countries, over a period of seven centuries and more. Consequently, it is misleading to systematize what to begin with derives from authorities whose sayings never were meant to be systematized. Still, we have valuable accounts of rabbinic theology, and, while subject to further refining and improvement, these works are illuminating. Foremost among them are the following: A. Schechter, *Some Aspects of Rabbinic Theology* (N.Y., 1936: Behrman House); George Foot Moore, *Judaism in the First Centuries of the Christian Era, The Age of the Tannaim* (Cambridge, 1954: Harvard University Press, Vols. I–III); Max Kadushin, *Worship and Ethics, A Study in Rabbinic Judaism* (Evanston, 1964: Northwestern University Press); Jacob Z. Lauterbach, *Rabbinic Essays* (Cincinnati, 1951: Hebrew Union College Press); and Louis Ginzberg, *On Jewish Law and Lore* (Philadelphia, 1955: Jewish Publication Society). The last-named work contains classic essays introducing the Palestinian Talmud (pp. 3–60) and on the allegorical interpretation of Scripture (pp. 127–52), among others.

Jewish mysticism, with roots in Talmudic Judaism, is masterfully laid forth in Gershom G. Scholem, *Major Trends in Jewish Mysticism* (N.Y.,

1954: Schocken), one of the most important works in the study of the history of Judaism.

For the bearing of archaeological discoveries on the study of ancient Judaism, I recommend Erwin R. Goodenough, *Jewish Symbols in the Greco-Roman Period* (N.Y., 1953 et seq., Bollingen Foundation, Vols. I–XIII).

By the Same Author

In addition to *History* and *Pharisees*, this writer's studies of Talmudic Judaism include the following: *A Life of Yohanan ben Zakkai* (Leiden, 1970, Second Edition, Completely Revised: E. J. Brill); *Development of a Legend, Studies on the Traditions Concerning Yohanan ben Zakkai* (Leiden, 1970: E. J. Brill); *Eliezer ben Hyrcanus, The Tradition and the Man* (Leiden, 1973: E. J. Brill, Vols. I–II); and *The Idea of Purity in Ancient Judaism* (The Haskell Lectures for 1973) (Leiden, 1973: E. J. Brill). In connection with the study of Talmudic literature and history, he has edited *The Formation of the Babylonian Talmud, Studies in the Achievements of Late Nineteenth and Twentieth Century Historical and Literary-Critical Research* (Leiden, 1970: E. J. Brill); and *The Modern Study of the Mishnah* (Leiden, 1973: E. J. Brill); as well as *A Soviet View of Talmudic Judaism, The Work of Yu A. Solodukho* (Leiden, 1973: E. J. Brill).

For beginners, the following textbooks may prove helpful: *Way of Torah: An Introduction to Judaism* (Encino, 1974: Dickenson), with its accompanying reader, *The Life of Torah* (Encino, 1974: Dickenson); for an anthology of Jewish theology, *Theology of Judaism: Classical Issues and Modern Perspectives* (N.Y., 1973: Ktav); and, for rabbinic Judaism in modern times, *American Judaism: Adventure in Modernity* (Englewood Cliffs, 1972: Prentice-Hall).

BIBLIOGRAPHY OF BOOKS AND ARTICLES SUITABLE FOR THE TEACHING OF POST-BIBLICAL JUDAISM OR UTILIZING ASPECTS OF IT IN COURSES OFFERED TO UNDERGRADUATES

Gordon Tucker

(° = available in paperback)

I.   *General*

— Ben Sasson, H. H. (ed.), *Jewish Society Through the Ages*, Schocken Books, 1972.

° — Bickerman, Elias, and Morton Smith, *The Ancient History of Western Civilization*, Harper and Row, 1976.

— Ehrlich, E. L., *A Concise History of Israel from the Earliest to the Destruction of the Temple in* A.D. 70, Harper Torchbooks.

° — Finkelstein, Louis (ed.), *The Jews: Their History, Culture and Religion*, Schocken Books, 1970, 1971.

— Grant, Michael, *The Jews in the Roman World*, Scribner's, 1973.

— Hadas, Moses, *Hellenistic Culture*, Columbia University Press, 1959.

° — Neusner, Jacob, *There We Sat Down*, Abingdon Press, 1972.

° — Schurer, Emil, *The History of the Jews in the Time of Jesus*, (rev. and ed. G. Vermes), T. and T. Clark, 1973.

— Schwartz, Leo W. (ed.), *Great Ages and Ideas of the Jewish People*, Random House, Modern Library, 1956.

° — Tcherikover, Victor, *Hellenistic Civilization and the Jews*, Atheneum, 1977.

II.   *From Temple to Synagogue*

° — Barrett, C. K., *The New Testament Background: Selected Documents*, Macmillan, 1957.

° — Bickerman, Elias, *From Ezra to the Last of the Maccabees*, Schocken, 1962.

° — Enslin, Morton, *Christian Beginnings*, Harper, 1938.

— Gutmann, J., *The Synagogue*, Ktav, 1975.

— Idelsohn, A. Z., *Jewish Liturgy and its Development*, Holt, 1932.

— Sandmel, Samuel, *Judaism and Christian Beginnings*, Oxford, 1978.

° — Schechter, Solomon, *Aspects of Rabbinic Theology*, Schocken, 1961.

III.	*Implications of Monotheism; Sectarianism and Exclusivity*

— Bamberger, Bernard, *Proselytism in the Talmudic Period*, Ktav, 1968.

— Finkelstein, Louis, *The Pharisees*, Jewish Publication Society, 1962.

° — Heinemann, J. (ed.), *Three Jewish Philosophers*, Jewish Publication Society, (Lewy on Philo).

— Jonas, Hans, *The Gnostic Religion*, Beacon Press, 1958.

— Josephus, *Against Apion*, in *Josephus, With an English Translation*, H. St. J. Thackeray, R. Marcus, and L. H. Feldman trans., G. P. Putnam's Sons, 1926–1965.

° — Josephus, *The Jewish War*, Penguin, 1969.

° — Neusner, Jacob, *From Politics to Piety: Pharisaic Judaism in New Testament Times*, Prentice Hall, 1972.

° — Nock, Arthur Darby, *Conversion*, 1961.

— Pagels, Elaine, *The Gnostic Gospels*, Vintage, 1981.

° — Parkes, James, *The Conflict of the Church and Synagogue*, World, 1961.

— Philo (Loeb Classics Edition), *Legatio ad Gaium, In Flaccum*.

— Sanders, E. P., *Paul and Palestinian Judaism*, SCM, 1977.

— Scholem, Gershom, *Jewish Gnosticism, Merkabah Mysticism, and Talmudic Tradition*, The Jewish Theological Seminary of America, 1960.

° — —————, *The Messianic Idea in Judaism*, Schocken.

° — Simon, Marcel, *Jewish Sects in the Time of Jesus*, J. H. Farley, trans., Fortress, 1980.

— Smith, Morton, "Palestinian Judaism in the First Century," in *Israel: Its Role in Civilization*, ed. Moshe Davis.

— Stone, Michael, *Scriptures, Sects and Visions: A Profile of Judaism from Ezra to the Jewish Revolts*, Collins, 1980.

— Stern, Menahem, *Greek and Latin Authors on Jews and Judaism*, Israel Academy of Sciences and Humanities, 1974 and 1980.

° — Vermes, Geza, (ed.), *The Dead Sea Scrolls in English*, Penguin, 1975.

— Wolfson, Harry Austryn, *From Philo to Spinoza*, Behrman House, 1977.

IV.   *Learning and Education*

° — Goldin, Judah, *The Living Talmud*, New American Library, 1957.

— Marrou, H. I., *A History of Education in Antiquity*, Sheed and Ward, 1956.

— Neusner, Jacob, *History and Torah*, Vallentine, Mitchell, 1965.

— Josephus, *Against Apion* (see above under III).

— Safrai, S., "Elementary Education in the Talmudic Period," in *Jewish Society Through the Ages* (ed. Ben Sasson), Schocken Books, 1972.

V.   *Hermeneutics, Rabbinics*

— Cohn, Haim, *The Trial and Death of Jesus*, Harper and Row, 1971.

— Daube, David, *The Civil Law of the Mishnah*, Tulane, 1944.

— Goldin, J., "The Period of the Talmud," in *The Jews: Their History, Culture, and Religion* (see above under I).

— Cohen, Gerson D., "The Talmudic Age," in *Great Ages and Ideas of the Jewish People* (see above under I)

° — Mielziner, Moses, *Introduction to the Talmud*, Bloch, 1968.

° — Montefiore, C. G., and H. Loewe, *A Rabbinic Anthology*, Schocken Books, 1974.

TEACHING COURSES IN GREEK AND ROMAN CIVILIZATIONS AND CLASSICAL MYTHOLOGY

Mark Morford
The Ohio State University

One of the signs of the post-McLuhan age in which we live is the decline of courses in literatures taught in English translation. Twenty years ago these courses would attract enrollments of 150 or 200 for Greek or Roman literature, yet now even in a huge State University, where the courses are still part of the Basic Education Requirements, an average enrollment will be 30 students for a course given but once a year. At the same time courses with a large visual element have proliferated. Typically these are titled Greek (or Roman) Civilization, and they involve a mix of historical, archaeological, and artistic materials as well as a certain amount of literary works read in translation. These courses were popular when first introduced (about 10–15 years ago in many institutions) and have managed to retain respectable enrollments over the years, despite increasing competition from similar courses in other fields. In many institutions, however, Classical Mythology has remained the staple of any program in Classical Civilizations, drawing huge numbers of students term after term. It is here that students without any previous knowledge of the ancient world are likely to be introduced to the thought and literature of ancient Greece and Rome, and a surprising number go on to study other courses in the Classics, in many cases including study of the ancient languages. However much we may profess our allegiance to the languages and literature of the Classical cultures, it is Mythology that is most likely to be both our savior and our burden.

The discrepancy between the focus of professional training (and research interests) of most Classics teachers and the interests of the students poses dilemmas that are hard to solve and are not often squarely faced. Two fundamental problems concern firstly the place of courses in Classical civilizations in a liberal arts curriculum, and secondly their intellectual quality. The problems are epitomized in a student evaluation turned in to the present writer at the end of a course in Classical Mythology: "I hated this course. I expected to be told stories, and you made me *think*." Let us agree that these courses are not justified if they merely convey information, without requiring creative or critical thought. In most cases they may not be an end in themselves, but will involve to some extent (often a comparatively small one) consideration of the achievements of the Classical peoples in relation to our own and other later cultures. They make peculiar demands on their instructors, who must be trained in the whole range of the Classics, yet must be very selective in the presentation of course material. It is, however, the intellectual quality of these courses that offers the most important challenge, and achievement of this goal is a fundamental principle in the observations that follow.

The types of course mentioned in the first paragraph of this essay will be found for the most part in institutions that have a program in Classics or faculty trained in the Classics. At a large University, typically, the whole range of such courses will be offered regularly, and in addition there will be programs in the Classical languages, Ancient History, and Ancient Archaeology and Art. The materials that will be discussed below were developed for the purposes of such a program, but one purpose of this essay is to show how such approaches to instruction can be useful for courses in institutions that do not have a fully developed program in the Classics. The commonest context for study of Classical civilizations in such institutions is as a component in a Survey of Western Civilization. The time available to cover the Classical cultures from Homer to Justinian may be as little as a few weeks, and often the instructor has been trained in a non-classical field (e.g. English, Modern History, or Social Studies). Both in these cases and in the case of instructors with Classical degrees, the survey course is generally but a small part of a heavy teaching load in quite widely differing fields. A second typical context is in colleges where whole courses are devoted to Classical Civilizations, but constitute the whole Classical program. For example, at the regional campuses of the Ohio State University the two-year undergraduate curriculum includes courses in Greek and Roman Civilizations, but allows no formal offerings in the Latin or Greek languages, beyond what the instructors can fit into their schedule over and above their regular course assignments. In other institutions these courses may be subordinate to some non-Classical major program or be more or less integrated with courses in non-Classical fields. Finally, courses in Classical Civilizations may have a formal relationship to interdisciplinary programs, for example, programs in Biblical Studies, in Ancient History, or in Comparative Studies or Humanities.

The greatest problems in the design of courses and the selection of materials are likely to be faced by instructors in programs where the Classics have a subordinate or incidental role. They are especially severe for the very large number of instructors who have no colleagues in their discipline with whom they can share the burden of teaching the ancient world and from whom they can obtain practical help and intellectual stimulation. On the other hand faculty in the large, well-staffed and well-funded programs, have almost an *embarras de richesses*. Can ways be devised to share this wealth?

Can the resources of the large Departments of Classics be channeled in some way for the use and advantage of faculty who are burdened with the task of maintaining a Classical presence in an indifferent environment? The following approaches will suggest some practical answers.

Let us take Classical Mythology first. At the Ohio State University the enormous numbers of students studying the subject (approximately two thousand every year, year after year) bring as many problems as advantages. The basic problem is how to maintain academic quality. Students come with vastly different levels of sophistication and motivation (especially noticeable at a university that has virtually an open-admissions policy), and the presence of 750 students in one class section means problems in quality and consistency in testing and grading, as well as the more obvious problems of student-instructor interaction when the instructor is but a distant "talking head." If the course is not to degenerate into a passive experience for the student, creative thinking is necessary to ensure proper quality of instruction and a proper challenge for the student. In testing this will mean insistence upon essay-writing, possibly in conjunction with multiple-choice testing. The latter is abhorrent to the present writer, but he recognizes that it is a practical solution to the problem of testing large numbers of students, especially if the computer can be used for grading, thereby freeing up staff time for evaluation of essays. In courses with small enrollments there is no justification for the use of multiple-choice testing. Of greater concern, however, is the proper selection and presentation of materials, and here the transfer of the resources of the large departments to help the more limited program is quite possible. At the Ohio State University the faculty has developed a battery of materials designed to increase the range of course-materials but at the same time to allow greater flexibility for different instructors' particular approaches to the subject, and to ensure more positive involvement by the student in the process of instruction. The key to this development is the skillful mix of lecture (i.e. material presented by the instructor to the class *en masse*, a context in which the student has a comparatively passive role) and of materials studied *individually*, in the student's own time and at the student's own pace. Even in institutions where resources are limited the materials about to be described can be used with judicious selection and adaptation. They do not necessarily require the use of a sophisticated Learning Center, and they certainly do not require a massive budget for equipment and staff.

At the Ohio State University materials were developed to supplement the formal lectures in Classical Mythology. First a textbook was written by the present writer and his colleague, Robert J. Lenardon. In the part dealing with the Gods it was found possible and appropriate to translate many passages from the Greek, for example, most of the major Homeric Hymns. On the other hand in dealing with saga, where the literary tradition is far more copious and diverse, it was found necessary to have a smaller proportion of the original sources and to rely more on summaries. We have noticed that even G. S. Kirk, who has dismissed such summaries as "the paraphrase industry," was compelled to adopt this method in his excellent book on Greek Mythology.

With the textbook as a resource common to all students in the class the instructor has a given set of materials upon which to base his or her lectures. This is very important, yet it is an easily-overlooked aspect of developing good materials for courses in civilizations. Too often such courses have too much time (and time is the most valuable commodity in this context) devoted to studying materials that can be more efficiently studied individually and in out-of-class time. The instructor, then, is free to lecture on aspects of mythology that are of especial interest to him (from here on the masculine pronoun will be used without any chauvinistic intent). Examples of particular emphases have been on the Classical tradition in literature and art; Classical mythology and music; interpretations of mythology; mythology and other sciences, e.g. psychology; mythology and comparative religions.

In addition to the textbook, a body of audio-visual materials has been developed to supplement both the written word and the classroom lectures. These consist of a printed study-guide, which includes a summary of a taped commentary, with space for the student to write his own notes, tables and other summary information, lists of significant names and other terms, and lists of learning-objectives. The study-guide is used in conjunction with a taped commentary and a set of slides. The student, in ideal circumstances, studies these materials in an individual carrel at his own pace, advancing the slides at a signal on the tape, stopping the tape or reviewing it or the slides as he wishes, or coordinating the audio-visual materials with the textbook and lecture materials. The tapes, study-guide, and slides are the work of Professor John Davis, and further information about them may be obtained from him at the Ohio State University. Our experience has been very favorable with these materials in the twelve years since they were developed, in terms of intrinsic intellectual interests, student motivation and enjoyment, and improvement of student knowledge of the subject. They have allowed for a wider range of material to be presented, most especially in the areas of art and music (particularly opera), and they have undoubtedly increased the enjoyment of students. It should be emphasized once more that these materials do not require the learning center and well-equipped carrels that a well-funded program at a State University can support. They may easily be studied in media centers such as many institutions have in their Library or Learning Resource Center; they may be studied in one or two simply-equipped learning stations or carrels (as was the case at the Ohio State University for one year of piloting, when 70 students used two carrels in a converted faculty office), or they may be used selectively in class, although this mode obviously militates against the principle of freeing up class time for other activities. Many teachers have developed their own materials, and have found the experience of selection and production stimulating and enjoyable. The ready availability of simple yet sophisticated equipment at a low price puts a range of materials within comparatively easy reach. Great flexibility can be achieved with a cassette tape-recorder, a carrousel projector and a screen, together with a duplicating-machine for running off brief study-guides, should one not wish to use Professor Davis's printed book. In sum, a well-integrated set of materials will enormously increase the range of study available to the instructor who otherwise would be limited by the time and space of the lecture-hall, yet it will not, and never should, replace the primary method of instruction, that is, the spoken words of the instructor.

Roman and Greek Civilizations:

The same instructional principles apply in these areas, although there are some important differences in particular problems. There is no adequate modern textbook in either field that can act as a reliable resource throughout a reasonably comprehensive course. The subject is broader than Classical Mythology, so that the problem of selectivity becomes even more crucial; finally, no one teacher can cover the field. Once the instructor has decided upon the focus of his course and has selected his subjects, he is free then to integrate the lectures and supporting materials as he wishes. In the program at the Ohio State University the principles of integration of lectures with printed study-guide, taped commentary, and slides, have been followed. The materials in Roman Civilization are rather more sophisticated than those in Mythology, in part thanks to the support of the National Endowment for the Humanities. This has meant a generous use of graphics specially drawn for the program, the clearance of copyright permissions, and a professional standard of reproduction for the tapes and slides. In the Greek Civilization materials there is no taped commentary, but a script has been provided from which an instructor may make his own tapes, and the study guide materials are provided in an unbound package, suitable for inclusion in a loose-leaf notebook, rather than in a bound and printed volume. The aim here is to provide as much flexibility as possible in the use of the materials in widely varying instructional contexts. The program is described in greater detail in the article reproduced below as Appendix 1.

Reference has been made above to the problem of selection of course material. The authors of the Ohio State program decided to begin with general surveys of the history of Greek and Roman civilizations, which have proved valuable and popular with students. The other materials are divided into separate units, which include art, architecture, city planning, the topography of Rome and Athens, Greek and Roman temples and theaters, and different aspects of daily life. There are many other areas of study that would lend themselves well to audio-visual treatment—for example, the town of Pompeii; a comprehensive survey of daily life; coins, inscriptions, and other evidence from ancient monuments; the position of women and children in Greek and Roman societies; the army, athletics and other games, rituals and entertainments—and many other subjects. Again, it is possible for the creative instructor to develop his own materials at little cost, with careful planning and selection and with the expenditure of considerable time in preparation. The Ohio State materials are too extensive to be practical in their entirety for any one course, still less for a section of a survey course in Western Civilization. But they do provide a body of material from which discriminating choices may be made, and great flexibility can be achieved in their use to supplement lectures and assigned readings. It should also be noted that there are many areas of study in ancient civilizations that do not lend themselves to the audio-visual approach, for example, Greek and Roman law and legal procedure, philosophy, and many aspects of Greek and Roman religion. If the instructor, however, has integrated the audio-visual materials and assigned readings with his lectures, he should be the more free to spend time on at least some of these important subjects, which too often are left out of a comprehensive course because of limitations of time. Finally, the published materials make available to instructors in limited programs with limited resources the resources and research of scholars in major graduate institutions.

The principles of the programs described above and in Appendix I are simple and not necessarily costly. They aim at flexibility, an essential principle in an area of study where choices must be made from a large amount of material for study. They encourage the active participation of the student in the instructional process, while increasing his enjoyment and usually improving his motivation. They allow for systematic testing and consolidation. Above all, they increase the range and flexibility of subject matter in courses whose scope would otherwise overwhelm all but the most disciplined instructor. Instructors in all types of institutions will find that they can develop comparatively simple yet sophisticated supplemental materials for their own use, or they can select from published materials such as those described here. They will certainly find that both approaches will extend the range of their courses, and they also will find that their control of the subject-matter will be improved by the disciplined use of materials carefully selected and prepared. Above all their students will learn more, enjoy more, and remember more.

APPENDIX 1:

Individualized Materials
in Roman and Greek Civilizations°

There has been a burst of activity in the last decade in the production and marketing of slides, films and tapes that deal with aspects of ancient civilizations. In this article one of the most sophisticated of these audio-visual programs will be described, with the purpose of explaining to teachers at the college and high school levels the principles upon which instructional aids of this sort should be designed and used.

In 1975, a grant of $159,000 was made to The Ohio State University for the development of a program of slides, tapes and printed study-guides in Roman and Greek civilizations. The program began its development in January 1976, and was completed during 1980. The Roman materials were published in April 1980, and the Greek materials will be available early in 1982. Members of the Departments of Classics and History were authors of the materials, and the program was directed by me, as Project Supervisor and author of the proposal, and by Professor John Davis, who was responsible for coordination and editing of materials and for negotiations with the publishers. The project team stayed together for the whole period of the project, no mean achievement over five years of often complicated problems as well as stimulating challenges. From the Department of History Professors Jack Balcer and Timothy Gregory were authors of the units on Greek and Roman history respectively; from the Classics Department Professors Charles Babcock and Mark Morford wrote the units on Roman Civilization and Professor Stephen Tracy (together with Professor Balcer) wrote the units on Greek Civilization. The materials were reviewed upon their completion by Professor Gwyn Morgan, of the University of Texas at Austin, whose wide knowledge and provocative but kindly criticism led to substantial improvement. The materials are published by the Charles Merrill Co., Alum Creek Drive, Columbus, Ohio 43216, attention of Ms. Jeanette Bosworth, to whom interested readers should write for further information.

The principle upon which the program is founded is the desirability of making available to students comprehensive materials for which time would not be sufficient in the average classroom lecture-course, to be studied individually at the student's own pace. The materials, it must be emphasized, are not designed to replace the instructor's responsibilities, but to supplement work in the classroom. Our experience with courses in other areas of Classical study had already shown the effectiveness of tapes, slides, and study-guides in learning-centers with individual carrels, and in 1975 it seemed appropriate to extend this type of instructional support to broader courses in Roman and

°From *The Classical Outlook*, Volume 59, Number 4, May-June 1982.

Greek civilizations. The development of the materials, and now their actual use in courses, has proved that our hopes were well-founded.

Each of the two civilizations was subdivided into five or six units, the first in each being a survey respectively of Roman history (through the fall of the Empire) and Greek history (through 146 B.C.). The historical surveys have proved to be valuable as an introduction for students not familiar with the history of the ancient world, and they allow the instructor to devote more time to aspects of civilization as opposed to a summary of historical developments. These units are different in approach from the others because of their chronological emphasis, and their success with students has dissipated the doubts of the project team as to the feasibility of compressing surveys of ancient history into 90 minutes of spoken commentary. The subject matter of the other units was chosen in part for its visual potentialities, in part because of the interests of the particular authors, in part because some at least of these areas require specialist knowledge or research that cannot readily be undertaken by instructors who do not have access to a good graduate library. Other areas could have been chosen—for example, several users have questioned the absence of a unit on Women in the Ancient World. In the case of some other well-known areas not selected, such as Pompeii and the Roman House, most of the relevant subject-matter has been covered incidentally in existing units. Pompeii, for example, is treated in the unit on City-planning and its monuments figure prominently there and in the units on Roman art, architecture, and engineering, while the Roman House is dealt with in the unit on architecture and engineering.

The following is a summary of the materials:

I.   *Roman Civilization*

Unit I (Gregory):	Roman History	185 slides and 25 black and white figures in the study-guide
Unit II (Babcock and Morford):	The Forum and Palatine	197 slides and 52 figures
Unit III (Morford):	Roman City-Planning	93 slides and 27 figures
Unit IV (Morford):	Roman Art	177 slides and 53 figures
Unit V (Babcock):	Roman Architecture and Engineering	205 slides and 58 figures

II.   *Greek Civilization:*

Unit I (Balcer):	Greek History	207 slides and 76 figures

Unit II (Tracy):	The Bronze Age	83 slides and 22 figures
Unit III (Balcer):	Greek City-Planning	58 slides and 14 figures
Unit IV (Tracy):	Topography and Monuments of Athens	90 slides and 34 figures
Unit V (Balcer and Tracy):	Greek Architecture: Temple and Theater	116 slides and 26 figures
Unit VI (Tracy):	Greek Art: Painting and Sculpture	118 slides and 8 figures

The three components of the materials were designed to be integrated, and this feature of the program is one that distinguishes it from almost all others currently available. Most teachers of the Classics are familiar with the classroom use of slides, and a number make some use also of films with a soundtrack or of taped commentaries. Very few, however, will have used study-guides beyond brief summary hand-outs for classroom reference. The study-guide for Roman Civilization runs to some 270 printed pages. In it each unit contains a list of Learning Objectives, which includes all the names, technical terms, and other details that the students will be hearing on the taped commentary. It also includes a list of study-questions, given both in summary form (e.g. "Learn where and when the following events took place") and in essay-subject form (e.g. "Discuss the causes of conflict between the emperors and the Senate in the first century A.D."). The primary purpose of these lists is to help the student focus on the significant aspects of each unit. The main part of the study-guide for each unit consists of an outline of the taped commentary, so printed as to leave space for students' notes between each paragraph of material, while all maps, charts, plans, tables and a generous selection of works of art have been included in black and white figures along with the outline. At the end of the volume is a fairly substantial bibliography of works in English for further reading (a very few works in Italian and German are also included where they are fundamental, for example Lugli's *Itinerario di Roma antica*), a list of the visuals together with credits and corresponding number in the study-guide for those so reproduced, and, finally, a subject-index. The study-guide is not the script itself (which is available from the publisher as a Teacher's Guide), nor is it a separate volume to be used without the other materials. It is a thorough and clearly-organized text to complement the audio-visual materials.

The slides are the most prominent part of these materials and are most likely to be used in a variety of contexts other than that for which they were

designed. The largest number are photographs of architectural and archaeological monuments and sites, reconstructions of buildings, and other
monuments, works of art and coins. A second category consists of graphics of
charts, time-lines, diagrams, plans, maps, line-reconstructions, and tables.
These graphics are the most significant original feature of the materials: they
were prepared in the studio of The Ohio State University's Teaching Aids
Laboratory and the artists were Mr. Gregory Jones, Mrs. Cathy O'Neil, and
Miss Rebecca Hall. Most of the nearly 400 graphics are original, drawn to the
specifications of the authors, while in other cases a published plan or diagram
was adapted. In all cases the artist and author worked closely together. This
was a time-consuming and administratively very difficult process, and any
who are planning the development of similar materials should be warned of
the problems that the process entails. The end product, however, justifies the
painstaking process of creation, and in several cases—for example, the
graphics of the Garden Court of Nero's Domus Transitoria—the graphic is a
new and worthy contribution to the literature. Where possible the graphics
were photographed in color, while the reproductions in the study-guide are in
black and white.

A third category of visuals is reconstructions of monuments, city-
complexes, or historical events, drawn three-dimensionally and in color. Most
of these were drawn by the artists of the Cinecraft Company of Cleveland,
and again were created in cooperation with the authors. They have proved
some of the most difficult materials to create and evaluate: on the whole
reconstructions of cities have fared the best, although controversial features
such as color of building materials or design of roofs have not always turned
out to every viewer's satisfaction, while reconstructions of historical events
(e.g. battles or scenes in Roman assemblies) do not always succeed in bringing
the scene to life for the student, at least in the way intended, and several were
withdrawn in the final stages of development. A trivial anecdote will illustrate
some of the problems in this area: a reconstruction of a busy intersection in the
Roman city of Gerasa (Jerash) was required and the author particularly asked
for "camels, dogs and other animals" to be part of the scene. The final product
has no camels or dogs, and as a result the graphic has lost much of its liveliness,
to say nothing of its oriental atmosphere. All in all, it may be said, the graphics
are a significant and unique feature of the materials and have already proved
their worth as aids to instruction.

The photographs of all visuals, topographical, artistic, archaeological and
graphic, are of excellent quality, the result of meticulous supervision by
Professor Davis. Holders of copyright have been generous with their
permissions, and here we must acknowledge especially the generosity of
Professor William MacDonald of Smith College, who made his unrivalled
private collection available to the authors and gave generously of his time and
wisdom, and of Miss Karen Einaudi, Curator of Fototeca Unione at the
American Academy in Rome who made her materials available to us with

unlimited generosity and patience and at minimal cost. Indeed, the publication of the Fototeca's resources in microfiche (some 16,000 black and white frames) was a very fortunate event for the project and the purchase of the fiches saved the authors many hours of labor in their research.

Those who intend to produce materials of their own should be well forewarned of the administrative and budgetary problems inherent in such programs. Mention has already been made of the difficulties in coordinating the production of graphics, and the time involved can accumulate to a very expensive amount. The Roman graphics required an average of about seven hours each and the Greek nearly twice that amount: multiply that by an hourly wage and one can realize how costly the process can be. In producing slide materials the question of copyright is paramount. While many of the archaeological and topographical visuals were photographs taken by the authors, who did not claim copyright fees, a large number were copyrighted. This was especially the case in the two Art units, for which the permissions for color reproductions sometimes ran as high as $120 for a single use. Not all copyright holders were as rapacious, and we owe a lot to the generosity of scholars such as Professors MacDonald, James Packer (Northwestern University) and Raymond Schoder (Loyola University of Chicago), whose superb photographs were granted to us for modest copyright fees. One could hardly ask for a better example of cooperation in the work of scholarly research, generously given and mutually enjoyed. Further, academic institutions such as the American Numismatic Society and the American Academy in Rome (where the Fototeca Unione is located) made their resources readily available, in the latter case without charge for copyright fees. Besides the budgetary complexities of copyright, the sheer amount of correspondence is daunting. Many of our photographs came from museums and sites in distant parts of the world, and the project's secretarial staff became expert at communicating with museum staffs in Germany, Italy, France, Britain, Tunisia, Greece, and places even further afield. In these times when the question of copyright for instructional purposes is likely to become quite vexed and is certain to involve major litigation, it cannot be too strongly emphasized that the careful clearing of copyright permissions is an essential, inescapable feature of the development of visual instructional materials. It can be seen from what has been said here that the final price of about 50–60 cents per slide is a bargain!

By far the simplest task of our preparation was the production of the taped commentaries. Originally we had planned to be Procrustean in fitting our commentary to the 30 minutes of an average cassette tape. In the event, however, we were allowed flexibility of time, so that the units vary considerably in length, from about 22 minutes for the Roman city-planning to 90 minutes for the surveys of History. The Roman tapes were spoken by a professional actor, who was coached by Professor Davis in the pronunciation of Latin names and technical terms, and the product is of professional quality, as the authors learned when the tapes that they had made for the piloting stages of development were contrasted with the published tapes. The commentary is extremely compressed, and it would be virtually impossible for a student to take in everything at a single hearing. The program was ideally designed for use in a learning center equipped with individual carrels, in which each carrel has a cassette tape-player and a carrousel slide-projector. The student controls the pace at which the program is played and displayed, and he or she may stop, advance, or replay the tape, as well as advance or repeat the slides. The tape has signals to indicate the appropriate moment at which to advance to the next slide. In these conditions the student will typically sit at the carrel with headphones on (this minor fact alone gives students a sense of privacy and security in studying the materials), open the study-guide to the unit being studied, and play the tape and advance the slides with pauses for review, related reading, the taking of notes (often in the study-guide itself), or reflection. The time required for the average 30-minute module will be around 45 minutes, so that time and a half is a good guideline to aim at in planning student time required for a learning center.

This, then, is the ideal way of using the materials, and it has been proved effective by years of experience. It has the obvious advantages of self-paced individualized study; in addition it ensures adequate consolidation of new subject-matter, which is introduced in a systematic and thorough manner. Finally, it does not detract from the instructor's freedom to teach the course as he or she wishes. There are so many ways of integrating the materials into a course that much thought should be given to the correct selection and use of the materials. For example, an instructor may require students to study the survey of Roman History, but not lecture on it in class. The proper "integration" would be to make reference to historical material covered in the survey in such a way that students' familiarity from their individual study becomes a positive factor in the process of learning. In other cases materials studied may supplement other aspects (or even the same aspects) of a subject dealt with in class. For example, classroom lectures on Roman sculpture or Greek temples may be reinforced by the materials studied individually. The important principle should be that the materials should not be allowed to substitute for the teacher's responsibilities: they should supplement and reinforce, and always be integrated with the rest of the course.

It has become clear since publication of the Roman materials that comparatively few teachers are willing to use the materials exactly as designed. They have been used at a variety of institutions of varying academic levels—secondary schools, two-year and four-year colleges, universities, public libraries. Thus teachers have exercised flexibility in choosing materials for their own particular needs, and the necessity for discrimination in their use cannot be overstated. The materials are very concentrated. In the average course it is unlikely that time or energy can be found for students to study more than one unit in a week, and in the most likely context of use, which is as part of a comprehensive course on Western Civilization, teachers will be compelled to be selective. The materials as designed do have enough flexibility to meet this need. It does seem, however, that most teachers are less willing to use the materials for individualized study (even where a well-equipped learning-center exists) than to select slides for classroom display with commentary (usually informal) from the teacher. Recognizing this the publishers have decided to issue the Greek materials without the taped commentary, providing instead a script from which the teacher can make a tape or give a commentary in the classroom. The Greek study-guide also will be more flexible than the substantial Roman volume. In its place the purchaser will obtain with the slides and script a set of master-copies for hand-outs, which will include the learning objectives, outlines and black and white graphics that would have been published in the study-guide had it been issued in book form. In this way the publishers aim to increase the flexibility of materials by allowing the teacher greater freedom to choose how to present the materials.

There have been lengthy discussions between the project directors and the publishers over the format and pricing of the final product. The marketing of the Roman materials as a whole has proved too costly for most schools, departments, and individuals, and it has now been agreed that they should be made available on a unit by unit basis. The Greek materials will also be marketed this way. This change has long been sought by the project staff and many other Classicists, and we are most happy that the inflexible marketing formulae of the last two years have given way to one that better meets the needs of teachers and students. Given the volatile conditions of the textbook market we cannot state a price here for each unit, and intending users should write directly to the publishers.

What conclusions should we draw from the experience of creating these materials? For the most part positive ones, let it be stated immediately. The problems that have made the project so much more demanding than the staff had foreseen are very largely concerned with administration, budget, and marketing, and it is important that they not be underestimated by those who are thinking of developing their own materials. On the other hand, the academic and instructional goals of the project have proved attainable. Complex materials have been developed at a high level of Classical scholarship and the technical quality of the actual visuals, tapes, and study-guides is superior. They have proved flexible for teachers and students, and will be even more so with the new marketing principles. They have made available to students and teachers specialized materials that otherwise might never have been used in actual classes: thus the resources of graduate research institutions have been brought before a wider audience. Breadth of coverage in the study of Roman and Greek civilizations has been increased without sacrifice of depth. The pedagogical principles of the program are sound, in that individualized, self-paced study has been made possible for students of differing abilities and interests, while the quality of learning has been improved, if the criteria of student enjoyment and improved grades are valid. A program of this sort makes exhausting demands on its creators and users, and it is this aspect that perhaps is least well appreciated by those who have not thought deeply about the use of audio-visual materials. If teachers and students accept the challenge posed by good materials rightly used, then they will find that their enjoyment and their knowledge of classical civilizations will be significantly enhanced. Here is a case where modern technology can be a potent ally in our presentation of the ancient world.

APPENDIX 2:

Sample pages from *Aspects of Roman Civilization*, Study-guide, (Charles Merrill Co., Columbus, Ohio 1980), pp. 123–27.

(Sample Page 123)

G.   Military colonies (*coloniae*) were important in the development of Roman city planning, especially from 275–25 B.C.   **FIGURE 3–6**

1. They were founded to control, settle, and defend conquered territory.

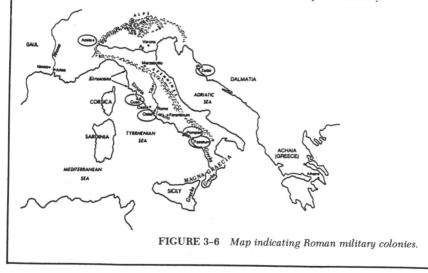

FIGURE 3-6   *Map indicating Roman military colonies.*

(Sample Page 124)

   2. The land belonging to a *colonia* was distributed to its citizens for their support.

   3. A commission supervised the founding of a colony.

      a. it conducted a survey dividing the territory into rectangular plots (*centuriae*), each ca. 125 acres, or 50 hectares, in size. Each side of an average square *centuria* was 710 meters.

      b. this division is called *centuriation*.

      c. Roman centuriation often has determined the layout of land, even to the present day.

      d. surveying the colony.

FIGURE
3-7

         (1) the surveying instrument was the *groma*, a cross-shaped bracket suspended from a central shaft. The center of the bracket was above the exact center of the area to be surveyed.

         (2) from the ends of the cross, four plumb lines were dropped from which sightings for the grid were taken.

FIGURE 3-7 *Groma*
(*after Bradford*).

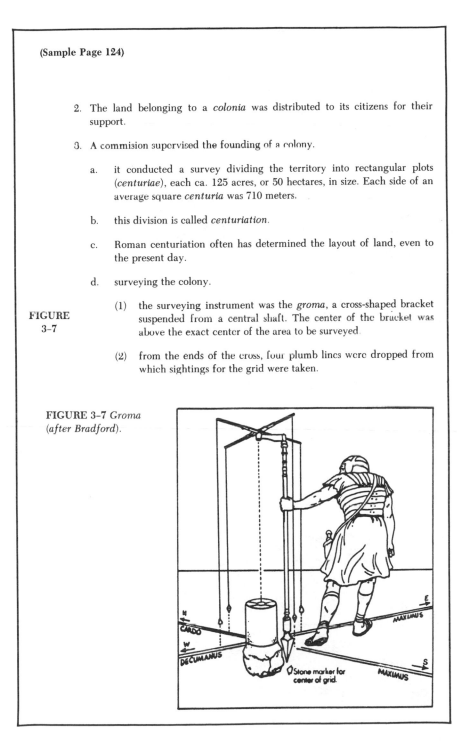

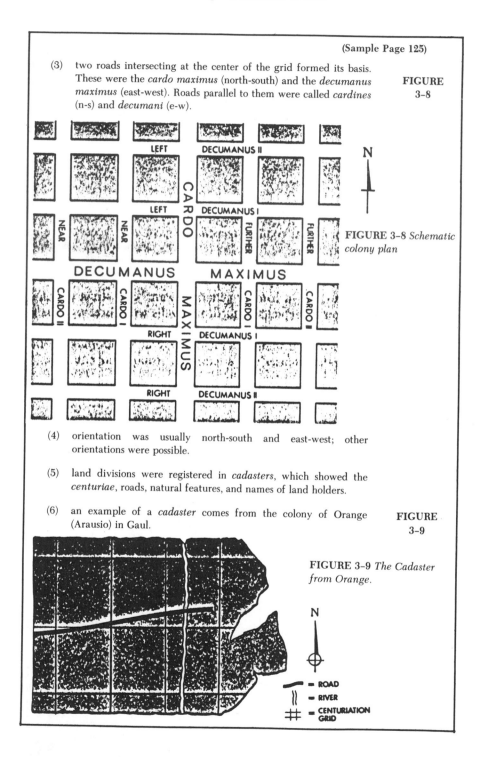

(Sample Page 125)

(3)   two roads intersecting at the center of the grid formed its basis. These were the *cardo maximus* (north-south) and the *decumanus maximus* (east-west). Roads parallel to them were called *cardines* (n-s) and *decumani* (e-w).   **FIGURE 3-8**

FIGURE 3-8 *Schematic colony plan*

(4)   orientation was usually north-south and east-west; other orientations were possible.

(5)   land divisions were registered in *cadasters*, which showed the *centuriae*, roads, natural features, and names of land holders.

(6)   an example of a *cadaster* comes from the colony of Orange (Arausio) in Gaul.   **FIGURE 3-9**

FIGURE 3-9 *The Cadaster from Orange.*

= ROAD
= RIVER
= CENTURIATION GRID

(Sample Page 126)

e.   after the survey, the *colonia* was founded by the ploughing of a furrow along the line of the future city walls.

(1)   this was a religious act marking the line of the *pomerium* (religious boundary) of the town.

(2)   A *pomerial* road sometimes ran immediately within the wall.

(3)   the pomerial road (*intervallum*) gave easy access to all parts of town for defenders.

FIGURE 3-13

f.   basic features of a *colonia* generally were: grid street systems, aligned with centuriation of dependent territory; walls with three or four principal gates; a pomerial road (*intervallum*); central market place (*forum*), with assembly hall (*basilica*) and temple; a citadel (*arx* or *Capitolium*) in the highest part, with separate defenses and a temple; a rectangular city plan.

FIGURE 3-10

(1)   an early *colonia* is at Ostia, ca 350 B.C.

(2)   the later city at Ostia expanded from the original fortified rectangular settlement (*castrum*).

FIGURE 3-11

g.   colonies were related to army camps in layout.

FIGURE 3-10 *Ostia.*

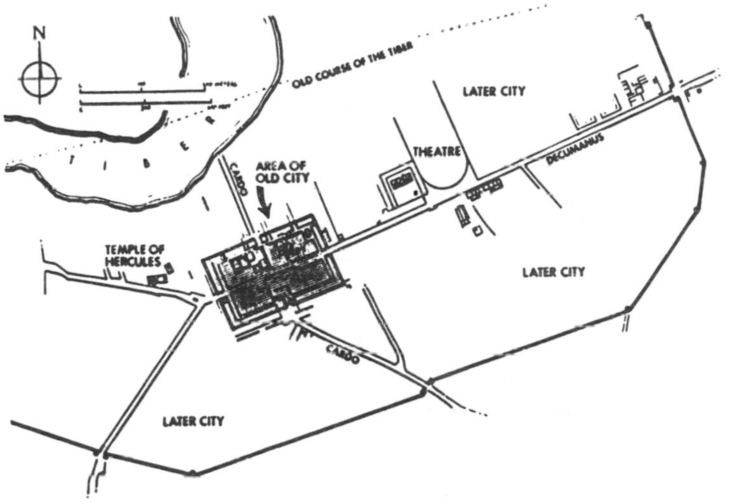

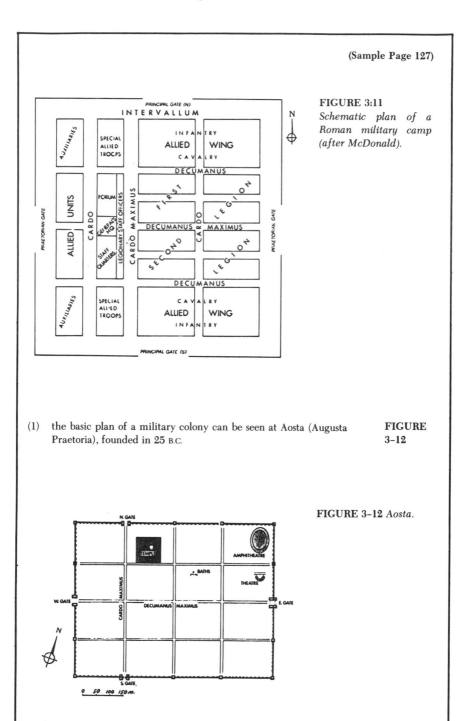

(Sample Page 127)

FIGURE 3:11
Schematic plan of a Roman military camp (after McDonald).

(1)   the basic plan of a military colony can be seen at Aosta (Augusta Praetoria), founded in 25 B.C.

FIGURE 3–12

FIGURE 3–12 *Aosta.*

APPENDIX 3:

Sample pages from Audio Script for *Aspects of Roman Civilization,* (Charles Merrill Co., Columbus, Ohio, 1980), pages 148–53. These pages are the script for the taped commentary to accompany pages 123–27 of the Study-guide (see Appendix 2).

(Sample Page 148)

3–10 (TONE) Most important in the development of Roman city planning was the creation of *coloniae*, military colonies, especially in the period from 275 to 25 B.C., with the purpose of settling conquered territory and defending it. A *colonia* was a fortified city controlling surrounding territory that was distributed to the citizens for their support.

(Sample Page 149)

FRAME 3–11   (TONE) A commission divided up the territory and
distributed it, supervising every aspect of founding
the colony. In this scene from a medieval manuscript
a nine-man commission is shown in session,
discussing plans and allotments. The Chairman is
shown at the upper right with his title written in
Latin above.
　　　　Basic to the division was a survey, called
centuriation,

3–12   (TONE) by which the land was subdivided into
rectangular or square plots (*centuriae*) each
containing about 125 acres (50 hectares). Roman
centuriation has often determined the layout of land
even to the present day, as seen in this illustration.

3–13   (TONE) This view of Zadar in Yugoslavia shows
clearly the Roman *colonia* on a peninsula with its
centuriated territory on the mainland having the
same alignment. Each square has a side of 710
meters.

FRAME 3-14 (TONE) The principal surveying instrument was the *groma*, a cross-shaped bracket suspended from a central shaft: the center of the bracket was above the exact center of the area to be surveyed. From the ends of the cross four plumb-lines were dropped from which the sightings were taken: two roads intersecting at the center formed the basis of the grid. These were called the *cardo maximus* and *decumanus maximus*, and roads parallel to them were called *cardines* and *decumani*. Any orientation was allowed, but usually *cardines* ran north-south, *decumani* east-west.

3-15 (TONE) In a town the principal north to south street was the *cardo maximus*, and the principal east to west street the *decumanus maximus*.

Land divisions were recorded in registers, called *cadasters*,

3-16 (TONE) which showed the *centuriae*, with the dividing roads, natural features such as rivers, and the names of the land holders.

FRAME 3–17   (TONE) Here is the detail of the lower fragment
from the previous slide with a simplified diagram of
its main features without the land holders' names
and the numbers of each *centuria*. This cadaster was
the register of the colony of Orange (Arausio) in
Gaul (Hold for three seconds).

3–18   (TONE) After the survey the *colonia* was founded
when the chief commissioner ploughed a furrow
along the line of the city walls, lifting it where the
gates were to be. This ploughing was a religious act,
and the trench marked the *pomerium* or religious
boundary of the town. Within the wall a "pomerial"
road sometimes ran, to give easy access for defenders
to all parts of the town.

        The basic features of the plans of colonies
seen, for example, at Cosa

3–19   (TONE) were a grid-system of streets, aligned with
the centuriation of dependent territory; walls with
three or four principal gates; often a pomerial road
(also called *intervallum*); a central forum (or market
place) with basilica (or assembly hall) and temple;
often a citadel in the highest part, with its own
defenses and temple. The basic plan was rectangular:

(Sample Page 152)

FRAME 3–20 (TONE) an early example is found at Ostia (around 350 B.C.), where the later city expanded from the original, rectangular, fortified settlement or *castrum*.

3–21 (TONE) The word *castrum* is a military term and reminds us that colonies were military foundations. Therefore there was a similarity between the planning of colonies and the layout of a Roman camp which was said by one Roman historian to be "like a city." In this plan of an army camp with two legions features familiar to us from colonies are prominent: the orthogonal plan, the terms *cardo* and *decumanus*, and the *intervallum* running next to the outer defences. The Roman army used a more or less standard camp-plan wherever an army was on the move and it should be compared to the basic plan of military colonies.

(Sample Page 153)

FRAME 3–22   (TONE) The basic colony-plan is seen excellently in Aosta (the Roman Augusta Praetoria), founded in 25 B.C. As in the previous plan of a camp, the *cardo maximus* runs well to the west (left) of the center of the *castrum*. Thus the north and south gates are also placed off-center. Note also the placing of the ampitheatre away from the center of population, to avoid large crowds massing within the central city.

3–23   (TONE) The plan can still be seen in the modern town. (Hold three seconds)

BIBLIOGRAPHY

Classical Mythology:

The basic bibliographical aid is:
John J. Peradotto, *Classical Mythology: An Annotated Bibliographical Survey*, American Philological Association, 1973. Obtainable from Scholars Press, P. O. Box 4869, Hampden Station, Baltimore, MD 21211.
Basic textbook:
Mark Morford and Robert J. Lenardon, *Classical Mythology*, New York, Longmans, Second edition, 1977.
The most useful book for comparative approaches to the interpretation of Classical mythology:
T. A. Sebeok, ed., *Myth: A Symposium*, Bloomington, Indiana University Press, 1971.
For the Classical Tradition and Classical Mythology see:
Douglas Bush, *Mythology and the Renaissance Tradition in English Poetry*, New York, Norton, 1963; and *idem*, *Mythology and the Romantic Tradition in English Poetry*, New York, Norton, 1963.
J. Seznec, *The Survival of the Pagan Gods*, Princeton, N.J., Princeton University Press, 1972.
For further bibliography see Peradotto, whose listing includes excellent critical evaluations, and the brief bibliographies in Morford & Lenardon.

Greek Civilization:

A full bibliography will be published in the forthcoming Ohio State Greek Civilization materials, available May, 1982, from the Charles Merrill Co., Alum Creek Drive, Columbus, Ohio 43216.

Roman Civilization:

The bibliography from the Study-guide of the Ohio State materials in Roman Civilization is attached on the following pages. It is reproduced from pages 243-46 of the Study-guide to *Aspects of Roman Civilization* (Columbus, Ohio: Charles Merrill Co., 1980).

Roman History°

GENERAL BIBLIOGRAPHY:
Adcock, F. E. *Roman Political Ideas and Practices.* Ann Arbor: University of Michigan Press, 1959.
Badian, Ernst. *Foreign Clientelae.* Oxford: Clarendon Press, 1958.
Balsdon, J. P. V. D. *Life and Leisure in Ancient Rome.* London: Bodley Head, 1969.

°Ancient Authors: The Penguin paperbacks and the Loeb Classical Library provide numerous translations of Roman (and some Greek) authors who serve as primary sources for Roman history. Some of the more important are: Historians—Polybius, Sallust, Livy, Tacitus; Orators, Philosophers, Essayists—Caesar, Cicero, Petronius, Seneca, Pliny (letters), Augustine; Poets—Vergil, Horace, Juvenal; Biographers—Plutarch, Suetonius.

Bloch, R. *The Origins of Rome*. London: Thames & Hudson, 1960.

Bowersock, G. W. *Augustus and the Greek World*. Oxford, Clarendon Press, 1965.

Brunt, P. A. *Italian Manpower, 225 B.C.–A.D. 14*. London: Oxford University Press, 1971.

—————. *Social Conflicts in the Roman Republic*. London: Chatto & Windus, 1970.

Crook, J. A. *Consilium Principis*. Cambridge: Cambridge University Press, 1955.

—————. *Law and Life of Rome*. Ithaca: Cornell University Press, 1977.

Gjerstad, Einar. *Early Rome*. 6 volumes. Lund: C. W. K. Gleerup, 1953–73.

Grant, M. *Roman History from Coins*. Cambridge: Cambridge University Press, 1958.

Gruen, E. S. *The Last Generation of the Roman Republic*. Berkeley: University of California Press, 1974.

Hammond, M. *The Antonine Monarchy*. Rome: American Academy in Rome, 1959.

Jones, A. H. M. *The Later Roman Empire*. Oxford: B. Blackwell, 1962.

Millar, F. *The Roman Empire and its Neighbors*. New York: Delacorte Press, 1967.

Pallottino, M. *The Etruscans*. Bloomington: Indiana University Press, 1975.

Rostovtzeff, M. *The Social and Economic History of the Roman Empire*. 2nd ed. Oxford: Clarendon Press, 1957.

Salmon, E. T. *Roman Colonization under the Republic*. Ithaca: Cornell University Press, 1969.

Scullard, H. H. *From the Gracchi to Nero*. 2nd ed. London: Methuen, 1963.

Sherwin-White, A. N. *The Roman Citizenship*. 2nd ed. Oxford: Clarendon Press, 1973.

Syme, R. *The Roman Revolution*. Oxford: Clarendon Press, 1939.

Taylor, L. R. *Party Politics in the Age of Caesar*. Berkeley: University of California Press, 1949.

TEXTBOOKS:

Boak, A. E. R., and Sinnigen, W. G. A. *A History of Rome to A.D. 565*. 5th ed. New York: Macmillan, 1965.

Cary, M., ed. *Methuen's History of the Greek and Roman World*. London: Methuen; New York: Barnes & Noble. Vol. IV: Scullard, H. H. *A History of the Roman World, 753–146 B.C.* 3rd ed., 1961. Vol. V: Marsh, F. B. Revised by Scullard, H. H. *A History of the Roman World, 146–30 B.C.* 3rd ed., 1963. Vol. VI: Salmon, E. T. *A History of the Roman World, 30 B.C.–A.D.138*. 5th ed., 1966. Vol. VII: Parker, H. D. M. Revised by Warmington, B. M. *A History of the Roman World, A.D. 138–337*. 2nd ed., 1958.

Cary, M., and Scullard, H. H. *A History of Rome*. 3rd ed. New York: St. Martin's Press, 1975.

Hammond, N. G. L., and Scullard, H. H. *Oxford Classical Dictionary*. 2nd ed. Oxford: Clarendon Press, 1970.

The Roman volumes of the *Cambridge Ancient History* are now somewhat dated but remain the single most comprehensive of the histories: Vol. VII: *Hellenistic Monarchies and the Rise of Rome*, 1928. Vol. VIII: *Rome and the Mediterranean 218–133 B.C.*, 1930. Vol. IX: *Roman Republic 133–44 B.C.*, 1932. Vol. X: *Augustan Empire 44 B.C.–A.D. 70*, 1934. Vol. XI: *Imperial Peace A.D. 70–192*, 1936. Vol. XII: *Imperial Crisis and Recovery A.D. 193–324*, 1939.

SOURCEBOOK:

Lewis, N., and Reinhold, M. *Roman Civilization*. 2 vols. New York: Harper Torchbooks, Harper & Row, 1955.

Roman City Planning: The City of Rome (Forum and Palatine)

Boëthius, A., and Ward-Perkins, J. B. *Etruscan and Roman Architecture*. Pelican History of Art. Harmondsworth: Penguin, 1970.

Brown, F. E. "La protostoria della Regia." *Rendiconti della Pontificia Accademia Romana di Archeologia* 47 (1974–75): 15–36.

Cary, M., and Scullard, H. H. *A History of Rome*. 3rd ed. New York: St. Martin's Press, 1975.

Coarelli, F. *Guida archeologica di Roma*. Verona: Mondadori, 1974.

Dudley, D. R. *Urbs Roma. A source book of classical texts on the city and its monuments*. London: Phaidon, 1967.

Gjerstad, E. *Early Rome VI*. Lund: *Acta Instituti Romani Regni Sueciae*, 1973.

Grant, M. *The Roman Forum*. New York: Weidenfeld & Nicolson, 1970.

Lugli, G. *Itinerario di Roma antica*. Rome: Bardi, 1975.

——————. *Roma antica. Il centro monumentale*. Rome: Bardi, 1946.

——————. *Monumenti minori del Foro Romano*. Rome: Bardi, 1947.

MacDonald, W. L. *The Architecture of the Roman Empire I, An Introductory Study*. New Haven: Yale University Press, 1965.

Nash, E. *Pictorial Dictionary of Ancient Rome*. 2 vols., rev. London: Thames & Hudson, 1968

Platner, S. B., and Ashby, T. *A Topographical Dictionary of Ancient Rome*. London: Oxford University Press, 1929.

Richardson, Jr., L. "Cosa and Rome: Comitium and Curia." *Archaeology* 10 (1957): 49–55.

Russell, J. "The origin and development of republican Forums." *Phoenix* 22 (1968): 304–36.

Stillwell, R., MacDonald, W. L., and McAllisher, M. H. *Princeton Encyclopedia of Classical Sites*. Princeton: Princeton University Press, 1976.

Van Deman, E. B. *The Atrium Vestae*. Washington: Carnegie Institution, 1909.

——————. "The Sullan Forum." *Journal of Roman Studies* 12 (1922): 1–31.

Van Deman, E. B. "The Sacra Via of Nero." *Memoirs of the American Academy in Rome* 5 (1925): 115–26.

Vitruvius, *The Ten Books on Architecture*. Translated by M. H. Morgan. New York: Dover, 1960.

Zanker, Paul. *Forum Augustum. Das Bildprogramm*. Monumenta Artis Antiquae II. Tubingen: Wasmuth, no date.

——————. *Forum Romanum. Die Neugestaltung durch Augustus*. Rome: Deluca, 1972.

Roman City Planning: Italy and the Provinces

GENERAL WORKS:

Banti, L. *The Etruscan Cities and their Culture*. London: Batsford, 1968.

Boëthius, A., and Ward-Perkins, J. B. *Etruscan and Roman Architecture*. Harmondsworth and Baltimore: Penguin Books, 1970.

Bradford, J. *Ancient Landscapes*. London: Bell & Son, 1957.

Dilke, O. A. W. *The Roman Land Surveyors*. Newton Abbott: David & Charles, 1971.

Lyttleton, M. *Baroque Architecture in Classical Antiquity*. London: Thames & Hudson, 1974.

McKendrick, P. "Roman Town Planning." *Archaeology* 9 (1956): 128–33.

Salmon, E. T. *Roman Colonization under the Republic*. Ithaca: Cornell University Press, and London: Thames & Hudson, 1969.

Stillwell, R., MacDonald, W. L., and McAllisher, M. H. *The Princeton Encyclopedia of Classical Sites*. Princeton: Princeton University Press, 1976.

Ward-Perkins, J. B. *Cities of Ancient Greece and Italy: Planning in Classical Antiquity*. New York: Braziller, 1974.

——————. "Early Roman Towns in Italy," *Town Planning Review* 26 (1955): 127–54.

SPECIFIC SUBJECTS AND SITES:

Bandinelli, R. Bianchi. *The Buried City: Excavations at Leptis Magna*. New York: Praeger, 1966.

Brown, F. E. "Cosa I: History and Topography." *Memoirs of the American Academy in Rome* 20 (1951).

Browning, Iain. *Petra*. London: Chatto & Windus, 1973.

Harding, G. L. *The Antiquities of Jordan*. Guildford and London: Lutterworth Press, 1959 and 1967.

Kraeling, C. *Gerasa*. New Haven: Yale University Press, 1938.

McCann, A. M., and Lewis, J. D. "The Ancient Port of Cosa." *Archaeology* 23 (1970): 200–211.

Merrifield, R. *Roman London*. London: Cassell, and New York: Praeger, 1969.

Roman Art

Bandinelli, R. Bianchi. *Rome, the Center of Power: Roman Art to* A.D. *200*. London: Thames & Hudson, 1970.

——————. *Rome, the Late Empire: Roman Art* A.D. *200 to 400*. London: Thames & Hudson, 1971.

Brendel, O. *Prolegomena to the Study of Roman Arts*. New Haven: Yale University Press, 1979.

Brilliant, R. *Roman Art*. London and New York: Phaidon, 1974.

Dorigo, W. *Late Roman Painting*. London: Kreager, 1971.

Hanfmann, G. M. A. *Roman Art*. London and Greenwich, Conn: New York Graphic Society, 1964.

Jex-Blake, K., and Sellers, E. *The Elder Pliny's Chapters on the History of Art*. London, 1896, and Chicago: Ares, 1974.

Kaehler, H. *The Art of Rome and her Empire*. New York: Crown Publishers, 1963.

L'Orange, H. P. *Art Forms and Civic Life in the Late Roman Empire*. Princeton: Princeton University Press, 1965.

Pollitt, J. J. *The Art of Rome* (Sources and Documents in Translation). Englewood Cliffs, N.J.: Prentice-Hall, 1966.

Strong, D. E. *Roman Art*. Edited by J. M. C. Toynbee. Harmondsworth: Penguin Books, 1976.

Toynbee, J. M. C. *The Art of the Romans*. London: Thames & Hudson, and New York: Praeger, 1965.

Vermeule, C. C. *Roman Imperial Art in Greece and Asia Minor*. Cambridge: Harvard University Press, 1968.

——————. *Greek Sculpture and Roman Taste*. Ann Arbor: Michigan University Press, 1977.

Wheeler, R. E. Mortimer. *Roman Art and Architecture*. London: Thames & Hudson, and New York: Praeger, 1964.

SPECIFIC WORKS AND AREAS:

Colledge, M. A. *The Art of Palmyra*. London: Thames & Hudson, and Ithaca: Cornell University Press, 1976.

Dawson, C. M. *Romano-Campanian Mythological Landscape Painting*. New Haven: Yale University Press, 1944.

Fischer, Peter. *Mosaic: History and Technique*. London: Thames & Hudson, 1971.

Ingholt, H. "The Prima Porta Statue of Augustus." *Archaeology* 22 (1969): 176–87, 204–18.

Richter, G. M. A. *Engraved Gems of the Romans*. London: Phaidon, 1971.

Rossi, L. *Trajan's Column and the Dacian Wars*. London: Thames & Hudson, and Ithaca: Cornell University Press, 1971.

Strong, D. E. *Greek and Roman Gold and Silver Plate*. London: Thames & Hudson, and Ithaca: Cornell University Press, 1966.

——————. *Roman Imperial Sculpture*. London: A. Tiranti, 1961.

Toynbee, J. M. C. *Animals in Roman Life and Art*. London: Thames & Hudson, and Ithaca: Cornell University Press, 1973.

Ward-Perkins, J. B. "The Art of the Several Age." *Proceedings of the British Academy* 37 (1951): 269–304.

Roman Architecture and Engineering

Ashby, T. *The Aqueducts of Ancient Rome*. Oxford: Clarendon Press, 1935; reprint ed., Washington: McGrath, no date.

Blake, M. E. *Roman Construction in Italy from the Prehistoric Period to Augustus*. Washington: Carnegie Institution, 1947.

——————. *Roman Construction in Italy from Tiberius through the Flavians*. Washington: Carnegie Institution, 1959.

Blake, M. E., and Taylor, D. *Roman Construction in Italy from Nerva through Antonines*. Philadelphia: American Philolsophical Society, 1973.

Boëthius, A., and Ward Perkins, J. B. *Etruscan and Roman Architecture* Pelican History of Art. Harmondsworth: Penguin, 1970.

Brown, F. E. *Roman Architecture*. New York: Prentice-Hall International, 1961.

——————. "Vitruvius and Liberal Art of Architecture." *Bucknell Review* 11 (1963): 99–107.

Burstall, A. F. *A History of Mechanical Engineering*. Cambridge: M.I.T. Press, 1965.

Cozzo, G. *Il Colosseo*. Rome: Palombi, 1971.

Daumas, N. *A History of Technology and Invention. Progress through the Ages. I: The Origins of Technological Civilization*. New York: Crown, 1969.

De Camp, L. Sprague. *The Ancient Engineers*. Cambridge: M.I.T. Press, 1970.

Drachmann, A. G. *The Mechanical Technology of Greek and Roman Antiquity*. Copenhagen: Munksgaard, and Madison: University of Wisconsin Press, 1963.

Grant, M. *Cities of Vesuvius*. New York: Macmillan, 1971.

Harris, C. M. *Historic Architecture Sourcebook*. New York: McGraw-Hill, 1977.

Hodges, H. *Technology in the Ancient World*. New York: Knopf, 1970.

Kirby, R. S., et al. *Engineering in History*. New York: McGraw-Hill, 1956.

Kostof, Spiro, ed. *The Architect*. New York: Oxford University Press, 1977.

Landels, J. G. *Engineering in the Ancient World*. Berkeley and Los Angeles: University of California Press, 1977.

La Rocca, E., deVos, M., and deVos, A. *Guida archeologica di Pompeii*. Verona: Mondadori, 1076.

MacDonald, W. L. *The Architecture of the Roman Empire I. An Introductory Study*. New Haven: Yale University Press, 1965.

——————. *The Pantheon. Design, Meaning and Progeny*. Cambridge: Harvard University Press, 1976.

McKay, A. G. *Houses, Villas and Palaces in the Roman World*. Ithaca. Cornell University Press, 1975.

Pannell, J. P. M. *An Illustrated History of Civil Engineering*. London: Thames & Hudson, 1964.

Richmond, I. A. *The City Wall of Imperial Rome*. Oxford: Clarendon Press, 1930; reprint ed., College Park, Md., 1971.

Sandström, G. E. *Man the Builder*. New York: McGraw-Hill, 1970.

Singer, C. et al. *A History of Technology, Vol. II: The Mediterranean Civilizations and the Middle Ages c. 700 B.C. to A.D. 1500*. Oxford: Clarendon Press, 1957.

Smith, N. "Roman Hydraulic Technology." *Scientific American* 238 (1978): 154–61.

Stillwell, R., MacDonald, W. L., and McAllisher, M.H. *The Princeton Encyclopedia of Classical Sites*. Princeton: Princeton University Press, 1976.

Van Deman, E. *The Building of the Roman Aqueducts*. Washington: Carnegic Institution, 1937; reprint ed., Washington: McGrath, 1973.

Vitruvius. *The Ten Books of Architecture*. Translated by M. H. Morgan. New York. Dover, 1960.

Wheeler, M. *Roman Art and Architecture*. New York: Thames & Hudson, 1964.

Greek Civilization°°

GENERAL BIBLIOGRAPHY
Burn, A. R. *The Pelican History of Greece*. Harmondsworth, 1966.
——————————. *A Traveller's History of Greece*. London, 1965.
——————————. *Pericles and Athens*, New York, 1962.
Bury, J. B. and Meiggs, Russell. *A History of Greece to the Death of Alexander the Great*, 4th ed. New York, 1975.
Dodds, E. R. *The Greeks and the Irrational*. Berkeley, 1966.
Ehrenberg, Victor. *Man, State and Deity: Essays in Ancient History*. London, 1974.
Ferguson, John. *The Heritage of Hellenism*. London, 1973.
Finley, M. I. *Aspects of Antiquity*. New York, 1969.
Hood, Sinclair. *The Home of the Heroes: The Aegean before the Greeks*. London, 1967.
Kitto, H. D. F. *The Greeks*. Harmondsworth, 1951.
Robinson, Charles A., Jr. *Athens in the Age of Pericles*. Norman, 1959.

Monographs and Special Studies (in chronological order by subject). An asterisk (°) indicates a book written for beginning students. The others are more specialized.

°Cadogan, Gerald. *Palaces of Minoan Crete*. London, 1976.
°Hood, Sinclair. *The Minoans*. New York, 1971.
°Willetts, R. F. *The Civilization of Ancient Crete*. Berkeley, 1977.
°Chadwick, John. *The Mycenaean World*. Cambridge, 1976.
°Vermeule, Emily. *Greece in the Bronze Age*. Chicago, 1964.
°Hooker, J. T. *Mycenaean Greece*. London, 1976.
Palmer, Leonard R. *Mycenaeans and Minoans*, 2nd. ed. New York, 1965.
Eliade, Mircea. *A History of Religious Ideas*. Vol. 1. *From the Stone Age to the Eleusinian Mysteries*. Chicago, 1978.
°Guthrie, W. K. C. *The Greeks and their Gods*. London, 1950.
Mylonas, George, *Eleusis*. Princeton, 1961.
Parke, H. W. *Greek Oracles*. London, 1969.
°Rose, H. J. *Ancient Greek Religion*. London, 1946.
°Murray, Gilbert. *Five Stages of Greek Religion*. New York, 1951.
Desborough, V. R. d'A. *The Greek Dark Ages*. London, 1972.
Snodgrass, A. M. *The Dark Age of Greece*. Edinburgh, 1971.
°Coldstream, J. N. *Geometric Greece*. London, 1977.
Walcot, Peter. *Hesiod and the Near East*. Cardiff, 1966.
Jeffrey, L. H. *Archaic Greece: The City-States c. 700–500 B.C.* London, 1976.
°Starr, Chester. *The Origins of Greek Civilization*. New York, 1961.
°Finley, M. I. *The World of Odysseus*. 2nd ed. London, 1977.
Page, Denys. *History and the Homeric Iliad*. Berkeley, 1959.
Kirk, Geoffrey. *Homer and the Epic*. Cambridge, 1965.
Huxley, George L. *The Early Ionians*. London, 1966.
Graham, A. J. *Colony and Mother City in Ancient Greece*. Manchester, 1964.
°Andrewes, A. *The Greek Tyrants*. London, 1956.

———————————

°°The Penguin paperbacks and the Loeb Classical Library provide numerous translations of Greek (and some Roman) authors who serve as primary sources for Greek civilization. Some of the more important are: Historians—Herodotus, Thucydides, Xenophon, Diodorus Siculus, Arrian; Orators, Philosophers, Essayists—Demosthenes, Plato, Aristotle, Theophrastus, [Xenophon]; Poets and Dramatists—Homer, Aeschylus, Sophocles, Euripides, Aristophanes; Biographers—Pultarch, Nepos.

Lloyd, G. E. R. *Early Greek Science: Thales to Aristotle.* London, 1970.
Michell, H. *Sparta.* Cambridge, 1964.
° Jones, A. H. M. *Sparta.* Cambridge, Mass., 1968.
Huxley, G. L. *Early Sparta.* London, 1962.
Kelly, Thomas. *A History of Argos to 500 B.C..* Minneapolis, 1976.
Roebuck, Carl. *Ionian Trade and Colonization.* New York, 1962.
° Burn, A. R. *Persia and the Greeks.* New York, 1962.
° Fornara, Charles. *Herodotus.* Oxford, 1971.
° Meiggs, Russell. *The Athenian Empire.* Oxford, 1972.
Hignett, Charles. *History of the Athenian Constitution.* London, 1952.
Adcock, F. E. *Thucydides and His History.* Cambridge, 1963.
° Finley, John. *Thucydides.* Ann Arbor, 1963.
° Grene, David. *Greek Political Theory.* Chicago, 1950.
° Finley, John. *Three Essays on Thucydides.* Cambridge, Mass., 1967.
deRomilly, Jacqueline. *Thucydides and Athenian Imperialism.* Oxford, 1963.
Woodhead, A. Geoffrey. *Thucydides on the Nature of Power.* Cambridge, Mass., 1970.
° Finley, John. *Four Stages of Greek Thought.* Stanford, 1966.
° Anderson, J. K. *Xenophon.* London, 1974.
° Lesky, Albin. *Greek Tragedy.* London, 1965.
Dover, K. J. *Aristophanic Comedy.* London, 1972.
Mosse, Claude. *Athens in Decline 404–86 B.C.* London, 1973.
° Cawkwell, George. *Philip of Macedon.* London, 1978.
Ellis, J. R. *Philip II and Macedonian Imperialism.* London, 1976.
° Hamilton, J. R. *Alexander the Great.* London, 1973.
Wilcken, Ulrich. *Alexander the Great.* New York, 1967.
° Adcock, F. E. *The Greek and Macedonian Art of War.* Berkeley, 1957.
Russell, D. A. *Plutarch.* London, 1972.
Eddy, Samuel. *The King is Dead.* London, 1961.
French, A. *The Growth of the Athenian Economy.* London, 1964.
° Austin, M. M. and Vidal-Naquet. *Economic and Social History of Ancient Greece.* London, 1977.
Guthrie, W. K. C. *The Sophists.* Cambridge, 1971.
Guthrie, W. K. C. *Socrates.* Cambridge, 1971.
° Baldrey, H. C. *The Unity of Mankind in Greek Thought.* Cambridge, 1965.
° Brown, Truesdell S. *The Greek Historians.* Lexington, 1973.
° Peters, Frank E. *The Harvest of Hellenism.* New York, 1970.
° Hadas, Moses. *Hellenistic Culture.* New York, 1955.
Wells, C. Bradford. *Alexander and the Hellenistic World.* Toronto, 1970.
Stadter, Philip A. *Arrian of Nicomedia.* Chapel Hill, 1980.
° Ferguson, William Scott. *Hellenistic Athens.* London, 1911.

Bronze Age

GENERAL WORKS: CRETE
Cadogan, G. *Palaces of Minoan Crete.* London, 1976.
Evans, J. A. *The Palace of Minos at Knossos,* I–IV and Index. New York, 1921–36. Reprinted, 1964.
Graham, J. W. *The Palaces of Crete.* Princeton, 1962.
Higgins, R. *The Archaeology of Minoan Crete.* New York, 1973.
Hood, S. *The Minoans.* New York, 1971.
Hutchinson, R. W. *Prehistoric Crete.* Baltimore, 1968.
Pendelbury, J. D. S. *The Archaeology of Crete.* New York, 1965.

GENERAL WORKS: MAINLAND GREECE
Alsop, J. *From the Silent Earth*. New York, 1964.
Chadwick, J. *The Mycenaean World*. New York, 1976.
Mylonas, G. *Mycenae and the Mycenaean Age*. Princeton, 1966.
Samuel, A. E. *The Mycenaeans in History*. Englewood Cliffs, 1966.
Schliemann, H. *Mycenae*, 1880. Reprinted New York, 1967.
Taylour, W. *The Mycenaeans*. London, 1964.
Vermeule, E. T. *Greece in the Bronze Age*. Chicago, 1964.

GENERAL WORKS
Hood, S. *The Home of the Heroes*. New York, 1967.
Marinatos, S. and Hirmer, M. *Crete and Mycenae*. New York, 1960.
Palmer, L. R. *Mycenaeans and Minoans*. London, 1965.

ART
Demargne, P. *The Birth of Greek Art*. New York, 1964.
Higgins, R. *Minoan and Mycenaean Art*. New York, 197.

LINEAR B
Chadwick, J. *The Decipherment of Linear B*. New York, 1958.

Greek City-Planning

Coulton, J. J. *The Architectural Development of the Greek Stoa*. Oxford, 1976.
Hanfmann, George M. A. *From Croesus to Constantine: The Cities of Western Asia Minor and Their Arts*. Ann Arbor, 1975.
Ward-Perkins, J. B. *Cities of Ancient Greece and Italy: Planning in Classical Antiquity*. New York, 1974.
Wycherley, R. E. *How the Greeks Built Cities*. London, 1962.

The Topography and Monuments of Athens

GENERAL WORKS
Rossiter, S. *The Blue Guides: Greece*. 2nd ed. London, 1973.
Travlos, J. *Pictorial Dictionary of Ancient Athens*. New York, 1971.
Wycherley, R. E. *The Stones of Athens*. Princeton, 1978.

ARCHITECTURE
Dinsmoor, W. B. *The Architecture of Ancient Greece*. New York, 1950.
Lawrence, A. *Greek Architecture*. Harmondsworth, 1957.
Robertson, D. S. *Greek and Roman Architecture*. 2nd ed. Cambridge, 1945.

SPECIFIC SITES
Hopper, R. J. *The Acropolis*. London, 1971.
Thompson, H. A. and others. *The Athenian Agora*. 3rd ed. Athens, 1976.
Thompson, H. A. and Wycherley, R. E. *The Athenian Agora XIV, The Agora of Athens, The History, Shape, and Uses of an Ancient City Center*. Princeton, 1972.

The Greek Temple

Bruno, Vincent J. (ed.) *The Parthenon*. New York, 1975.
Dinsmoor, William Bell. *The Architecture of Ancient Greece*. New York, 1975 (reprint).
Lawrence, A. W. *Greek Architecture*. Harmondsworth, 1957.
Melas, Evi (ed.) *Temples and Sanctuaries of Ancient Greece*. London, 1973.

Scully, Vincent. *The Earth, the Temple, and the Gods: Greek Sacred Architecture.* New York, 1968.
Seltman, Charles. *The Twelve Olympians.* New York, 1960.
Yavis, Constantine G. *Greek Altars: Origins and Typology.* St. Louis, 1949.

The Greek Theater

GENERAL WORKS
Arnott, P. D. *An Introduction to the Greek Theater.* Bloomington, 1967.
Bieber, M. *The History of the Greek and Roman Theater.* Princeton, 1961.
Lesky, A. *Greek Tragedy.* London, 1965.
Whitman, C. H. *Aristophanes and the Comic Hero.* Cambridge, Mass., 1964.

THE THEATER OF DIONYSUS
Pickard-Cambridge, A. W. *The Theatre of Dionysus in Athens,* Oxford, 1946.
————. *The Dramatic Festivals of Athens,* 2nd ed. Revised by J. Gould and D. M. Lewis, Oxford, 1968.

The Art of Greece

GENERAL WORKS
Boardman, J. *Greek Art.* New York, 1965.
Richter, G. *A Handbook of Greek Art.* New York, 1967.
Boardman, J., Dorig, J., Fuchs, W., and Hirmer, M. *Greek Art and Architecture.* New York
Charbonneaux, J., Martin, R., Villard, F. *Archaic Greek Art.* New York, 1971.
————. *Classical Greek Art.* New York, 1972.
————. *Hellenistic Art.* New York, 1973.
Carpenter, R. *The Esthetic Basis of Greek Art.* Bloomington, 1959.

VASE PAINTING
Arias, R. E. and Hirmer, M. *A History of Greek Vase Painting.* London, 1962.
Boardman, J. *A Handbook of Athenian Black Figure Vases.* London, 1974.
————. *Athenian Red Figure Vases, A Handbook.* London, 1975.

SCULPTURE
Ashmole, B. *Architecture and Sculptor in Classical Greece.* New York, 1972.
Lullies, R., and Hirmer, M. *Greek Sculpture.* New York, 1957.
Robertson, M. and Frantz, A. *The Parthenon Frieze.* London, 1975.
Yalouris, N. *The Elgin Marbles of the Parthenon.* New York, 1967.

DATE DUE

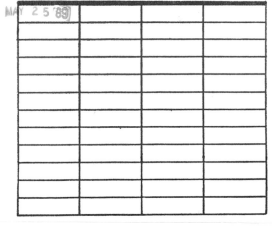

MAY 2 5 '89			